CHINESE ESPRESSO

Chinese Espresso

CONTESTED RACE AND
CONVIVIAL SPACE IN
CONTEMPORARY ITALY

GRAZIA TING DENG

PRINCETON UNIVERSITY PRESS

PRINCETON & OXFORD

Published by Princeton University Press
41 William Street, Princeton, New Jersey 08540
99 Banbury Road, Oxford OX2 6JX

press.princeton.edu

All Rights Reserved

ISBN 978-0-691-24578-2
ISBN (pbk.) 978-0-691-24579-9
ISBN (e-book) 978-0-691-25561-3

British Library Cataloging-in-Publication Data is available

Editorial: Fred Appel and James Collier
Production Editorial: Jill Harris
Cover Design: Chris Ferrante
Production: Lauren Reese
Publicity: William Pagdatoon

Cover images: Adobe Stock

This book has been composed in Arno

10 9 8 7 6 5 4 3 2 1

To all my teachers
across three continents.

CONTENTS

ACKNOWLEDGMENTS

THIS BOOK IS THE RESULT of countless espressos and cappuccinos that I drank and brewed in Bologna and elsewhere in Italy. I would first like to thank the baristas and their customers of all nationalities who shared their experiences and stories with me. I am also indebted to the many Chinese families who allowed me to conduct research in their coffee bars, put up with my endless questions, taught or otherwise shared their barista skills, and welcomed me into their lives. Several other Chinese interlocutors whose families were not engaged with the coffee bar businesses have also generously shared with me their life stories and perceptions of Chinese experiences in Italy and have allowed me access to their family and social networks. I am delighted to have witnessed their important life moments over the last decade: finishing school, getting married, starting new businesses or careers, and becoming parents or grandparents. While I use pseudonyms to identify all my Chinese interlocutors, I do wish to acknowledge and express my profound gratitude for their immense support and sincere friendship throughout my research. My thanks extend to the *Chiesa Evangelica Cinese in Italia di Bologna*, the Associna (*Associazione Seconde Generazioni Cinesi*), and the *Associazione Bar Cinesi in Italia* for helping me to build and to extend my networks of interlocutors. Special thanks go to Tianzuo Li for initially scoping out Bologna as a promising field site for the study of Chinese-owned coffee bars when I was still in the early stage of project design in Hong Kong. Many thanks go to my Chinese friends in Cesena for their hospitality and for sharing with me one of the most memorable Lunar New Years of my life.

A number of native Bolognese and other Italians whom I knew beyond the coffee bars also greatly facilitated my research. My heartfelt gratitude goes to the Minghetti family and the Fabbri family for their incredible hospitality and family-like care. This was all made possible thanks to Mara Mori's initial introductions through the *Intercultura* (AFS Italy) networks. Both families provided me with a home during my first year of fieldwork and throughout all my return trips. I miss the good wines, food, and laughs that I shared with them, their extended families, and their friends. I would also like to express my warm thanks to Janna Carioli for her generous support and friendship. She thoughtfully showed me the changing neighborhood where she lived, introduced to me several local bureaucrats and intellectuals for interviews, and invited me over for meals, social gatherings, and house parties so that I could connect with people useful to my research. Laura Lepore, Stefano Ratti, Rossella Roncati, and Daniele Massaccesi generously shared with me their observations of and experiences with the transformations of coffee bars in their own cities or towns. I particularly thank Andrea Resca for allowing me to read the unpublished thesis for his *Laurea* on Chinese communities in Bologna in the early 1990s. Very special thanks go to Simone Marini who took me to the emergency room one dramatic night when I broke my arm, and to my excellent and generous physiotherapist Massimo for his professional treatment which far exceeded the limits of my health plan.

This book took its embryonic form as my PhD dissertation at The Chinese University of Hong Kong. My deepest thanks go to Joseph Bosco for supporting me in every aspect of my research from the research plan, to fieldwork, and then on through the writing process. He taught me how to observe and think anthropologically and guided my growth as a serious anthropologist. I am also deeply grateful to Sealing Cheng for her intellectual imagination and perceptive vision, which helped me to think and write with greater clarity. Her warm encouragement and thoughtful advice were crucial to keeping my writing program on schedule. She also deserves credit for the title of the book. In addition, I am grateful to my other committee members—Gordon Mathews and Sidney Cheung—as well as to my external examiner Mette Thunø for providing me with helpful insights throughout this project. My gratitude extends to Teresa Kuan, Matthew West, Danning Wang, Yu Huang, and Wai-Chi Chee for nurturing my intellectual growth, alongside my thesis committee. A debt is owed to Erika Evasdottir for brainstorming my book proposal and revision plans while we sat in a café in Central for an entire evening after her busy workday. Special thanks go to Ju-Chen Chen for the numerous intellectual conversations we had, but more importantly for her unflagging support as a dear friend.

I did much of the writing and rewriting of this book while at Brown University, which proved crucial to my intellectual formation. The Population Studies and Training Center provided me with superb institutional support and an incredibly productive working environment that allowed me to focus on my research and writing. As a postdoctoral researcher, I became part of a wonderful community composed of anthropologists, sociologists, economists, demographers, and historians. I owe my most profound gratitude to David Kertzer, who selflessly and carefully reviewed several drafts of this book in great detail. His relentless support and profound engagement have helped shape my project's final incarnation. I am very grateful also to Katherine Mason for her trenchant feedback on each draft chapter of the manuscript and for invaluable ideas shared in our discussions of my work. I also benefited from Michael White's graduate seminar "Migration and Population Distribution," which I sat in on, as well as the many conversations we had within and beyond our office space at Mencoff Hall. Evelyn Hu-DeHart offered her firm support and unfailing care in guiding me to grow academically. Brown University's PSTC Migration Working Group, which Andrea Flores and Kevin Escudero convened, also provided me with extremely helpful feedback. Particular thanks are due to Andrea Flores for reading several draft chapters of the manuscript and for her precious support, both intellectual and personal. Jessaca Leinaweaver also read a draft chapter and provided me with rich feedback. Susan Short, Zhenchao Qian, and Massimo Riva were unstinting in their support for my work. The students in my Fall 2021 Anthropology of the Chinese Diaspora class inspired me with new thoughts on this project in critical ways.

Several Italian scholars also offered their help. I am indebted to Antonella Ceccagno for precious feedback, especially for inviting me to conduct my major fieldwork between 2014 and 2015 under the auspices of the University of Bologna and for her mentorship, which cleared bureaucratic hurdles to enable my long stay in Italy. I am similarly indebted to Asher Colombo for facilitating my fieldwork in Bologna, for inviting me to discuss my work in his classes, and for sharing his insightful thoughts, brilliant sense of humor, and loyal friendship over the years. My gratitude goes as well to Matteo Legrenzi, Alessandra Gribaldo, Maurizio Bergamaschi, Giuseppe Scandurra, Dario Tuorto, and Rossella Ghigi for their conversations and suggestions at various points along the way. I benefited from these social scientists not only because of their intellectual acuity, but also from their lived experiences as native Italians.

Visits to Harvard University and the University of Wisconsin-Madison during my doctoral dissertation writing also greatly contributed to this work. I owe an enormous debt to Michael Herzfeld for his thought-provoking insights in our numerous conversations, very often over great food and wines, not only in Cambridge, Massachusetts, but also in many other places around the world where we met for conferences, fieldwork, and workshops over the years. His relentless encouragement, openness, and support have brightened my path along this anthropological adventure. I thank Yongming Zhou for his wonderfully perceptive input on my research questions and for generous advice on my academic growth. I also appreciate Michael Puett and Shelly Chan for their invigorating conversations.

I feel fortunate to have had the opportunity to be part of several outstanding international communities of scholars. Mentors, colleagues, and friends working on the Chinese migration to Europe and the Chinese diaspora more broadly have shaped my thinking and inspired my work. I thank in particular Chee-Beng Tan, Nanlai Cao, Daniele Brigadoi Cologna, Valentina Pedone, Massimo Bressan, Tu Lan, Pál Nyíri, Cheryl Mei-ting Schmitz, Derek Sheridan, Minghuan Li, Simeng Wang, and Diego Luis. I am also grateful to have met and engaged with many wonderful fellow-students, colleagues, and friends whom I met in classes and offices, during fieldwork, or at conferences in Asia, in Europe, and in North America. They include Yichen Rao, Elena Nichini, Lai Wo, Ping-hsiu Alice Lin, Alan Tse, Isabel Briz Hernández, Ruslan Yusupov, Changgeng Yuan, Edwin Schmitt, Philip Demgenski, Man-Kei Tam, Perseus Cheung, Ling Ding, Ka-Kin Cheuk, Jacopo Scarin, John Skutlin, Fiori Berhane, Stefano Portelli, Hua Yu, Jiangjiang Wu, Bo Wang, Yukun Zeng, Dong Dong, Pu Hao, Marty Alexander, Tianjiao Liu, and Clare Wan. Many have become my life-long friends, and I thank them for their sparkling ideas and intellectual companionship, which helped me enormously in getting through the ups and downs of this long project. Special thanks go to Gil Hizi for his sharp and meticulous reading of my entire manuscript. I also presented my work in progress at a variety of conference sessions, invited lectures, seminars, and workshops and I would like to acknowledge the organizers and audiences for making this book a better one. I am especially grateful to the Emerging Scholars Program on "Migration Matters: Ethnicity, Race, Labor, and Politics across Borders" that Ayşe Parla organized at Boston University's Department of Anthropology.

I appreciate financial support from several institutions that made possible my research and writing for this book, including the IJURR Foundation (previously the Foundation for Urban and Regional Studies), the Chinese University of Hong Kong, and Brown University. Earlier versions of some of the materials in this book appeared in the following articles: "*I Cinesi* among Others: The Contested Racial Perceptions among Chinese Migrants in Italy" in *Journal of Ethnic and Migration Studies* (Advance online publication 2023); "A Chinese Woman's Journey to the 'West': Ethnographic Knowledge Production amid Ambiguous Power Dynamics" in *Ethnography* (Advance online publication 2022); and "Chinese Immigrant Entrepreneurship in Italy's Coffee Bars: Demographic Transformation and Historical Contingency" in *International Migration* 58 (3): 87–100 (2020).

I feel privileged and honored to publish this book with Princeton University Press. I thank Fred Appel for his steadfast support and editorial guidance. Two readers, Elizabeth Krause and Lilith Mahmud, whose identities were only revealed at the end of this process, offered generous comments and incisive suggestions that helped transform the manuscript into a more refined product. My thanks extend to Eva Jaunzems for her copyediting that gave the language a more natural flow and cadence, Chris Ferrante for her terrific cover design, James Collier for his highly effective editorial assistance, and all the other editorial, production, and marketing staff, including Jill Harris, Susan Clark, Lauren Reese, and William Pagdatoon, for their professionalism and expertise. I also appreciate the Equity, Inclusion and Belonging Council for supporting and trusting in this project, along with Princeton University Press's Global Equity Grant.

I could not have carried out this lengthy project without the care and generosity of a great many friends beyond the immediate orbit of my intellectual communities. I am privileged to be grounded in multiple linguistic communities that prepared me to take on my fieldwork. I owe gratitude to my Italian language teachers and research mentors in Bejing, Shanghai, and Trento, Italy, including Jianmin Tang, Jianhua Wang, Ebe Cecinelli, Yujing Zhang, Ying Xu, Yonghong Zhou, Lili Zhou, Mi Zhang, Qigao Huang, Tianqing Wang, Serenella Baggio, Sabrina Francesconi, Raffaella Lenzi, and Tiziano Giongo. I am particularly indebted to those friends and their families who generously opened their homes or found a free bed for me when I traveled to their cities for research or conferences, including Mosa Pan, Massimiliano Zeni, Coco Shen, Yanjie Wu, Ying Qiu, Xiaochan Lai, Huikai Lin, Jianing Ji, Yuan Li, Cornelia Herzfeld, and Stefano Anzelotti. Deep thanks are due also to the many friends who cheered me up and stayed by my side during the challenging pandemic when we were stuck in Providence, Rhode Island. In particular I thank Alessandro Moghrabi, Brooke Grasberger, Diego Luis, Vera Rosen-Bernstein, Aaron Jacobs, Pablo a Marca, Stacey Murrell, Ji Soo Hong, Jorge Rosario Rosario, Fernando Norat, Emily Roche, Ann Daly, Julia Gettle, Mahmoud Nowara, Milen Ivanov, and Simeon Simeonov for their intellectual companionship that has deeply influenced my way of thinking, and for their emotional support that cheered me along the road toward the project's end. Their care, friendship, and solidarity remain a treasured part of my life.

Finally, I would like to thank my parents Guifeng Huang and Hongguan Deng. They never compromised my education throughout my teenage years, which were the most difficult and uncertain times of their lives as laid off workers in China. If I am today a strong and independent woman who can embrace whatever challenges come my way, it is almost entirely thanks to them. I owe a huge debt of gratitude to my husband, James Wang, whose love, support, and wisdom made the book possible. He was at my side throughout the entire rewriting process, reading countless drafts and cheering and inspiring me in my hardest moments. Our discussions often took me outside my anthropological comfort zone and enabled me to think more historically and holistically.

This book has taken a decade-long journey across three continents from its inception to this final product. Its travels reflect my own journey of learning about the Chinese diaspora and about what it means to be a diasporic Chinese. Countless people whom I met at different stages of my life have influenced me to become who I am. I call them my teachers, and this book is dedicated to all of them. Thank you for lighting my path to my diasporic past, present and future.

Cappuccino Time

"*DING!*" THE BROWN-COLORED glass door slides open with a bell-like sound. Only when I have come all the way inside does it return to its original position, separating the interior space from the outside world. The aroma of freshly ground coffee beans permeates the air and mixes with the fragrance of reheated *panini* sandwiches. An Italian radio plays some nostalgic light music, but I cannot place the song or the singer. Sugar, milk, cocoa, tissue boxes, and two small dishes of free snacks are on the bar counter that I face. Some breadcrumbs are scattered across its surface. Next to the cash register is a small pile of leaflets and flyers advertising a jazz night, a neighborhood festival, a massage center . . . , all old ads, nothing new. Behind the counter is a four-tiered shelf with a rich collection of beverages—some alcoholic, some not—and an assortment of cups and glasses. Three columns of *gratta e vinci* or "scratch and win" cards hang on the left side of the shelf next to the espresso machine.

This is an ordinary coffee bar serving neighbors, passersby, and those who work nearby in the city of Bologna. Brown is the leitmotif of the décor, which looks dated but is well maintained. The furniture is a bright brown, the square ceramic floor tiles wheat-colored. The surfaces of the bar counter and the square dining tables are a rosy-brown marble, and pictures in chocolate-colored frames hang on the golden-oak wood panels of the walls. The ceiling is an exception. It is painted white with several carefully placed recessed lamps that lend brightness to this compact windowless space. Some newly added Christmas decorations make the space even cozier. A plastic Christmas tree stands in the left corner. Next to it, atop a cupboard, are three large gift baskets covered with red cloth. Green and red tinsel streamers hang from the ceiling.

It is nearly 10 am. A wave of customers has already come and gone, but Luca's coffee bar is still quite busy, as several late risers trickle in for breakfast.[1] One young couple stands to the left side of the L-shaped bar counter and orders the classic local breakfast: cappuccino and a croissant, or *brioche*, as people in Bologna usually call it. Their baby sleeps quietly in a stroller. A middle-aged man loiters in front of the bread cabinet, undecided as to which croissant he should choose. Meanwhile a young female care worker pushes a wheelchair-bound elderly woman out of the dining room. They stop briefly to play the slot machine next to the entrance. Sitting alone in the corner of the dining room with an espresso on the table is an elderly man thumbing through a newspaper.

Among all of the faces, some familiar and some not, I notice three men who have already become my coffee bar friends: Gigi, Raffel, and Alberto. Gigi sits in his usual seat to the right of the narrow corridor near the entrance. His left arm rests on the narrow hall table that holds an empty espresso cup and a copy of the latest *Il Resto del Carlino*, a local *bolognese* newspaper. "*Ciao* [hello], Ting Ting!" He greets me first, calling me by my Chinese name. Doubling the monosyllabic given name produces a diminutive commonly used among Chinese families and friends. Gigi has learned it from a Chinese woman who runs a clothing store near his rented apartment. Never married, this Italian man in his fifties makes a living as a construction worker. He has been frequenting this coffee bar for decades. More often than not, he just sits alone and looks around.

Raffel is playing on a slot machine at the right corner of the entrance. This Bangladeshi man in his late twenties is a trader in foodstuffs. He rises before dawn every day to deliver fresh vegetables and fruits to the green groceries managed by his fellow

Bangladeshi immigrants. Luca's coffee bar is where he often hangs out with friends or just passes time alone during daylight hours. He turns his head to give me an absentminded *"ciao"* and then quickly turns back to the machine. Maybe those hens on the screen will lay some golden eggs for him today. I read from his knitted eyebrows that he must already have lost hundreds of euros this morning. Then, just at that moment, I hear a stream of clattering sounds coming from the slot machine. Coins are dropping. "Bravo, Raffel!" I congratulate him. He replies with a big smile and says, "Thanks, but I have to stop playing!" Each time I see him, he repeats these words in fluent but strongly accented Italian. He has to save money, he explains to me, so that he can get married one day when he returns to his country.

Alberto greets me with a nod. He takes his espresso as he stands next to the bread cabinet. Originally from Southern Italy, in his late forties, he has lived in Bologna for more than twenty years. He had also worked in Germany, where his brother owns an Italian restaurant, but he decided to return to Italy after several years because he did not like the German climate. As a chef in a nearby restaurant, he often comes to Luca's to take a break or meet friends for a beer. He told me that, in his professional opinion as someone experienced in the food service business, Luca's is the best in Bologna.

"Ciao, Grazia!" At that moment, Lina walks back to the bar counter from the dining room, holding a round tray with several dirty cups and dishes on it. *"Un cappuccio per te* [A cappuccino for you]?" She asks me while putting the tableware into the cleaning basket. In Bologna, it is common to say *cappuccio,* instead of *cappuccino,* which is literally a diminutive form of the former word in Italian. Receiving my confirmation, she begins the series of routine steps that go into coffee making, steps that she repeats hundreds of times each day. Her skilled movements and the hissing sound made by the steam in the milk tell me it will be a delicious cappuccino, as usual.

Meanwhile, I ask her about their Christmas schedule, indicating the announcement hanging on the shelf. "Are you closing for two and a half days for Christmas? Does your father know about it?" She gives me an affirmative nod. Finally, she will get the chance to take a "long" break from work. Alberto interjects into our conversation: "I told you, this family is the best! They are very well integrated into *la cultura italiana* [Italian culture]."

Hearing the compliments, Lina compresses her lips in a shy smile. I watch her pouring creamy milk into the fresh espresso, forming a white heart in the center of the foam. Gigi glances at the cappuccino from his seat and comments, "*Brava*, right? This Chinese family is *stupenda* [fantastic]!"

Yes, this family is Chinese. They use Italian names in this neighborhood bar that they purchased four years ago. The owner, whom I call Uncle Gumin, is "Luca" to his customers, while his eldest daughter Ensi is "Lina."

"*Bravissima* [Very well done]!" I echo the pleasantries that are repeated every day in this convivial little coffee bar community. I pour a packet of brown sugar into the cup and watch it sink slowly into the liquid. After stirring it well with a teaspoon, I take hold of the large cup and sip the warm and creamy cappuccino.

CHINESE ESPRESSO

1

The Paradox of Chinese Espresso

COFFEE BARS ARE UBIQUITOUS in urban Italy.[1] They are liberally distributed across all kinds of urban spaces: in piazzas and along sidewalks, in *centri storici* (historic centers) and peripheral *quartieri* (neighborhoods), in both tourist zones and residential areas. And they are found not only in cities, but also in provincial towns and villages. All offer as their most quintessential commodity, Italian-style espresso-based coffees. But unlike Starbucks or other independent specialty coffeehouses in the United States or in China, which focus on coffee consumption, a typical coffee bar in Italy is a hybrid establishment serving as a bar, a convenience store, and often as a game room as well. These are places where urban dwellers, whether native Italians or recent immigrants, can have breakfast, take a break from working or walking, pass their leisure time, or simply use the restroom after buying a bottle of water or a cup of coffee. A coffee bar is also a place where people can meet friends, get up-to-date local news, and enjoy the sense of belonging to a community. The nearly 150,000 *bars*—one for every 400 people—thus constitute a fundamental part of the urban landscape of contemporary Italy and play an integral in the lives of its people.[2]

Coffee bars were a fresh and foreign cultural experience for me when I was an exchange student writing my Master's thesis in socio-historical linguistics at the University of Trento between 2005 and 2006. It was my first visit to Italy and my first time outside of China. During my ten-month stay in that Alpine city, I had few interactions with my co-nationals beyond the university circle. They were as mysterious to me—an international student from the same country—as to native Italians. I knew of a clothing shop run by a young Chinese couple close to my dorm, but I never went inside. My Italian friends brought me to a couple of Chinese restaurants, but I did not like their Italianized dishes. I visited Via Paolo Sarpi in Milan and Piazza Vittorio in Rome, both of which were known in Italy for their high concentrations of Chinese residents and their cheap consumer-goods shops and ethnic restaurants. Some Chinese academic friends who had lived in Italy longer than me told me that there were actually many more Chinese residents in Italy. They were immigrant workers hidden in small factories where they both worked and lived and thus became almost invisible to urban dwellers.

Back then, I had never encountered a Chinese barista or heard Italian friends talk about Chinese ownership of coffee bars. I could not even imagine any kind of connection between Chinese immigrants, largely marginalized and detached from Italy's urban life, and the omnipresent coffee bars at the heart of its urban culture. I was astonished when, in 2012, I heard by chance that many coffee bars in Italy had in fact been taken over by Chinese people. This contradicted my own experiences of Italy. My intuition told me that this phenomenon might make for a fascinating ethnographic study for my doctoral dissertation, and I almost immediately decided to pursue research on the topic.

As my project proceeded, I learned that there had been a few sporadic cases of Chinese ownership of coffee bars in Italy in the early 2000s, or even before that. Their rapid spread however coincided with the onset of the Great Recession of 2008. The FIPE's annual reports reveal that since then more coffee bars had closed than were opened each year.[3] However, as a counter to these closures, foreign ownership had rapidly expanded in Northern and Central Italy during that same period. In 2008, around 5,000 coffee bars, comprising 6.6 percent of the total number in Italy, were owned by people who were not born in the country. Ten years later, the percentage had risen to around 10 percent. Among the coffee bars classed as *imprese individuali* or "sole proprietorships," which is the form of enterprise with the highest level of foreign ownership, some Northern regions reported numbers as high as 20 percent. Over the same period, the numbers of foreign workers had also grown considerably and, by 2018, nearly a quarter of employees in the coffee bar sector were born outside Italy. The Chinese were not the only foreign-born owners of Italian bars. I also encountered coffee bars managed by Russians, Moroccans, and Romanians, among others. But Chinese management was and still is the most visible due to Chinese baristas' obvious phenotypical differences and their large market share. Coffee bars managed by Chinese people have become quite common in both large cities and provincial towns and in city centers as well as residential areas.

This fact has touched a raw nerve in native Italians who associate the increasing Chinese presence in this niche with the growth of Chinese transnational investment in Italy more broadly. Many Italians express admiration for China, once a poor developing country that has emerged as an economic superpower seemingly almost overnight, while Italy has remained mired in economic stagnation. At the same time, I noticed that even Italians who historically identified with the left often resented China for "buying up" Italy with supposedly problematic money which, in their eyes, was invariably linked to suspicious economic activities or money laundering operations. With few exceptions, both left- and right-wing media have, with remarkable consistency, used provocative headlines and claimed an "invasion" of Chinese capital into the Italian economy.[4] Their coverage spans the entire range of the Chinese economic presence in Italy, from large companies in the energy industry, banks, and infrastructure sectors, down to small businesses such as coffee bars, restaurants, barbershops, and dollar stores. They share similar concerns about the rapid growth of Chinese enterprises and worries about *i cinesi* (the Chinese) becoming the *padroni* (bosses) of more and more Italian workers, and maybe one day even the *padrone* (boss) of the entire country. These discourses often equate Chinese people with China in the same racialized category, regardless of the fact that many Chinese residents have lived in Italy for decades and have children who were born or have grown up in Italy.

The anxiety many Italians feel about the supposed loss of Italian culture on this very local level further exacerbates the controversy over Chinese ownership and management of coffee bars. The "coffee bar is not just any place," a news article claimed.

> It has a soul, sometimes very deep roots, and branches that cover the communities of a territory or of a single area. A life, even a very intense one, takes place around the coffee bar, and this is why we can consider the coffee bar as a garrison of relationships, human relations and civility. It is a precious and intangible heritage that we cannot waste or abandon in our daily life.[5]

Alongside its provocative anti-Chinese tone, this article highlights the integral role of coffee bars in shaping Italy's urban cultures and local identities and argues for resistance to Chinese ownership due to its allegedly alien character. However, the article describes coffee bars in Italy as if they were ahistorical and takes no account of Italians' diverse class, gender, generation, and other social backgrounds. Like other public discourses I heard and read, it also ignores the increasing foreign-born populations in Italy who today form an important part of the clientele of coffee bars. Like many Italians, these immigrants frequent coffee bars as part of their life style and as a venue for building social relationships.

Another piece published in a local newspaper based in Ravenna, a UNESCO seaside city known for its mosaic art, recounted stories of how two Italian coffee bar owners reacted differently "when China approached."[6] The one who sold his business to a Chinese family was described almost as a traitor to his country, despite having expressed his reluctance in the face of a colossal global power from the "Orient." The other owner, who refused a Chinese family's offer, was depicted as a patriot whose rejection of the Chinese buyers was an honorable action taken for the sake of conserving local identity, cultural heritage, and national patrimony. The owner was quoted as saying:

I would rather give up my business to an Italian, even better to someone from the Romagna region. This isn't an ideological choice, but simply because I want to see my small *bar tabaccheria* [tobacco bar] in the hands of someone familiar, someone who can maintain the characteristic convivial atmosphere of a meeting place for the town.

This owner emphasized the "non-ideological" character of her decision. However, her words were certainly ideologically charged, even racist. Race is a "sliding signifier."[7] It is a social and discursive construct invented to justify human differences and inequalities rather than to signify anything inherent in a person's physical or biological aspect. People of Chinese descent and other East Asians have been historically racialized as perpetual foreigners and unassimilable Others in white-dominant societies, where national identities have always been associated with whiteness.[8] In this contemporary case, the owner assumed that the Chinese family, unable to understand Italian culture, would not maintain the "authentic" cultural environment of an Italian social space. She made it clear also that people of Chinese descent, regardless of their citizenship, were not Italians in her eyes, as if culture were a geographically bounded and immutable concept. Yet, according to Italian law, only Italian or EU citizens are allowed to purchase tobacco shops, which implies that there was at least one member in that Chinese family who held Italian citizenship.

The owner's words expressed a common skepticism that many Italians share about Chinese baristas' ability to manage coffee bars. She mentioned wanting to sell her business to "someone familiar," on the grounds that local knowledge was critical for maintaining the social functioning of her tobacco bar as a community social

center. This notion is furthered by the social and cultural implications of espresso, the staple commodity of an Italian coffee bar.
Together with its variant, cappuccino, espresso is widely considered Italy's national beverage and internationally recognized as a
product that is a symbol of *Italianità* (Italian-ness).[9] How could a
person of Chinese descent, who presumably came from a totally
alien culture, possibly make an authentic Italian coffee? This is one
of the first questions that some curious Italians raise, while others
simply pose it as a rhetorical question to which they already know
the answer: They cannot.

This controversy and the resistance and skepticism it provokes,
however, contradict the reality of Chinese-managed coffee bars
and their seemingly convivial atmospheres, as we saw it described
in Luca's (Uncle Gumin's) coffee bar in the Prelude. It seems in
fact that, despite the racial and ethnic tensions exhibited in heated
public discussions and in the media, Chinese baristas have managed to fare quite successfully in intercultural encounters with
their local customers. It also appears that Italian consumers, albeit
perhaps reluctantly, are getting used to coffee made by Chinese
baristas, even while sighing over the "invasion" of the *orientali*.

Chinese Espresso and Convivial Bricolage

This book investigates the conditions, mechanisms, and implications behind the rapid spread of Chinese-managed coffee bars in
Northern and Central Italy since the economic downturn of 2008.
The project stems from my initial curiosity over why and how Chinese coffee bar owners, supposedly cultural aliens, could manage
a business model regarded by Italians as rooted in a distinctively
Italian taste and constituting a uniquely Italian social space. I have
this puzzle in mind when I refer in this book to the paradox of
Chinese Espresso. The two terms initially seem to be mutually
exclusive. Espresso coffee is, after all, an Italian national icon. Nevertheless, I use the juxtaposition of the two terms to challenge
taken-for-granted perceptions that attach national and cultural at-

tributes to this particular beverage, regardless of its complicated colonial history and current global commodification. Meanwhile, many native Italians and other local populations in Italy have gradually come to regard espresso coffee made by Chinese baristas, as well as Chinese-managed coffee bars, as a new normal. The story of Chinese Espresso is to my mind emblematic of lives in pluralistic, postmodern, and postcolonial urban societies. In this case, racialized immigrants, presumably embodying irreducible and incommensurable cultural differences, nevertheless assume fundamental roles and positions of taste production and place-making that would normally be expected to heavily reward only persons long-rooted in local culture and the national identity. It exposes also the paradox between the apparent multi-racial and multi-ethnic conviviality that prevails in the everyday life of a specific urban space and the hostility against immigrants prevalent in a wider, white-dominant European society.

I see the Chinese Espresso described in this book as a kind of everyday convivial bricolage. The concept of "bricolage," which denotes the practice of making do with whatever is at hand, has been used by philosophers, cultural theorists, and anthropologists in explaining culture-making and identity formation. Claude Lévi-Strauss first used this concept as a metaphor in *Wild Thought* to depict the ways in which mythical thought, an intellectual process in opposition to scientific thought, is made. He noted that both contingency and inevitable constraints characterize bricolage, to which mythical thought is analogous. They arise because the bricoleurs' "universe of instruments is closed," which "restricts their freedom of maneuver."[10] In this sense, bricolage implies a compromise which "enables the formation of novel systems of meaning."[11] Michel De Certeau further developed this concept in his theory of practice. For him, "bricolage" as "the poetic ways of making do" constitutes a form of social resistance, or "tactics" in his own words, by which common people appropriate, manipulate, and re-use the institutions and structures of power, such as language, place, and social order, in their everyday practices for their own interests.[12] Gilles Deleuze and Félix Guattari have instead understood bricolage as a mode of desiring-production; all humans, as desiring subjects, are in their view bricoleurs.[13] Building on these French theorists' interpretations, I define "convivial bricolage" as an interdependent and collaborative social practice by which immigrant subjects cultivate urban conviviality. Chinese Espresso thus produces a collective tapestry woven over time by convivial bricoleurs in their everyday social, cultural, and racial encounters that is characterized by contingency and compromise. This contingency in turn establishes boundaries on the conviviality that they cultivate.

Conviviality is thus central to this book in that it examines how people contrive to live together in an era of unprecedented mobility. The concept of "conviviality"—the art of living together—has its roots in the idealized notion of the *convivència* between Jews, Muslims, and Christians in medieval Iberia. Since the 2010s, this concept has been increasingly used to describe cohabitation and interactions across differences within everyday urban lives.[14] This alluring concept raises fundamental questions about "what constitutes a 'good' society when that society is diverse."[15] In the European scholarship of migration, the concept of "conviviality" serves as both an analytical and methodological tool for understanding social interactions and urban encounters between natives and newcomers in an increasingly heterogeneous Europe.[16] It also represents a kind of "virtuous aspiration" that seeks an alternative to both xenophobic and liberal multiculturalist discourses by imagining social possibilities for more inclusive immigrant reception in Europe.[17] Yet, regardless of its professed ideals, the discourse of conviviality risks downplaying structural inequalities within Europe, all the while reproducing a form of racial discourse that emphasizes cultural harmony and essentialist ideas of difference.[18] In this book, I instead use the concept of conviviality to denote a contingent and situational social reality that resilient immigrant subjects learn to deploy and cultivate to maintain their precarious livelihoods in the face of economic austerity and structural inequalities. Stepping away from a Eurocentric lens, this book provides a narrative from the immigrants' perspective, exploring how these new city-makers perceive and live within a European society while confronting various forms of difference.[19]

In an aging Europe, immigrants participate actively in urban development and in the fashioning of local people's everyday lives. In the case of Italy, some have become caretakers for Italian pensioners within the shifting environment of neoliberal welfare reform, in spite of not being recognized as "ethical citizens."[20] Others have undertaken social solidarity initiatives and formed networks for improving local livelihoods and promoting radical political change despite the increasing hostility directed against them.[21] A large number of newcomers operate market stands or storefront businesses that have transformed the urban landscape and neighborhood life.[22] Both established and more recent residents in each of these specific "meeting places" have forged a particular constellation of relationships and understandings that integrate the global and the local.[23] The Chinese-managed coffee bars that are the subject of this study, however, mark a new frontier of immigrant participation in local urban lives, for coffee bars have been construed as central to Italian culture, and in almost all cases they predate Chinese ownership as convivial urban spaces. Yet, quite unexpectedly, it would seem that these purported racial and cultural aliens have managed to preserve the convivial sociality of their establishments.

Coffee bars are first of all a space of economic production. This small-scale business niche, characterized by self-employed family management, is now being passed down along class lines that cross racial and ethnic boundaries. Chinese and other immigrants are incorporated, voluntarily or reluctantly, into this established niche, which offers both laborers and entrepreneurs new opportunities within the globalized labor market regime. Chinese entrepreneurship in Italy's coffee bars also highlights, once again, the fact that kinship, social networks, and other factors typically associated with immigrants' ethnicity and considered crucial in "traditional" immigrant entrepreneurship still play important roles in the capital and knowledge accumulation that is essential for running this new niche.[24] It shows as well that beliefs and values, sentiments and affects, human relations, as well as other non-economic factors, continue to operate as forces that enable, constrain, and shape production, albeit in some new ways.[25] In this process, the capitalist production that shapes local taste further integrates immigrant labor in taste-making at the local level, while immigrant subjects in turn "make taste public" through everyday practices in specific premises of sociality.[26]

Coffee bars are also a space of social relations. They constitute a new form of "contact zone" where local populations, both Italians and immigrants, with their own sets of identities converge, meet, and interact with one another in the course of their everyday social encounters and within the context of "highly asymmetrical relations of power."[27] Like other immigrant subjects in Italy, Chinese baristas demonstrate their own subjectivities rather than appearing merely as disadvantaged social victims who are unilaterally racialized, oppressed, and disempowered within the country's social reality of structural inequalities and its rigid immigration and citizenship regime.[28] They have not only claimed urban space, but have also cultivated their own ways to maintaining and regulating it for their own purposes and aspirations.[29] In this process they have, in collaboration with other urban populations, whether considered desirable or not, constructed convivial spaces through the "frictions of encounter."[30]

Coffee bars also serve as a crucial terrain in which ordinary people learn, re-envision, and transform racial hierarchies. As a study of regional racial formation in suburban California shows, multi-racial local residents can experience and imagine the multiple proximities that ostensibly blur fixed boundaries.[31] Those sites of everyday life thus serve as places where local residents develop a particular kind of situated knowledge and form transformative understandings of race, ethnicity, and identity. The Chinese-managed coffee bars that I studied likewise became for me an instructive global-in-the-local site. I observed how every-day convivial bricolage was produced in practice within a locally embedded social institution, seeking to understand how Chinese baristas perceived, negotiated, and ultimately helped reproduce existing racial formations and hierarchies so as to maintain con-vivial sociality.

My analysis was also more broadly situated on two larger scales of social context. I looked at Italy as a white-dominant European country experiencing a growing body of anti-immigrant policies, while at the same time confronting several new dilemmas—low fertility rates, an aging population, and increasing immigration, all of which further challenge its mythologies of whiteness and homogeneity.[32] Here, I located convivial bricolage in the seem-ingly contradictory national contexts of population dynamics around culture and race as translated into everyday practice. The third context was our increasingly globalized world, in which re-cent Chinese diasporas and China's geopolitical and economic rise challenge the white-dominant racial ideology and world order. At this most comprehensive, transnational level, Chinese Espresso emerges as part of a broader web of cultural and racial dynamics.

From these three levels of social context, I endeavored to un-ravel the paradox of Chinese Espresso around three central ethno-graphic questions: First: why and how did the espresso believed by many to be quintessentially Italian come to be served increas-ingly by Chinese baristas in Chinese-owned coffee bars? Second: how were Chinese baristas coming together with other local pop-ulations, both native Italians and recent immigrants, with whom they were presumably mutually exclusive socially, to perpetuate an existing form of convivial local culture? Third: how did Chi-nese baristas in Italy form their own racial understandings in their everyday social encounters with diverse local populations? By fo-cusing on the intersectional production of taste, place, and race, the "biography" of Chinese Espresso that I present in this book thus brings to light the cultural dynamics, immigrant encounters,

and racial formations around everyday places and practices of
seemingly little importance.[33]

Race, Italian Style

Razza or "race" is not a common topic of discussion in everyday
Italy. Many Italians think of race as an American fixation or "problem." I have rarely heard Italians use words like *bianco* (white) or
nero (black) to describe people in the same way as we hear them
used in the United States, although the perception that Italians are
white is in the ascendent in Italian rhetoric nowadays.[34] Instead,
cultura or "culture" is the preferred concept that native Italians use
to talk about difference. Yet, while avoiding the taboo of speaking
of race, this "culture" discourse does not prevent native Italians
from noticing race and categorizing *italiani* and *immigrati* along
classic racial lines.[35] It would, therefore, be fair to say that Italy's
racial formations conflate culture, nation, and race.[36] Immigration
is "par excellence, the name of race."[37] The widespread discourses
of cultural differences between *italiani* and *immigrati* serve to
explain social inequalities as the result of biological differences
rather than structural inequalities.[38] They function to legitimate
and justify perceptions of recent immigrants as more backward
and less civilized. This form of racism provides an ideological de-
vice that neatly harmonizes with populist discourses and alarmist
rhetoric that warn of dangers inherent in the erosion of national
and cultural boundaries by *stranieri* or "foreigners."[39]

This colonial evolutionary notion of culture, embedded in Eurocentric liberal values of progress, modernity, and rationality, has
contributed to the historical production of racism in Italy.[40] Despite its inclusionary promises of Enlightenment and humanism,
such a liberal system of values has its roots in white supremacy
and racism directed against non-white populations. The Italian
state claims itself to be a "cultural power," celebrated for centuries
with artistic superlatives and this notion of "cultural power" is the
very logic that has structured modern Italy as a nation-state.[41] In

this context, native Italians celebrate as common sense the idea that *la cultura italiana* or "Italian culture" is built upon the ancient and venerable Roman foundations that gave birth to European civilization and enabled the Renaissance. In her ethnographic project on the Freemasons in contemporary Italy, anthropologist Lilith Mahmud reveals that the dominant discourse of *cultura*, in the sense of high culture, reified the inheritable nature of culture, maintaining that it was inculcated by family and home, rather than achievable through formal educational training such as might be available to anyone.[42] This preserves systems of distinction based on the social and cultural capital of the usually white Italian family. In the same vein, media reports and popular discourses often describe the low birth rate of native Italians in contrast to the higher birth rates of recent immigrants as a "crisis" and spread panic about the demise of the Italian "race" and European culture generally.[43] An ethnographic study of the Italian transnational fashion industry in China presents another clear example of how this logic functions in the real world. The study found that Italian managers perceived *italianità* as "intuitive, a result of growing up in Italy," something that was culturally conditioned and could not be taught in a classroom.[44]

As Italy sought to construct *italianità* as connoting racial, cultural, and moral superiority, its external colonies and the Italian South became the first metaphorical and symbolic representations of Italy's marginal and racial Others.[45] Both Italy's liberal and fascist regimes launched a series of imperialist projects in the Horn of Africa, North Africa, and the Balkans, which aimed to bring Italy into the company of the wealthier, more industrialized, and more powerful European nations. Having colonies was seen as a fundamental feature of Europeanness and therefore modernity in the colonial logic of the late nineteenth and early twentieth centuries.[46] In addition, colonization abroad would, it was thought, help to flatten Italy's internal differences based on race, class, and gender, as "Italians united as nationals and as Europeans" against their colonies and the colonized Others.[47]

At the same time, internal Orientalist tropes associated Southern Italy with images of clientelism, corruption, crime, and backwardness.[48] Southern Italy became a sort of imagined colonized subject. It was often referred to as "Africa," and Southerners were "Africans" or "Moroccans." Colonial Africa thus served as a "governing metaphor" through which it was possible to make sense of Southern Italy as well.[49] Documentaries and newsreels of the 1970s often described internal migrants from Southern Italy to the more developed North as *immigrati*, as if Southern Italians were in fact foreigners from outside the national borders.

Italy's history of colonialism was largely erased or at least obfuscated in post-WWII Italian national culture.[50] In broad consensus, political conservatives, liberals, and even communists rewrote Italy's colonial and fascist history emphasizing its anti-fascist tradition, insisting that fascism was only a historical aberration in the country's long liberal and humanist tradition.[51] The construction of *italianità* thus centered on a positive image of the Italians as *brava gente*, "good, kind people," who were to be viewed in the collective memory as victims of war and fascism.[52] The combination of denial with a sort of alleged kindness and humanity that underlay this rewriting has not only covered up Italy's brutal colonial regime in its African colonies and downplayed the country's fascist history, but has also provided a cultural justification for ignoring and denying the escalating racism against non-white residents in contemporary Italy.[53]

Since the mid-1970s, millions of new arrivals, both immigrants and refugees, from over one hundred countries have settled in Italy, especially in the Northern industrial districts, where they satisfy an increasing demand for flexible and low-cost labor. Nowadays, Italy hosts one of the most diverse foreign populations in Europe, even as the country has gradually become less attractive to certain immigrants due to the enduring economic recession that began in 2008.[54] These newcomers, mainly "different" in appearance and religious and cultural practices, have "naturally" replaced Southerners and have become new "problems" in the Italian nationalist discourse. A new nationalist rhetoric has re-cast pre-1980 Italy as a racially and ethnically homogenous nation-state, as if the racialization of Southern Italians had never occurred. New racial fault-lines further facilitate the scapegoating of *immigrati* as responsible for the economic recession of 2008 and the subsequent austerity, while disempowering and breaking up the working class from below.[55]

The growing anti-immigrant and populist rhetoric often assumes that newcomers "from outside the racially circumscribed national 'community'" have a natural bent toward criminality.[56] They are presumed to be members of mafia-like underground organizations that endanger public security and ultimately erode the Italian national identity. For instance, the term *marocchini*, which originally denoted people from Morocco, has had its meaning extended as a racial pejorative that signifies North Africans more broadly and has come to be associated with drug dealing and crime.[57] Discourses on drugs and prostitution, once seen as harms brought by Southerners, are now cast as something non-Italian in nature. Pervasive stereotypes of immigrant criminality highlight a commitment to law as a new national identity differentiating Italians from *immigrati*.[58] As postcolonial theorist Paul Gilroy has suggested, the law as a national institution "symbolizes the imagined community of the nation and expresses the fundamental unity and equality of its citizens."[59]

Italy's restrictive immigration and citizenship policies at both the national and local levels have also contributed directly to the social exclusion of recent immigrants.[60] Its legislative regime that regulates entries of immigrants through predefined quotas and specific sponsorship by the employers has proved to be ineffective, as most of these newcomers work in small family businesses, or as seasonal or occasional workers in Italy's vast array of informal economies.[61] Large numbers of undocumented immigrants thus entered Italy with a tourist visa or illegally. To obtain a *permesso di soggiorno* (residence permit), however, one needs to have a labor contract for regular employment. The link between a residence permit and a labor contract thus further limits the opportunities of foreign workers, forcing them to remain in what are most often subordinate positions within informal labor markets. While earlier immigrants could still rely on the periodic amnesties offered up until 2012 to legalize their residency, many more recent comers find themselves trapped in criminal networks.[62] Earlier in the 1990s, Marzio Barbagli's research suggests that the significant increase of criminal cases committed by immigrants in Italy was also connected to the difficult social realities and "relative deprivation" that they faced.[63] Italy's policies on naturalization are in fact among the most restrictive in the European Union. People who can prove that they have an Italian ancestor who emigrated from Italy after Italian Unification (1861–1870) have the right to claim Italian citizenship immediately. In contrast, a citizen from a country outside of the EU must prove ten years of uninterrupted legal residence in Italy and in addition pass a language exam to qualify for citizenship. Italian-born children of foreign citizens must go through the same naturalization process to obtain Italian citizenship, and the application has to be submitted within a year of their reaching the age of eighteen. Terms for hyphenated identities, such as *sino-italiano* (Chinese-Italian) that correspond to "Chinese-American" in the United States have only just begun to be used in some progressive and activist circles in recent years and are not in general use throughout the country.

Italy's problematization of immigrants is also related in part to the project of defending "Fortress Europe," a term that symbolizes the European Union's wider border control regime.[64] Protecting Italians from non-white immigrants demonstrates Italy's compliance with this objective.[65] The word *extracomunitari* (extra-communitarians or non-EU members), initially used by the EU legislative bureaucracy to refer to individuals coming from countries not belonging to the EU, has become an ambiguous term to denote those who are "outside the community" in its more literal sense.[66] It is now a stigmatizing social label that implies the social exclusion of non-white immigrants from countries outside of the

EU. White Swiss and Americans are never labeled *extracomunitari*, even though neither Switzerland nor the United States belongs to the EU. People of different nationalities among the *extracomunitari* are further labeled, grouped, and differentially categorized based on fixed stereotypes.[67] Some are more integrated, some more trustworthy, others are more dangerous, and still others are more hardworking. However, unlike the United States, Italy has no stereotypical concept of a "model minority."

China is the third most common country of origin of non-EU residents in Italy, after Morocco and Albania.[68] Chinese residents, seen as both physically and culturally distinct from native Italians, are firmly categorized as *extracomunitari*. Indeed, the entire history of Chinese migration to Italy demonstrates "persistent racism" against Chinese people.[69] While the term *i cinesi* tends to racialize the entire Chinese population and erase internal differences within their ranks, the racialization of Chinese residents has its own peculiar features. Native Italians often describe Chinese workers or small entrepreneurs in the service industry as *simpatici* (nice, friendly), smiling, and hardworking, qualities regarded as typically *orientali*. Yet, the same Italians may also believe that Chinese entrepreneurship, with its visibly growing economic power in Italy, must have been achieved through unfair competition and underground *trucchi* (tricks) that often sacrifice quality and involve counterfeiting, thereby destroying local economies. Money laundering, tax evasion, and *lavoro nero* (unreported employment) are also typically charged against Chinese entrepreneurs. In contrast to the label "Made in Italy," which signifies good quality, *prodotti cinesi* or "Chinese products" are synonymous with low-quality merchandise. A neighborhood with highly visible Chinese populations, workshops, restaurants, shops, and other ethnic businesses in Prato—a Tuscan textile city and a center of the "Made in Italy" fast fashion industry—has become a ghetto-like "Chinatown" in the eyes of local *pratesi* and a "Chinese problem" to be "fixed" if the city is to maintain its *italianità*.[70] There, Chinese residents face a hostile social climate, negative and racist portrayals in the local media and from native Italians, as well as a range of everyday forms of racism and marginalization.[71]

As an Italian anthropologist friend of mine sarcastically commented, "One Chinese is exotic; many Chinese are immigrants." But, no matter whether one or many, no matter their citizenship, and no matter how attached they might be to Italy, the racialized Chinese are "matter out of place" in Mary Douglas's phrase.[72] The Italian Orientalist gaze perceives China as culturally formidable, economically ambitious, and geopolitically threatening, and people of Chinese descent as unassimilable. Such perceptions fit comfortably within broader anti-immigrant and nationalist discourses on cultural differences and immigration problems. Meanwhile, over the past four decades, Chinese residents have become one of the most prosperous and economically powerful ethnic and immigrant groups in Italy. The increasing number of "Oriental" faces as well as their products and their storefront enterprises are so visible as to constitute an integral part of the urban landscape and urban life. This development, which is part and parcel of China's rise as a global economic power, looks like a countercurrent to Italy's chronic economic stagnation. In the populist-nationalist discourse, "China's threat" has now taken on a new guise that merges admiration and resentment.

New Frontiers of Chinese Migration

The well-known Chinese TV drama series *Wenzhou Yi Jia Ren* (literally, "A Wenzhou Family"), broadcast by China Central Television in 2012, tells the story of a family from the rural Wenzhou region of southern Zhejiang Province on the southeast coast of China. The family progresses from extreme poverty to material success through entrepreneurial effort, overcoming hardships within and beyond the national border during China's Reform and Opening Up era in the 1980s. The series tells a "Legend of Entrepreneurship" (which is also the drama's English title) that showcases the social transformation of contemporary China from an impoverished third-world country to a global economic super-power, a narrative in full accord with the state's official account of the reform period. The drama thus glorifies the "Wenzhou spirit" as the Zeitgeist of post-Mao China's struggle for development and prosperity. Indeed, the rural hinterlands of southern Zhejing, including Wenzhou and its neighboring Qingtian County, are the places of origin of most Chinese baristas in Italy. [73]

There is a reason why this Chinese TV drama chose a Wenzhou story to exemplify "rising up." People from Wenzhou are well-known within China as migrant merchants, traders, and artisans. Due to environmental and socioeconomic circumstances, Wenzhou generated numerous surplus agricultural laborers who were historically engaged in migratory labor and mercantile activities, a trend that was only briefly disrupted during the Maoist era. When China's state policy turned towards a market economy in 1978, Wenzhou was the first area to react by embracing a privatized economy, which later was dubbed the "Wenzhou Model."[74] Numerous migrants from the hinterlands of Southern Zhejiang became a "floating population" in search of employment and business opportunities and established migrant settlements in China's urban centers.[75] Many others, encouraged by both central and local government policies, instead reached Europe and other parts of the world where they sought new economic trajectories.[76] Kinship and native-place networks, crucial for many other migrant groups as well, are their primary means for organizing their travels, economic activities, and social lives.[77] Through wide-ranging transnational networks, they are able to occupy economic niches that fit into the local ecologies of their destinations, from *baihuo* shops in Cape Verde, to wholesale markets in Brazil, and from coffee bars in Italy to lingerie shops in Egypt.[78]

The recent Chinese arrivals with whom I spoke are aware of the region's reputation for emigration and small-scale entrepreneurship. They often emphasize and take pride in their supposed cosmopolitan sensibility that is associated with their regional identity as merchants. As people from there often claim, "we," Wenzhouese (or sometimes more generally Zhejiangese) "go wherever there is business," and we are able to "do business with anyone" and to "manage any business." This claim echoes Li Zhang's ethnographic study of Wenzhou migrants in Beijing in the 1990s.[79] While long-time urbanites in Beijing categorized rural migrants as a "floating population" and described them as dirty, uncivil, provincial, and backwards, Wenzhou migrants highlighted their flexibility, self-reliance, industriousness, vitality, determination, and bravery. All these self-identified positive qualities, as Li Zhang argued, served as a counter-discourse on urban belonging that transcended a fixed locality and allowed them to self-fashion spatial mobility as a way of life, while drawing boundaries from other urbanites.

For my Chinese interlocutors from Southern Zhejiang, baristas or not, the coffee bar business was nothing special, simply one of many small enterprises through which their families were able to *zhuanqian* (make money) in Italy and elsewhere. But, if we look back at the modern history of emigration from China, a cosmopolitan sensibility was by no means unique to people from Wenzhou. The model of entrepreneurial migration was typical of people from three *qiaoxiang* (emigrants' hometowns) provinces—Zhejiang, Fujian, Guangdong—all on the southeast coast of China.[80] In these areas, petty capitalism has historically been what historian Hill Gates has referred to as "China's motor" for both the state and the society.[81] Numerous rural laborers from these *qiaoxiang* left voluntarily or were forced to leave their homes and seek a living as *huagong* (Chinese laborers) or *huashang* (Chinese merchants) in other parts of the world.[82] These Chinese emigrants developed economic niches in colonial Southeast Asia beginning in the 1500s, in the settler-colonial societies of the Americas and Australasia by the mid-1800s, and more recently in Europe in the early twentieth century.[83]

Unlike the "old" emigrants, "new" Chinese emigrants—those who arrived after 1978—are inextricably linked to China's growing participation in the global economy. The Chinese managers and entrepreneurs who today are involved in the transnational capital-

ism of fast fashion in China like to highlight their cosmopolitanism or "worldly knowledge," which "encompasses their abilities to
transcend culture to embrace the seemingly universal aspects of
capitalist business practices."[84] More than describing a business
strategy, this discourse provides a cultural explanation for the economic success of both Chinese emigrants and of China itself as a
rising economic power. It reveals a newfound cultural confidence
that Chinese entrepreneurs feel in their ability to navigate global
capitalism. Yet, one thing is missing from this cultural explanation.
It does not yet give us a broader structural perspective in which to
contextualize the international mobility of labor amid economic
globalization and global capitalism.[85]

Chinese emigrants, mostly laborers and merchants, have participated in developing a global trading and production system
alongside European colonialists' global expansion since the six-
teenth century. Like other international migrations from the
Global South, the "new" Chinese mass emigration after 1978 was
also a response to the receiving societies' declining fertility and the
presence of segmented labor markets in which immigrants could
be employed.[86] While many aspired to become entrepreneurs,
these migrants were first of all laborers in pursuit of better economic opportunities through transnational mobility.[87]

Chinese and other migrant businesses are certainly not "new."
They have, however, become increasingly noticeable in Italian and
other European cities that have experienced mass immigration
since the 1980s. What is new in the Chinese-run coffee bar business in Italy is that, as a racialized immigrant group, Chinese labor
is fitting itself into an existing "traditional" niche at the core of
Italian culture, which was previously occupied by native Italian
merchants and laborers. Indeed, in an unprecedented step in the
history of outward Chinese migration, these Chinese laborers and
merchants can neither reliably use Chinese identity as a selling
point, nor depend on Chinese manufacturing and supply chains to
market cheap products. And this is not just happening in Italy. The
phenomenon of Chinese entrepreneurs submerging their ethnic

identity in order to pursue a business niche predicated on reproducing a local commodity culture and selling local taste to local
populations is also occurring in Spain, France, the Netherlands,
and elsewhere in Western Europe.[88]

The tale of Chinese Espresso also marks a new chapter in the
story of "Chinese among others," to echo historian Philipp Kuhn
in his book that extensively explores Chinese emigrants' experiences, hopes, and sorrows around the world.[89] In this global history some Chinese laborers and merchants strove to make a living
and survive hostility from host societies through residential segregation and in ethnic enclaves, such as with the many US Chinatowns.[90] Others acted as "middleman minorities" providing goods
and services to marginalized racial and ethnic groups, typically in
poor neighborhoods.[91] A clear social boundary was thus drawn
between themselves and other ethnic groups, towards whom they
held negative and prejudicial attitudes. A typical coffee bar in Italy
by contrast is neither an enclave business nor a middleman minority niche. It is a fundamental and long-established urban social
space and a "traditional" food sector, where Chinese baristas must
leverage all of their "integration capital" to connect, interact, and
live with others, willingly or reluctantly.[92]

Yet, like middleman minorities and other Chinese shopkeepers
in poorer countries across the globe, Chinese baristas in Italy also
face the predicament of being simultaneously economically privileged and socially vulnerable.[93] Their economic privilege often
coexists with legal and political vulnerability, as shown in an ethnographic study of the moral struggles between street-level bureaucrats and Chinese residents in Tanzania.[94] In South Africa, Chinese
residents have become targets of both a corrupt state and common
criminals, while they ambiguously shift between the identities of
whiteness and blackness.[95] In the United States, Chinese and other
Asian Americans, regardless of their socioeconomic status, have
long confronted anti-Asian racism and even violence aimed at
them. And, as many studies show, racial tensions also exist between
Asians and other disadvantaged American racial groups.[96]

The ambiguous power dynamics that Chinese baristas face in Italy are contextualized within a white-dominant country that has undergone a change in its demographic composition as a result of various forms of migration.[97] Racial encounters between Chinese immigrants and the dominant white Italian population are complicated by South-South encounters. Thus, the story of Chinese baristas producing an Italian nationalist commodity while preserving a distinctly Italian social space goes beyond a Eurocentric narrative about immigrant-host relations or a European society's reception of immigrants. This new narrative further complicates our understanding of racial formation within the shifting racial landscapes and realities of the Global North, in which an immigrant group, themselves subject to racialization, in turn racialize other groups.

Bologna as an Ethnographic Context

I visited Bologna several times during my exchange program in Trento. As a tourist, I was amazed by the city's well-preserved *centro storico* with its two medieval towers rising into the blue sky and its seemingly endless porticoes and eye-catching red rooftops. I was drawn to it as well as the site of the University of Bologna, the oldest university in the Western world. As a student from China, Bologna had another attraction for me, however, one that had nothing to do with what I read in my *Lonely Planet* travel guide. There was a Chinese grocery store just a fifteen-minute-walk from the railway station, and this became a must-go destination for me whenever I passed by Bologna by train. After I embarked upon this project for my Ph.D. dissertation, I learned that the *quartiere* just outside the *centro storico* where the Chinese grocer was located was called Bolognina or "little Bologna." It is notorious for its higher concentration of people with migrant backgrounds, including Chinese. Chinese speakers themselves refer to two long streets passing through this area as *zhongguo jie* (Chinese Streets) due to the high concentration of Chinese storefronts and residents found there.

What is not widely known among younger *bolognesi* is that there have been Chinese people living in the city since the 1920s. Local legends like that of the Sun family and their gas company Sun Gas, which was founded in the 1950s and provided residential gas, are now only conversation pieces, sometimes mentioned when elderly *bolognesi* recall their early, curious peeks into the city's mysterious *comunità cinese* (Chinese community).[98] The current Chinese population in Bologna, as in other parts of Italy, has its origins primarily in the mass migration from China that began in the mid-1980s. Registered Chinese citizens in the city of Bologna increased from 269 in 1986 to nearly 4,000 in 2016.[99] Most early comers worked in the textile manufacturing sector, but more recently a large number have moved to restaurants and other service industries, including coffee bars, and have relocated their homes nearer to their workplaces. Although the number of Chinese residents in Bologna is not particularly large, their presence in the city has become increasingly visible, alongside other nonwhite populations, due to their active engagement in the commercial and service industries that spread across the city.

A major urban center for centuries, Bologna is the seventh most populous city in Italy with a population of nearly 400,000 and a greater metropolitan area that hosts around one million inhabitants.[100] Its vigorous service-sector economy and the dynamic small enterprises in the industrial districts of surrounding areas, which are considered a core component of the so-called "Third Italy," have recruited numerous laborers from outside the area since the post-war era.[101] Indeed, Bologna is a city of migrants. By 2011, two-thirds of the registered residents of the city had some sort of migrant background, either domestic or from abroad.[102] The city was in fact one of the major destinations for internal mass migration from rural areas and from Southern Italy during the post-war economic boom in the 1950s and 1960s. More immigrants arrived in the mid- to late 1980s, and by 2016, the number of registered foreign citizens reached nearly 60,000 or 15 percent of the Bologna's population. Most came from Eastern Europe, North Africa, South

Asia, the Philippines, and China.[103] These more recent immigrants, like the earlier internal migrant workers, typically worked as either low-wage laborers or were self-employed small entrepreneurs in this aging, post-industrial city, where the local population was in demographic decline.[104]

Bologna is also known by a nickname, *la rossa* or "the Red," due originally to its many red brick towers and buildings. That moniker took on an additional political connotation in the twentieth century, as Bologna was run by the Italian Communist Party (PCI) from the end of the war until the party's dissolution in 1991.[105] Even in the 2018 and 2022 general elections, Bologna was one of the few electoral districts in which the center-left coalition, defeated nationally, was able to eke out a victory. This strong leftist tradition, however, has not spared newcomers from the effects of racism. David Kertzer's ethnographic study of a poor *quartiere* in Bologna during the 1970s shows that sentiments against Southern Italians, the major *immigrati* at that period, were strong enough to bridge the political schism between the Catholic Church and the Communist Party, thereby helping to promote a collective identity for Northerners.[106] Davide Però's study also reveals that while Bologna's left-leaning municipal administration often showcased the city as exemplary of their innovative, progressive, and inclusionary social policies toward materially disadvantaged and culturally marginalized people, including immigrants, these policies are not as supportive of integration and multiculturalism as their reputation might suggest.[107] Similarly, Bruno Riccio's study of Senegalese immigrants in Emilia-Romagna exposes the ambiguous immigration policies that operate there under a logic of closure and exclusion, even while the region claims to recognize the rights of newcomers.[108]

I chose Bologna as my field site specifically because its demographic, economic, and political contexts were well suited to an exploration of my primary interest; namely conviviality. More specifically, I wanted to learn how Chinese residents managed to live together with Italian and other local populations rather than in relative segregation. Like other cities across Northern and Central Italy, Bologna had experienced striking growth in the number of its foreign-owned coffee bars. The number reached 461 in 2011, taking in more than 16 percent of the 2,852 coffee bars operating in metropolitan Bologna that year. This percentage is higher than the national average (10.2 percent), but consistent with that in other regions in Northern and Central Italy.[109] While no available official statistics on the total number of Chinese ownerships is available, the Statistics Office at Bologna's Chamber of Commerce recorded that in 2014 half of the foreign-born "sole proprietorship" coffee bars were Chinese-owned. When I began my fieldwork in the same year, my estimate of the total number of Chinese-owned coffee bars was between 200 and 300, comprising ten percent of the total coffee bars in metropolitan Bologna.[110] And Chinese coffee bar ownership continued to increase until the Covid-19 pandemic. Some Chinese-owned establishments are located at the heart of Bologna's *centro storico*, where they target tourists and street shoppers and rely on their white employees to advertise their quality. Some are in the city's affluent neighborhoods and serve sophisticated drinks to well-off professionals. Still others are located in the university area and sell cheap alcoholic drinks to hard-pressed college students. I noticed, however, that most Chinese-owned coffee bars are *bar tradizionali* (traditional bars) located in working-class neighborhoods, in urban peripheries, and in provincial towns. Although other urban dwellers do stop or may even have their daily coffee rituals there, the patrons of these coffee bars are primarily marginalized people, including working-class men of different generations who often have migrant backgrounds both from within Italy and from beyond its national borders.

My ethnographic journey in Bologna started with fourteen months of intensive fieldwork between May 2014 and July 2015, and then continued in short annual visits that were only interrupted by the Covid-19 pandemic.[111] No longer a passerby, I explored emotions and relationships in the city and made myself live as a part of these discoveries. I established personal connections

FIGURE 1.1. A bar sign under Bologna's famous porticoes.
Note the "T" in the back advertising that this establishment also sells
tobacco products. (Photograph by author)

with many people, most of whom lived at the margins of society and whose everyday lives in no way resembled *la dolce vita* (the sweet life) that many foreign tourists like to imagine. Despite having been in Italy for many years or even their entire lives, the people whom I typically came to know in Chinese-managed coffee bars, whether they were owners or customers, had seen very little of this *Bel Paese* (the Beautiful Country, one of Italy's nicknames) and experienced Italy as something far less romantic and pleasant than the Italy foreign tourists enjoyed. These local inhabitants were often stuck in a street-corner bar, where they spent the bulk of their working, and even leisure hours either making or drinking Chinese Espresso, day after day. This ethnographic journey in Bologna thus became also my own quest to demystify the imaginary "destination Italy" that was and still is so deeply linked to a romanticized past with "a strong reputation for resisting commodification through historical preservation, artisanal craftsmanship, espresso hegemony, and the like."[112] It is an Italy that is intensely involved in globalization, just like most countries and regions throughout the world.

Ethnographer, Barista, and Bricoleur

As an anthropologist, I ask structural questions about the forces that undergird the social and cultural complexity of humans as they go through seemingly banal and trivial everyday experiences, and I try to make sense of these using my "sociological imagination."[113] Throughout the whole period of my intensive fieldwork, primarily in Bologna, I visited more than one hundred coffee bars, about sixty of which were owned and managed by Chinese people. As a young woman, I followed the local gendered social norms when I entered a coffee bar alone as a customer (more about this in Chapter Three). During those five or ten minutes of drinking a coffee or some other non-alcoholic beverage, I often initiated conversations with the barista. In this way, I could gain a general idea about the place, experience the whole process of the service, observe the composition of the customers, and in some cases hear stories about the coffee bar. However, it was almost impossible for me to simply sit with a cup of coffee for hours to observe the activities of the baristas and their customers, as few of them were a place like Starbucks where college students or young professionals could connect to Wi-Fi and sit alone with their laptops for hours.

When I had established a certain trust and built a relationship with the Chinese baristas and their families, their coffee bars became somewhat more accessible for my intensive fieldwork. I was able to regularly visit eight Chinese-owned coffee bars where I engaged with the Chinese baristas and their customers, either for at least two months or even throughout my entire fieldwork. Due to my Chinese appearance, some customers thought I was a friend or a relative of the family, or even a "girlfriend" when the barista was a young man. While consuming my drinks (in many cases offered for free by the Chinese owners), I watched how coffees and other products were produced and served. I observed interactions between Chinese baristas and their customers, and between customers from diverse social backgrounds. I also took opportunities to chat with the baristas when they were not serving their clientele. We spoke in Mandarin Chinese or Italian, depending on the Chinese baristas' preference. Our conversations were often interrupted by customers who joined our chats to give an opinion, make a joke, or just exchange some words of greeting. Similar to the experiences of Jane Cowan, who conducted research on gendered everyday sociability in the coffee bars of a Northern Greek town, I also made unexpected discoveries "after sharing endless cups of coffee," and I too often felt myself enmeshed in the "meanings and reciprocities" of such sociability.[114] To maintain the authentic vibe of our interactions, I decided not to record any conversations that happened at the bar counter. My only recordings were of one-on-one conversations where I sat down with my interlocutors in a more formal interview setting. I did take notes or simply jotted down key words on my smartphone during the intervals between our interactions, and then once I returned home, wrote more complete accounts of the day's observations. Quite often I also showed the notes to my interlocutors to confirm what they had said and what they meant.

In December 2014, I got a chance to move even closer to my subject matter. For four months I served as an informal and unpaid apprentice barista. In effect, I was transformed from a mere "participant observer" to an active "observing participant."[115] Apprenticeship was "both a mode of learning and a field method" that opened another door to ethnographic understanding.[116] It allowed me to gain first-hand knowledge about how Chinese baristas learned the manual skills needed to produce a local taste recognized as familiar by their diverse customers, and how they viewed their work and developed their business and management strategies. The experience also enabled me to build a closer relationship with the Chinese owner's family, as well as with other Chinese baristas, with whom I could share and discuss barista skills and from whom I could learn something about coffee bar management. Working as a barista further allowed me to interact directly with customers, build up a new type of relationship with them, and experience intercultural encounters.

I became part of a community that would serve my ethnographic goals by providing an instructive conceptual framework within which I could examine the ways in which established residents and newcomers convened at a very local level within a national border.[117] The coffee bars were first of all a sensory field where I engaged in an embodied sensory investigation of Chinese baristas' labor skills of taste-making.[118] They offered also an analytical social field at the intersection between a core local institution and an international migration. In short, I had found a productive setting for an investigation into conviviality and diversity. I was ready now to follow earlier ethnographies of encounters by giving attention to the "interactive and unequal dynamics of power that shape culture-making across relationships of difference" rather than merely focusing on "a single population or cultural group."[119]

These ethnographic encounters constitute "points of interpenetration and mediation at the center of the investigation."[120] In particular, I apply the "social poetics" approach to explore diverse aspects of verbal and non-verbal communications and interpersonal interactions in order to observe how meanings and relationships are constructed intersubjectively through conventions and inventions, compliance and infringement.[121]

Alongside Chinese-managed coffee bars, I was a part also of social networks centered around my two Italian host families and the *Chiesa Evangelica Cinese in Italia di Bologna* (Chinese Evangelical Christian Church of Bologna in Italy). These locations provided me with broader social contexts, where I probed the issues of exclusion, segregation, and non-encounters. The families—one *bolognese* for three generations, the other with a migration background from Southern Italy—furnished me, a guest family member, with opportunities to observe native Italian families' social and cultural activities. By participating in their daily lives, I obtained first-hand experience of their family life as it was embedded in the historical Italy, and as it played its role in the country's ongoing social transformation. I learned about their perceptions of culture, immigration, China, and other social issues, and of course I learned about their coffee bar consumption habits. Each was a piece of the larger picture and deepened my understanding of the social realities behind Chinese Espresso.

I got access to the community at the Chinese Evangelical Christian Church through the introduction of some Chinese Christian baristas, and this religious community introduced me to additional Chinese Christian families engaged in the coffee bar business. These Chinese Christians exemplified wider patterns of Chinese immigration to Italy, including migration trajectories, class composition, family values, professional distribution, and social exclusion.[122] They not only became the major Chinese social network through which I became acquainted with most of my key Chinese interlocutors, but also an important window into how Chinese residents in Bologna live their social and cultural lives outside business spaces, as well as how they construct their Chinese identity.

My everyday life in the "field" was thus split among three independent but simultaneously interrelated social locations. I frequently shifted between Italian middle-class families and multiracial working-class coffee bar communities and swung between the mainstream society of my Italian hosts and the marginalized Chinese immigrant community. Through these shifts and navigations, I learned how my different interlocutors perceived me, how they defined my positionality, and how that positionality was contested and negotiated in each of these social locations. In this way, my own intersectional positionality became both a particular methodological approach to understanding knowledge production and an epistemological representation of the structural inequalities under which my fieldwork experience was constructed.[123]

These experiences led me to rethink the issue of the "native" anthropologist. Some earlier reflexive accounts had already called into question the dichotomy between "native" and "non-native" by emphasizing each ethnographer's multiple identifications that would impact their fieldwork experiences and interpretation of cultural "texts."[124] Moreover, the notion of the "native" in anthropology is itself problematic as it is a product of the "West" and carries colonial connotations of the "othering" of non-white people.[125] The term "natives" conventionally refers to people and communities that are confined in places distant from "the metropolitan West" in the anthropological imagination.[126] The anthropological construction of the "native" and "otherness" thus spatializes cultural difference, in the same way as the anti-immigrant politics of nativism, which likewise assume an irreducible and incommensurable "difference" between the "foreign" cultures of immigrants and the "home" cultures of a host society.[127] So-called "native" anthropologists thus presumably enjoy linguistic advantages, cultural affinity, and an insider's "privileged" access to ethnographic truth when they study their own "skinfolk," cultures, "home societies," and co-national migrants.[128] In migration studies, this divide can readily lead to what Andreas Wimmer and Nina Glick Schiller have called a "methodological nationalism" that takes for granted ethno-national distinctions as primary boundaries on both methodological and analytical levels.[129] In my case, my shared nationality was not sufficient for my Chinese interlocutors to treat me as one of their own. In their eyes, I was one of the *liuxuesheng* (Chinese international students) who had different migration motivations, life trajectories, and educational backgrounds from their own. Nor did we share a regional identity, as I did not come from the same geographical area as they did.

I perceive myself as a "multiply inscribed" subject rather than an essentialized "Chinese woman" who enjoys "a kind of privileged nativism in the anti-hegemonic representation of difference."[130] As a "positioned subject," I was aware that my multiple identifications, including gender, race, ethnicity, social class, and age, among others, intersected with one another to shape an intricate relationship with my interlocutors.[131] My "Oriental" appearance announced my "difference" from both the biology and culture of Italians, even though I spoke fluent Italian. This essentialized "difference" further assigned me a racialized identity identical to that of my Chinese interlocutors, for we had shared experiences of various forms of discrimination and racism. As a woman, I encountered "male gazes" and "patriarchal gazes" that came not only from native Italian men, but also from older and younger Chinese men, as well as other male immigrants from varied national backgrounds. These gazes all formed "a part of the overall functioning of power," in Michel Foucault's words, that policed me and regulated my fieldwork practices.[132]

My experience of growing up in mainland China and doing my Ph.D. in Hong Kong, going to Europe for ethnographic fieldwork, and finally settling in the United States since my postdoctoral work, has provided me with a "multi-situated perspective" and transnational sensibilities that inform my anthropological inquiry.[133] I bring a decolonized and feminist lens, voice, and perspective to anthropological knowledge production built primarily on "the historically constructed divide between the West and the non-West."[134] This entire process reflects many years of my efforts in learning through the "frictions of encounter" with my diverse research subjects amid a web of structural inequalities and intricate power dynamics.[135] None of the putatively disempowering factors in my life—racial and ethnic identity, gender, and age—proved barriers to my ethnographic knowledge production. In this process, both personal emotions and interpersonal relationships helped me to unravel the complexity of others' social lives, values, ideologies, and ethics, and to understand how they reshaped new realities. Both structural inequality and empowering ethnographic moments, deliberately designed or not, have shaped my embodied experiences in the "field" and constitute key components of how I go about producing ethnographic knowledge. There was much serendipity—even at vulnerable moments—that came to my aid.[136] In this sense, *Chinese Espresso* is also a kind of bricolage, produced by ethnographic encounters characterized by contingency, compromises, and resistance. To echo Deleuze and Guattari's claim, we are all "bricoleurs."

The Organization of This Book

Chinese Espresso is a part of the ongoing story of Chinese baristas in Italy. After setting up the conceptual and contextual framework of the paradox around the very notion of Chinese Espresso, the following five chapters are planned to deliberately follow the protagonists' steps little by little, as they construct conviviality across differences. Chapter Two, "Becoming Baristas," investigates the availability of family labor, comparative ideologies of work and transformative aspirations, and other economic and non-economic factors that contributed to the transfer of ownership from Italians to Chinese in this very "niche" micro-enterprise. Chapter Three, "Situating Space," discusses how Chinese entrepreneurs categorize coffee bars and situate themselves in their variegated socialities, which are often marked by social class. Chapter Four, "Reproducing Taste," examines Chinese bricoleurs' manual and sensory labor in making mutually constituted taste and place. Chapter Five, "Performing Sociability," shifts the focus to baristas' emotional labor as they struggle with, but sometimes also strategically deploy cultural essentialism, stereotypes, and misunderstandings, as well as various forms of structural inequality, all the while attempting to convey hospitality in the quest for a convivial space. The final Chapter Six, "Contesting Racialization," probes Chinese baristas' racial formations within and beyond the convivial coffee bar community, as well as the limits of conviviality.

The three vignettes encapsulate the book's biography. "Cappuccino Time" in the Prelude and "Coffee Break" in the Intermezzo describe, in chronological sequence, two ethnographic moments in a typical coffee bar in Italy of the sort that anyone might experience. The Coda, "Closing Time," then updates the account with a survey of changes that I noticed over the years, suggesting that while the book must end, there is yet an unclear future ahead for Chinese Espresso.

2

Becoming Baristas

IN A SEASIDE TOWN SOUTH OF VENICE, a thirty-something Chinese woman is the new barista at a local coffee bar that serves the town's elderly residents. She is virtually an indentured worker who puts in long hours to pay off the debt that she owes to the underground, mafia-like Chinese organization that arranged for her journey to Italy and promised eventually to pay for her son's passage as well. This "Chinese mafia" seemingly controls various types of Chinese-operated businesses in Italy, ranging from restaurants to sweatshops and from wholesale businesses to coffee bars. In the beginning, the young mother barely spoke Italian and had few barista skills, but gradually her language and her skills improved. Meanwhile, she established a friendship with one of her regular *clienti* or customers, a recently widowed white fisherman, which hovered at the margins of romance. Their relationship, however, encountered strong opposition from both the local Italian and Chinese communities. The fisherman ultimately died alone of a broken heart, and the woman was transferred, once again by her mysterious Chinese bosses to another city where she at last is reunited with her son from China.

This is the plot of the Italian film *Io sono Li* (English title: *Shunli and the Poet*), which was released at the Venice Film Festival in 2011. Several Italian friends watched this award-winning film and recommended it to me as a must see. The film indeed sensitively captures how mutual distrust, prejudices, and stereotypes by both

Chinese immigrants and local Italian society present obstacles to multicultural conviviality between the two groups. However, in spite of its anti-racist and anti-xenophobic intent, it ironically adopts a racialized and Orientalist depiction of Chinese residents in Italy. Among its many racialized tropes, the mysterious Chinese underground organization echoes widespread rumors in Italy that the *mafia cinese* (Chinese mafia) is the mastermind behind the boom in the prosperity of Chinese business ventures in Italy and, more to our point, the reason why there are so many Chinese people running coffee bars.

I heard stories, rumors, and urban legends about this "Chinese mafia" from my Italian host families, from customers in the coffee bars, and from friends and the friends of friends. The first mention came a few days after my arrival in Bologna in May 2014. I was at a family reunion feast where I met my first Italian host Melissa's extended family. Hearing about my project, Melissa's father—a retired licensed land surveyor in his seventies—told me his theory: A mafia-like Chinese organization purchases coffee bars for purposes of money laundering, regardless of their profitability as bars *per se*. To further convince me, his wife, a retired chemist in her sixties, told me about a *bolognese* acquaintance who sold his business to some Chinese who offered "an amount to which he couldn't say no" with "a suitcase full of cash." Suspicion about Chinese buyers' sources of capital is also included in an FIPE report that addresses the increasing foreign ownership and declining Italian ownership of coffee bars in Italy.[1]

Rumors can create reality in the minds of people, rather than merely reflecting their existing social perceptions.[2] The word *mafia* is nowadays widely applied to transnational criminal organizations in the English-speaking world. Yet, this originally Italian word also offers a convenient and reductionist label for imagining old and new "subaltern" groups, to borrow Gramsci's word, within Italy's national borders and has been associated with political knowledge production in the service of anti-Southerner and anti-immigrant politics in Italy.[3] The *mafia cinese* was initially a metaphor for crime reporting created by Italian journalism in the 1990s and applied to interpret the mass migration from China involving human trafficking, undocumented labor, and other illicit economic activities.[4] It has since become the dominant interpretative lens through which Chinese residents' economic and social activities in Italy are interpreted. The discourse of the *mafia cinese* thus belongs to the wider genre of anti-immigrant politics and racism in Italy that has "ridden on the coat-tails of anti-southernism."[5] Old representations of Southern Italians were transposed onto the new immigrants who were now the imagined Other in contrast to *Italianità* or "Italian-ness."

My long-term fieldwork uncovered no evidence for the existence of any wide-reaching "Chinese mafia" networks that used coffee bars at camouflage.[6] What I instead discovered were Chinese immigrants' unfinished stories of "becoming," despite social, structural, and material obstacles.[7] In these stories, they emphasized their aspirational efforts and the hopes that sustained them through their persistent pursuit of a better life. Coffee bars were, it seems, one of the few businesses available and accessible to them at this historical moment. Many also confessed that they simply followed the successful examples of other Chinese immigrants. Yet, if one traces the Chinese-run businesses in Italy back to the early 2000s or even earlier, it turns out that at that time coffee bars were not even a remote option for potential Chinese immigrant entrepreneurs. The FIPE's annual report of 2008 described foreign ownership of bars, in particular by Chinese, as "real news in recent years." Indeed, most of the Chinese coffee bar owners I encountered in Bologna began their businesses after 2008, most of them after 2010. But only eleven years later, in 2021, one out of ten coffee bars in Italy were owned by Chinese residents and one out of six Chinese residents in Italy was working in this business niche.[8]

I was unable to determine who exactly was the first Chinese coffee bar owner in Italy. I did, however, meet several Chinese baristas who claimed to be the first or at least among the first Chinese to take up this business. Lisa was one of them. She and her husband had managed a coffee bar in the *centro storico* of Bologna since 2003. The couple spoke fluent Italian. "They even had a *bolognese* accent," according to some Italian customers. My conversations with them were always in Italian, as they could barely speak Mandarin Chinese. Yet, they told me that both of them could understand the Chinese dialect that their parents spoke. Lisa had migrated to Italy with her mother in 1988 when she was five years old, joining her father who had lived there for several years. It was in Italy that she received her primary and middle school education. She then went on to a secondary vocational school to study restaurant and hotel management, since her family was managing a Chinese restaurant at the time. Barista skills were included in her curriculum, but she did not start her own coffee bar business until she married a Chinese man with a similar migration background in 2003. An elderly Italian couple had managed a coffee bar close to Lisa's parents' restaurant for decades, and they wanted to sell the business and retire. The young Chinese couple bought it, and like the previous owners, they worked as baristas together with two hired Italian workers. When they were working, Lisa's parents-in-law took care of their three children, cooking for them and getting them off to school.

Most of the coffee bars in Italy are micro-enterprises, very often family-owned and managed. The FIPE's annual reports reveal that the average number of workers of each firm has consistently been less than four, including both self-employed and hired labor. With few exceptions, both the Chinese forerunners and the latecomers to this business typically acquired an established coffee bar, at least as their first venture, rather than opening a new one, and they usually maintained the business model of self-employed family management with little to no hired wage labor. This means that Chinese owners are not forming a new business niche but filling an existing one. They serve as a new generation of baristas supplanting the previous Italian generation. Thus, the mystery of Chinese Espresso is not simply why this niche has become such a popular one for Chinese residents in Italy, but also why it has been abandoned by native Italians. In other words, how did this "fill-in" model of immigrant entrepreneurship come into being?

The family ownership and management of coffee bar businesses is consistent with the "Made in Italy" model of small-scale industrialization and capitalist development that relies on cheap, flexible, and reciprocal kin labor.[9] In this business mode, kin-based social relations become the building blocks of capitalist value production.[10] This is a hybrid economic form, and it allows many small, independent coffee bars to survive despite their small profit margins, while larger-scale enterprises that rely on hired wage labor struggle.[11] Starbucks and other large transnational coffeehouse chains have thus remained marginal in Italy despite the country's huge coffee market.[12] The dependency on family labor, however, also can lead to instability and vulnerability. A family is often forced to terminate or sell their business when family members become unable or unwilling to work at the coffee bar. While in the past, other native Italians typically took over these businesses, now it is often foreign residents, and Chinese in particular, who are doing so.

My analysis employs a comparative lens to examine the transformation of ownership from Italians to the Chinese in this niche micro-enterprise. I focus on the changing availability of family labor for both the Italian and Chinese generations of coffee bar owners, as well as on the social formations in which this takes place. Rather than employing capital-centric theories of economics, I concentrate on ethnographically thick descriptions of individual families' social relations within households and within kin-based networks that shape economic decision-making and practices.[13] These family stories make clear the role of kinship systems, family structures, social relations, values, and ethics, as well as other non-economic forces in the formation of this new immigrant business niche. As I will show later in this chapter, micro-level economic activities and individual family stories are embedded in larger opportunity structures and sociological contexts.[14] Demographic changes in class and ethnic composition resulting from Italy's aging population and the arrival of immigrants, the shifting composition of its Chinese resident population, and economic restructuring on the level of both Chinese ethnic and national economies have all impacted the formation of the Chinese generation of baristas. These "convivial bricoleurs" have made do with the resources available to them to navigate through uncertainty and precarity. In the process they have created their own economic and social history and have given existential meaning to their lives in Italy.

A Vacated Niche

The Italian coffee bar business has been in a steady decline since the Great Recession of 2008, if not before. Over this period, thousands more coffee bar businesses closed than opened each year. The explanations for this decline are many and varied, but they are predominantly socioeconomic. Some Italian owners trapped in the rapid gentrification of Bologna and its surrounding peripheral areas provided me with financial figures chronicling the decreased profitability of their businesses due to the increasing costs of rent, labor, taxes, utilities, and other expenses. Some also complained of competition from supermarkets and shopping malls. These large-scale commercial enterprises with advantageous pricing undercut one of the traditional selling points of their coffee bars, namely easy access to food, drinks, and other consumables for people living and working around the establishments. Some coffee bars also faced competition from small grocery stores, typically migrant-run businesses, as they also sold bottled beers and other alcoholic drinks. Lastly, the economic downturn reduced both the number of customers and the level of their individual consumption.[15]

Many coffee bar owners have managed to stay in business, however, in spite of decreasing profitability. Marco is one of them. He runs a coffee bar on the street corner of the peripheral town outside of Bologna where I lived with my second Italian host family. It is a tiny *bar latteria* that focuses on both coffee and dairy products. There are only two tables with a few seats outdoors and no indoor seating at all. Marco told me that he purchased the business in the 1980s, but that it had been in existence since the 1960s. He has kept it going longer than any of the other five to six prior owners. From Monday to Friday this man in his late forties arrives at the bar at 5:20 am and leaves at 7:30 pm, except on Saturdays when he closes at 1 pm. Sunday is his only day off. On weekdays he pulls down the roller shutter for two hours from 1 pm to 3 pm, locking himself inside while he enjoys his lunch and often takes a nap.

"I have been lucky enough to continue my small *bar* without the need for an employee, otherwise nothing would be left for me," Marco told me in 2015. According to him, this *bar latteria* was the only one that survived of an original ten in the town. His "luck," however, had a great do with the reciprocal nature of his family-run business. Marco never married. His parents, who live in another neighborhood in the same town, send lunch to him every working day. They also help look after the business when he has a serious fever or tooth pain or when other things come up. Without the contribution of their unpaid labor, Marco's business would not be tenable. Marco has no intention of closing or selling his business. The *piacere* or "pleasure" that he finds in his barista job will, he believes, keep him content managing this otherwise *faticoso* (tiring, laborious) business for decades. Yet, he also admits that it will be increasingly difficult for him to continue as he gets older, as his parents are already well advanced in age.

Faticoso is a word I often heard younger-generation native Italians use to describe the self-employed coffee bar business. A coffee bar located in the central *piazza* of the small town where my first host family lived used to be managed by a Sicilian couple. After migrating to Northern Italy in the 1970s, the couple bought the business with savings that they had accumulated through several years of hard work. The coffee bar had been quite profitable, and they had stayed in the business for decades. When they reached the age of retirement, however, their daughter had no interest in continuing the business, because it was too *faticoso* and she would not have *tempo libero* (free time) to "go to the beach and on holidays." In the end, the daughter opened a new stationery shop with money obtained by selling the coffee bar to a Chinese family. Opening hours were shorter at a stationery shop and her family could "enjoy the weekends." Her understanding of *faticoso* relates to the temporal dimension of the relationship between work and leisure. It illustrates the strict capitalist demarcation of the domain of "work" from the domain of "life," whereby the former is a time of production and the latter of leisure.[16] The *tempo libero*, "holidays," and "weekends" that she wants are not possible in a condition of self-employment in a coffee bar business, where the longer time of production that is required conflicts with her imaginary of a good life with "free time."

This *faticoso* business, however, was once considered a good path towards economic autonomy by Italian internal rural migrants, Marco and the Sicilian couple among them. An oral history narrated by Angiolino Campagna illustrates the changing attitudes to work and time in Italy over a quarter of a century. In 1960, after marrying at the age of twenty-four, Angiolino and his wife finally joined those who left behind the countryside in order to "find less *faticoso* and more profitable jobs" in the city.[17] They received a loan and after careful evaluation bought a *bar osteria* with its own production of wines. He believed it was the "right road to offer a more suitable occupation for every member of the family," including himself, his wife, and his parents.[18] They kept the business open every day from 6 am to 2 am. The family worked twenty hours per day for twelve years, taking no break on weekends and public holidays until local government policy required them to keep the business closed one day per week. For Angiolino, managing a coffee bar was less *faticoso* than working in the field, even if sometimes the coffee bar environment gave him "an unpleasant sensation of suffocating."[19] He stayed in the business for twenty-four years, until his wife fell into ill health and his parents became too old to help out. He decided to sell the business, as his family composition was no longer adequate to provide the self-employed labor needed to maintain it.

A similar transformation in the values surrounding work is on-going in self-employed small businesses in Italy at large. Aging is an issue. By the time many business owners reach retirement age (or are already past it), their better-educated children have left the family business behind for greener pastures. Others simply do not want to continue the business, as it is incompatible with their notions of how to balance free time and labor. Such was the case with the artisans in a gentrified neighborhood of Rome. Their retirements often meant the demise of their artisanal businesses as they are hard-pressed to find young people, including their own offspring, who were interested in manual work and self-employment.[20] The FIPE has also documented the steady decline of the number of small restaurants, *bar gelateria* (ice cream bars), pastry shops, delicatessens, and other food-service businesses, many of which had survived for decades before their owners decided to retire. Some owners who were able to sell their businesses even stayed on as wage laborers working for new owners. Like the earlier generation, the new owners aspired to economic autonomy through migration and self-employment, but increasingly this took place in a transnational context.

A Family Story of Becoming

Uncle Gumin, called Luca in Italian, ran the coffee bar introduced in the Prelude. He was born in 1965 in a mountain village in Southern Zhejiang and spent most of his childhood and adolescence in the village during the Maoist era (1949–1976). Times were hard and his agricultural family was not able to afford a good education for him and his six siblings. He dropped out after completing primary school. Like many other young boys in the village, Uncle Gumin left home at the age of fifteen to make a living for himself. He followed a cotton-fluffing artisan to a province in South China and opened his own artisanal workshop after a few years. Ten years later, when he made the decision to go to Europe, he already had ten apprentices working for him. "The business was quite good at that time, but it was a low-ranking, small business," he recalled. "At that time, so many people were flooding into Europe. Everybody said Europe was full of opportunities and money to earn. My elder brother was already in Europe, so I decided to close down my small business and come to Europe as well."

In the autumn of 1994, Uncle Gumin finally set foot on Italian soil. He was twenty-nine years old. His wife and three children, aged six, two, and one, stayed behind in the village in China to live with his parents. Uncle Gumin had spent all the savings he had accumulated from the cotton-fluffing business plus a considerable sum borrowed from relatives to fund his journey or, as he called it, his *toudu* (literally "the stealing of passages"), which was achieved through payments to a human smuggling gang. I tried to retrace his working trajectory in Italy, but even he himself could not sort out the numerous jobs he had held, which city they were in, or in what order. Piecing together the fragments that he mentioned in different conversations, I discovered that he had passed through numerous Chinese-owned businesses, from a cramped workshop hidden in an ordinary residential building to the fast-paced kitchens of Chinese restaurants, and from working as an itinerant masseur on the beach hoping to be hailed by middle-class Italian sunbathers to peddling trinkets as he passed among the tables of local restaurants. This precarious life, typical of undocumented immigrants, went on for several years until his immigrant status was legalized through an amnesty in 1997. His newfound legality meant that his wife and three children would finally be able to join him in Bologna through family reunion visas obtained a year later. He also managed to get his driver's license by memorizing all the sample questions and pictures (he was barely able to read and speak Italian at that time). He rented a stall in a local market where he sold clothes, then bought it after several more years. He considered this market vending business, or *maisan* in his Southern Zhejiang dialect, as his first *shiye* (business or enterprise) in Italy.[21]

During his years working as a market vendor, Uncle Gumin never stopped looking for new and better business opportunities for his family. It wasn't until 2010, fifteen years after he arrived in Italy, however, that he bought his first coffee bar, at a time when his three children were old enough to contribute their labor to the family business. He claimed:

> I bought the business for my kids. They all grew up here. I have to think about them, find something for them to do. It is not easy for us Chinese to make a living here. We can only work for others or do our own small *shiye*. But what kind of business can we do with such a bad economic situation? I used to *maisan*, blown by the wind and scorched by the sun. It's fine for us old guys, but it is not a good job for the youths. . . . We don't have the skills to open a restaurant. We also don't have enough financial resources to run a big business. In the end, we decided to buy a *jiuba* [bar].

His three children became the main baristas in their new family-run business, while Uncle Gumin went back and forth between the coffee bar and the market stall. He played multiple roles in the new enterprise as a driver, cleaner, stocker, lunch deliverer, accountant, manager, coordinator, and also a barista when extra labor was needed for busy customer traffic or when his children had other plans at school, in the church, or with friends. His wife, who was not in good health, rarely showed up in the family business, unlike most Chinese wives in Italy whom I know, but was instead in charge of domestic work and occasionally helped her husband in the local market.

Ensi (Lina in Italian), Uncle Gumin's eldest child, was the primary worker in their business when I met the family in 2014. After she arrived in Italy at age ten, she was assigned to the fourth grade in a local primary school. As the elder sister, she had to help her two younger siblings adapt to Italian school, tutor them in their homework, and take care of them. She started going with Uncle Gumin to their family's market stand to *bangmang* or "help out" when she was still a middle school student. She told me she was a good student at school and had even enrolled in the University of Bologna, but then quit after a short time. I asked her why, but she only said it was due to her own personal reasons. At that time her psychological situation was not stable, and she was unable to continue her studies. I do not know how much of her decision was due to her mental health and how much it was because of her work responsibilities as the eldest child in the family. In spring 2015, she married a Chinese man to whom she was introduced through family friends. He had migrated to Italy at the age of sixteen. The young couple received financial support from the groom's parents and cash gifts from their relatives on both sides at their wedding, which they were to use to start up their own small business. They finally bought Uncle Gumin's coffee bar at a relatively good price. It had the added benefit that it was a business Ensi knew well. She told me that they bought the bar not because they liked this business, but because they needed to earn a living and it was among the very few choices they had.

Enhua, Ensi's younger sister, was six years old when she migrated to Italy. She completed her education in Italy and was able to speak and read both Italian and Mandarin Chinese very well. When I met her in 2014, she was in the final year of an undergraduate major in economics and working as a part-time barista for her family's business. As for her career plans, Enhua told me in fluent Mandarin Chinese interspersed with Italian words, "I would like to find a job in an *ufficio* (office) rather than working here. Otherwise, what would have been the point of studying in the university at all?" After her graduation, she went to work in a *studio commercialista* (accounting firm). However, only one year later, she quit the job to work full-time as a barista in her family-owned bar. Enhua told me dispiritedly: "It's hard to find a job outside. The economy is not good, and the salary is very low. Some colleagues have worked there for twenty years, but their salary is still less than 2,000 euros [per month].[22] There is no future there." Enhua was not the only child of Chinese immigrants who opted to stay self-employed in their small family business after obtaining their college degree. Apart from familial duty, the high unemployment rate, low salaries in Italy's white-collar labor market, and the country's uncertain economic environment combined to discourage them from moving on.

Uncle Gumin's youngest child Enbao is one year younger than his second sister Enhua. I met him in 2014, when, due to a previous interruption of his studies, he was finishing his last year in a night high school. He also worked as a part-time barista in the family's coffee bar. He told me his thoughts on his job in Italian, the language he spoke the most comfortably and fluently: "It's okay to work here for now, but not forever. In the future, I like the idea of traveling and working in other places, not necessarily in Italy but maybe also in China." One year later, he started college to study industrial design and then graduated with excellent grades before continuing his studies for a Master's degree. Even though he expressed to me many times his interest in studying in other places in Italy or abroad, he chose to stay in Bologna, where he could "help out" in his family's business.

From the Invisible to the Visible

The pioneering Chinese migratory flow to Italy took place in the interwar period. Several hundred young Chinese men arrived from France, where they had served as cheap labor or small merchants during the First World War and then had lost their jobs afterwards.[23] These Chinese men, originally agricultural laborers or small artisans from the mountainous hinterland of Southern Zhejiang, settled in Milan, Bologna, and Florence, as well as other major Italian cities. They ran their own small workshops in the textile and leather industries or made a living as street vendors.[24] Many started families with Italian women who were themselves new rural migrant workers, even though interracial marriage was discouraged and eventually prohibited by the fascist regime in the name of "defending the race."[25] The population of Chinese immigrants continued to rise until the outbreak of World War II, which was followed by a mass return migration to China in the 1940s. Around five hundred Chinese men remained in Italy, among whom two out of three were sent to fascist internment camps as "subjects of an enemy country."[26] Of those who survived the war, many returned to China while approximately a hundred others, especially those who had married Italian women, chose to remain in Italy.[27]

These Chinese-Italian families became the early sponsors of their relatives and fellow villagers who wanted to work in their family-run manufacturing workshops or restaurants. The number of the new arrivals was quite limited during the Maoist era due to state regulations against emigration.[28] The situation then changed dramatically with China's opening to the capitalist world in the late 1970s. Europe became a new and desirable land of opportunity, and increasing numbers of Chinese were eager to get in on those opportunities and "get rich quick" by linking themselves into the chain migration.[29] Some of them arrived in Europe with formal visas for work or family reunion, but many others like Uncle Gumin followed underground migration routes.[30] Nearly 200,000 Chinese citizens, mostly labor migrants, were registered to settle in Italy by 2011.[31] The number would be even bigger if undocumented immigrants were counted. The influx did not slow down until Italy's economic downturn in 2008. After that point, emigration was no longer seen as the best choice for Chinese unskilled labor, as economic conditions changed in both China and Italy. The number of Chinese citizens, however, has continued to increase, reaching a peak of nearly 334,000 in 2015. The increase was primarily a result of two factors: immigration for family reunification and the relatively higher birth rate of Chinese residents in Italy, keeping in mind that the Italy-born children of foreign citizens do not obtain Italian citizenship at birth.

Italy was not the only European destination for Chinese labor migrants entering Europe in the post-Mao period, but it was the most popular, followed by Spain and France. By 2011, nearly a quarter of all Chinese citizens living in the twenty-eight countries of the EU were settled in Italy.[32] Several of my Chinese interlocutors confessed that Italy was not their original destination; they had temporarily passed through other European countries. They eventually settled in Italy because its border controls were less stringent and its regularization process was easier and faster due to the amnesties offered to immigrants every few years between the 1980s to late 2000s. These Chinese residents in Italy were again primarily recent arrivals from Southern Zhejiang. The other two most common origin points, Fujian Province and *Dongbei* (Northeastern China), accounted for no more than 20 percent of the total Chinese population in Italy.[33] The situation was different in other European countries with colonial legacies in Asia and the Americas, such as Britain, France, the Netherlands, and Portugal. People of Chinese descent living in those countries came from a wider range of regions.[34]

That Italy became the primary destination for mass labor migration from Southern Zhejiang was not coincidental. The Wenzhou Model of self-employment in small household-based workshops was a perfect match, economically and socially, with the "Made in Italy" business model. Both were based on small-scale family capitalism and decentralized production.[35] "Made in Italy" brands, often manufactured in small, specialized, and well-networked family firms, especially in the fast fashion industry, were thirsty for cheap and flexible labor that could respond to rapid market changes. The Chinese-run subcontracting workshops that served this industry gradually began to cluster in *distretti industriali* or "industrial districts" common in Northern and Central Italy. Their Chinese self-employed owners usually did the same manual work and lived in the same workshops as their documented and undocumented wage laborers. Free board and lodging allowed the new arrivals to settle in quickly without having to deal on their own with a new cultural and linguistic environment. Such reciprocal work and living arrangements also allowed the Chinese-run workshops to be highly flexible at meeting manufacturing needs. "Invisible"

Chinese labor thus made it possible for "Made in Italy" products to become well-known and competitive in the global market, but this success came with a heavy price in the form of lost personal time and little private life.[36] Under these circumstances, childcare was often achieved through the transnational circulation of children, who would be sent to live with extended family in China.[37]

In addition to manufacturing industries, food services were also an early focus of Chinese family entrepreneurship. In fact, the earliest interpersonal interactions between Chinese residents and native Italians most often took place in Chinese restaurants. While there were a few earlier establishments in the major cities targeting local clients of the upper middle class, Chinese restaurants did not take off in earnest until the 1980s. Family-managed, with Italianized menus, and affordable prices, they caught the new fashion for *pasto fuori casa* (eating out) among middle-class urbanites enjoying a new round of economic prosperity. They were also a new *punto di riferimento* (reference place) where Italians could have an exotic experience with Chinese cuisine and Chinese people.[38] In 2003, however, an epidemic of SARS in South China proved disastrous. Some Chinese entrepreneurs estimate that as many as 90 percent of the Chinese restaurants in Italy went bankrupt due to racism and Sinophobia sparked by this new virus.[39] Chinese restaurateurs then began to search for alternate business models. They took many forms. Some owners still identified their restaurants as Chinese, others were re-christened as East Asian, Southeast Asian, Italian, or Fusion. Chinese-owned restaurant businesses now spread throughout the country from the largest city centers to the smallest towns, even if those dedicated solely to Chinese cuisine became a minority.

Together with restaurants, Chinese-run small-scale trade and service businesses have mushroomed in the new millennium. An increasing number of Chinese residents have left the "invisible" manufacturing workshops in peripheral industrial districts for open urban areas where they quite visibly operate storefront businesses. This move was enabled by the revocation of Italy's institutional ban on immigrant entrepreneurship. From 1990 to 1998, immigration law had prohibited the establishment of new self-employed micro-enterprises by immigrants originating from countries where Italian citizens did not enjoy reciprocal rights, China included. Import-export used to be an economic pathway for some earlier Chinese merchants by trading "Made in Italy" products to China and introducing to Italy the vast reserves of "Made in China" products.[40] Their companies were mostly concentrated in large urban centers, such as Milan, Rome, and Florence. Since the removal of the ban on new self-employment, many more Chinese entrepreneurs are engaged in small retail businesses, running market stands, garment shops, or cheap retail stores. Others entered the small-scale service sector, operating coffee bars, barbershops, and massage parlors that primarily targeted a non-Chinese clientele.

Self-Employment as a Way of Life

The first-generation Chinese immigrants who managed coffee bars typically migrated to Italy after the mid-1990s. Among those whom I encountered, most came from the rural hinterlands of Southern Zhejiang and a few from neighboring Fujian province. Many of these surplus rural laborers also had made internal migrations prior to emigrating. Some were wage workers, but more often they were artisans, vendors, or small business owners. In the tide of market-oriented economic reforms that swept over post-Mao China, they became a "floating population" in the cities. Though they now lived in cities, they could not rid themselves of the socially inferior label of *nongmin* (peasants) assigned by the Chinese state's *hukou* or "household registration" system.[41] Many artisans and merchants, including Uncle Gumin, closed up their small businesses later and travelled to Europe, sometimes in search of adventure, for their overseas aspirations were not always driven by extreme poverty or negative business performance. Rather, these cosmopolitan "desiring subjects" saw Europe as a promising land of new possibilities for not only economic prosperity, but also for social mobility.[42] From the mid-1990s on, China's official narratives equated international migration with modernity, progress, and even patriotism.[43] Transnational practice thus afforded not only the possibility of "capital accumulation," but also that of transforming their identities from backward *nongmin* to cosmopolitan *huaqiao* or "overseas Chinese."[44]

New arrivals from China typically began their immigrant lives in Italy by working in Chinese-owned workshops, restaurants, or other enterprises. As they acclimated to their new conditions of life, some kept on working as wage laborers, others became street peddlers, mobile beach massagers, or took on other self-employed informal businesses as a shortcut to economic mobility. It was unsurprising that those, like Uncle Gumin, who had experience and cultural capital as small entrepreneurs were among the most motivated to start up their own *shiye* (business, enterprise) once the opportunity arose. Self-employment was one of the few business models open to these marginalized foreign laborers hoping to achieve economic autonomy, either in post-Mao China or abroad.[45] It was also a way of avoiding the direct exploitation of their labor from other people and it allowed them more flexibility in time management. With the goal of autonomy in mind, these would-be immigrant entrepreneurs were commonly proactive in obtaining residence permits as soon as immigrant amnesties made this possible. Those who migrated to Italy between the mid-1990s and the late 2000s were no longer subject to restrictions on self-employment but it took time. It could take two to three years from emigration to the start-up of the first formal *shiye*, but more commonly the wait lasted five to six years. Over these years, in addition to accumulating initial capital for their small enterprises, they also had to work at paying back their emigration debts, legalizing their residency, sending remittances to their families in China, and eventually bringing their children to Italy.

Market vending was a popular start-up business for Chinese immigrants in Bologna striving to transform from undocumented workers into small entrepreneurs in the late 1990s and early 2000s. Many Chinese coffee bar owners worked as market vendors before entering the coffee bar businesses, or at least had some kind of related experience. Due to their frequent interactions with the shoppers, as well as the shorter working hours (many markets are only open for half a day), Uncle Gumin and many other Chinese market vendors gained not only satisfactory economic returns from this business, but also opportunities to learn Italian faster than those who worked in workshops or restaurant kitchens.[46] The market vending business, however, has been gradually abandoned by Chinese immigrants since the Great Recession of 2008. Consumers have much smaller budgets for buying clothes, shoes, and other consumer goods. More importantly, several Chinese interlocutors told me that the profits of Chinese merchants have been severely reduced by competition from big fast fashion brands as well as other non-Chinese market vendors.

Some Chinese coffee bar owners I encountered had once managed their own subcontracting workshops, but saw their businesses failing in the economic restructuring after 2008. The decline in profits pushed them to search out new entrepreneurial paths. A shoemaking workshop owner told me that many workshops had closed, due mainly to a shrinking volume of orders, cash flow problems, or labor shortages. Small workshops, usually those with fewer than ten workers, encountered great difficulties when trying to remain in the market.[47] By contrast, coffee bar sales were most often cash transactions that avoided the risk of payment delay or insolvency. Even if the business turned out to be insufficiently profitable, the owner could still sell it to someone else, thus reducing the potential for economic loss enough to make the risks involved in the business bearable.

Some coffee bar owners who had previously run other kinds of businesses had faced labor shortages in their previous firms, especially shortages of any kind of specialized labor that they required. New Chinese arrivals often strived to leave wage jobs to run their own small businesses as soon as several years of capital accumulation made this possible. Meanwhile, significantly fewer people were leaving China for Italy, too few to refill the bottom of the wage labor market. Registered Chinese enterprises in the form of *imprese individuali* or "sole proprietorships," which were typically self-employed small-scale family businesses, steadily increased by 25 percent to more than 52,000 over the eight years between 2012 to 2019, just before the Covid-19 outbreak.[48] Records also disclose that roughly one out of every six Chinese residents in the country had a business registered under their name when I was doing fieldwork in Italy between 2014 and 2015. One Chinese restaurant owner explained to me: "It is very hard to maintain a small restaurant if you aren't a chef yourself. It's not easy to find a new chef if one leaves." In comparison, the management of a coffee bar could consistently rely on self-employed family labor, thus negating the need for a higher number of hired workers.

For Chinese immigrants looking for a start-up business, the increasingly vacant coffee bar niche indeed provided a good opportunity. It was first of all a rather easy-to-access business from a financial perspective. The Chinese coffee bars that I contacted in Bologna reported in 2015 that the lowest purchase price for a bar was 80,000 euros, while the most expensive was 400,000 euros. I heard that one might have to pay 600,000 euros or even more to secure a coffee bar in Milan, but I also knew some Chinese families who had paid 50,000 euros for peripheral coffee bars in provincial towns. In many cases, the full amount did not have to be paid in one lump sum; it was possible to make an initial down payment, followed by monthly installments. Combining their own savings with financial support from "relatives and friends" could make a purchase possible. As far as I am aware, the income that a self-employed family earns from managing a coffee bar is usually better than what a wage laborer or market vendor would make. One Chinese family, for example, bought a small coffee bar in the middle of my 2015 fieldwork. The parents in their early forties managed it together with their seventeen-year-old daughter without hiring any paid labor. When I went back to Bologna in the summer of

2016, the family told me that the revenue they made after a year of management had surpassed the purchasing cost of 100,000 euros, although no labor costs were deducted.

My Chinese interlocutors, especially the first-generation immigrants, did not share middle-class Italians' perception of the coffee bar business as *faticoso*. My barista teacher Letai and his family are an example. The patrilineal family had bought two coffee bars. One, in a mountain town, was managed by Letai's older brother and his wife, while the other in the city center was managed by Letai and his mother. Letai's father in his fifties regularly brought dinner boxes to Letai when I was learning barista skills there. While Letai was eating in the dining room, his father would work temporarily as a barista. We had many conversations in those thirty-minutes while we were both standing behind the bar counter. Letai's parents, who had migrated to Italy one after the other in 1999 and 2000, tried street vending and restaurant businesses before establishing their coffee bar. They and Letai's brother, who reunited with them in Italy at the age of seventeen, had also worked in manufacturing workshops as wage laborers. Letai's father thought coffee bar management was not *xinku* [tiring, laborious], but quite *qingsong* (easy, relaxing), and it was a better job than managing a manufacturing workshop or doing street vending. As he explained it, when there was an order in a manufacturing workshop, both the *laoban* (boss) and the *gongren* (workers, employees) were "trapped" into "working without stop" for more than twelve hours per day. In a coffee bar, by contrast, "you only need to work when *keren* [guests, customers] come in," and "most of the time, you can just sit there doing whatever you want." Compared to street vending, working in a coffee bar was also more "comfortable," as "there was air conditioning." Letai shares his father's opinions. Given that all the work available to them is synonymous with long working hours, time spent in a comfortable coffee shop seems better than other options.

The word *xinku* has the same meaning as the Italian word *faticoso*. They can both be used to describe a job that is labor-intensive, time-consuming, or requires considerable energy. However, middle-class Italians stress the temporal dimension of coffee bar management as a negative and so, from their perspective, a coffee bar owner is trapped in the business without any leisure time. While I heard some Chinese coffee bar owners also complain about the long working hours, most of them did not speak of the work as *faticoso* or *xinku* in terms of work intensity. The time expended in a coffee shop was different in quality from the time that heavier labor consumed. Letai's father in particular emphasized that the intensity of work and the nature of the working environment were what mattered. He also did not make a distinction between working time and leisure time. In his understanding, "doing whatever you want" during working hours also constitutes leisure. Indeed, playing on their smartphones, chatting, reading digital books, and even watching TV dramas were common activities that Letai and many other Chinese baristas did to kill time between customers. When I was working as an apprentice barista at Letai's coffee bar, it was often the boredom rather than busyness that got me down during the long afternoons.

Children's Coming of Age

Emigration after the 1980s most often worked on a kind of family plan for Chinese immigrants from Southern Zhejiang. It might be undertaken to satisfy one's personal ambitions but, more often, it was for the sake of the family's well-being. Some unmarried young adults started families after settling in Italy, while many others had married and had one or more children prior to emigration. Some husbands left China first and had their wives and children apply later for family reunion visas to join them in Italy. Other couples emigrated together, leaving behind any children with their grandparents and only later bringing them to Italy via official channels once that became possible. While first-generation Chinese immigrants often arrived in Italy undocumented, their children rarely did so. This is also one of the major reasons why would-be Chinese entrepreneurs usually prefer to legalize their residency as soon as possible rather than remaining in Italy as undocumented immigrants. Many couples had their second or third child in Italy. The circulation of children between China and Italy was very common among the families engaged in the manufacturing industry in Prato. Anthropologist Elizabeth Krause has argued that it was a coping strategy to maintain mutual relations within their transnational households across generations, while also meeting the demand for flexible workers.[49] It was less common among the families in Bologna though. Some parents sent children born in Italy to their grandparents in China and then brought them back to Italy when they reached school age. Others, especially those who had storefront businesses, were able to raise children in Italy. While the parents were working for initial capital accumulation, their children grew up alongside them.

There is great diversity among the children of Chinese immigrants in Italy. The place of their birth and the age at which they arrived have a considerable impact on their educational level and career choices, even among children in the same family, as can be seen in the case of Uncle Gumin's children. Those who attended Italian primary schools, for even part of their elementary years, were better equipped to earn higher degrees and eventually find a job in the white-collar labor market. Some of them, however, were discouraged by Italy's uncertain economic environment and precarious labor market with its high rate of unemployment, and like Uncle Gumin's second daughter Enhua, they retreated to their family's small business. Many children joined their parents in Italy at some point in their teenage years, before age eighteen when they would no longer be eligible for family reunion visas. Several of my interlocutors in this category laughingly referred to themselves as the *1.5 dai* or "one-and-half generation" rather than the full *erdai* or "second generation" immigrants who were born, grew up, and received their complete school education in Italy. Some scholars have used the same term to refer to children of immigrants who straddle both the emigrant and immigrant societies yet are not fully part of either.[50]

For the "one-and-half-generation" children, making a living through self-employment was typically a better option than attempting to join the white-collar labor market. Language limitations hampered them in school and were an obstacle to continuing on to higher education. I did not encounter anyone who had received Italian language training in China. Few who started school in Italy in middle school went on to higher education. Some of them had received extracurricular language classes in school, but no bilingual education was available to them. They told me that it often took them at least two years to be able to handle ordinary everyday communication in Italian, and that this was not enough to cope with school materials, especially in high school, since their vocabulary range was insufficient. Some subjects were particularly difficult for them, such as history, Italian literature, and foreign languages. Many of them were held back after the first year of high school and ultimately dropped out after one or two years.[51] For those who enrolled directly in a high school education in Italy was only pro forma. My barista teacher Letai joined his parents in Bologna when he was fifteen years old. He enrolled in a *liceo linguistico* (linguistic high school) with the intention of learning Italian, but dropped out after just one year since the only subject he could pass was mathematics. He complained to me, saying, "I couldn't understand anything there! I wanted to learn Italian, but at that school I also needed to learn another two languages. How can I learn Italian, English, and Spanish all at the same time!"

The children of immigrants from Southern Zhejiang are a valuable source of labor in their small family economies, regardless of their education levels and future employment trajectories.[52] The older children, especially the first child, often face heavy pressure from their parents to perform their duties by *bangmang* or "helping out" in the family as early as the age of twelve or thirteen. They contribute by taking care of younger siblings, doing domestic chores, working beside their parents, and communicating with

Italian *commercialisti* (accountant and business consultants), suppliers, and other stakeholders and authorities. High school and even university students very often work as part-time baristas. A study of Chinese families running small restaurant businesses in the Netherlands in the 1980s reveals that the children either excelled in school or dropped out altogether as a result of their parents' rational calculations for maximizing family capital accumulation.[53] The parents in that study believed investment in education was worthwhile only if its expected benefits outweighed the loss of the child's labor. A Chinese Master's candidate, whose parents were market vendors, told me that her parents were resentful that she did not *bangmang* in the family. She finally got permission from them to continue higher education at the price of their financial support for her, so she had to pay for her college education by doing part-time jobs outside of her family business. Even for parents like Uncle Gumin, who claim to support his children's studies "until they don't want to continue," *bangmang* in the family business remains a "duty."

The labor of children appears to be especially valuable in coffee bar management. Baristas need relatively advanced Italian language competence and other forms of cultural capital to interact with their customers. As Uncle Gumin confessed to me, "Language is the key. My generation doesn't have enough language skills. We can handle basic communication, but it isn't enough. If our coffee bar were reliant only on me, it wouldn't survive." The Master's student I mentioned earlier also told me that her parents wanted to open a coffee bar, but that they could not without her *bangmang*. Children usually have better language competency and more education than their parents. They can read and speak better Italian and handle daily communication more easily as a result to having learned Italian at a young age or as a benefit of attending Italian schools, even if only for a few years. Moreover, all of these children have at least received a complete education from primary to middle school, whether in China or in Italy. In contrast, while some younger parents born in the 1970s had attended middle school in China, older parents, born in the 1960s or earlier often had only finished primary school, if that. Many of them do not have the ability to read Italian, so having their children work as baristas is critical to the success of their business.

Reciprocal Kin-Based Networks

One day in spring 2015, I had a conversation with Uncle Gumin in the storeroom of his family-owned coffee bar. A shelf full of bottled water and a single bed occupied most of the space, but it served other purposes as well. It was where he and his children had lunch, did homework, took breaks, and sometimes had a nap. While he talked to me, Uncle Gumin was eating lunch, some reheated stir-fried noodles with meat and vegetables that he had brought from home. He was recalling the old days when he had crossed the EU border and begun working as an undocumented immigrant in Italy. He had complicated feelings about those experiences, which he rarely mentioned to his three children and never discussed in detail. It had been painful, but he seemed to be proud of himself for having overcome those initial tribulations and satisfied with what he and his family had achieved through their migration. "You see, we are good now. The whole family lives together. My kids are all obedient. We have our own *shiye*—not a big one, but enough for a decent life. All the *ku* [bitterness] I ate has been rewarded." Every time our conversations reached a point like this, this short, slender man, the stern father of three children, his face lined with wrinkles, would give me a big smile and draw a long sigh of relief.

Uncle Gumin's sense of relief echoes a Chinese idiom: *xian ku hou tian* or "bitterness first, sweetness later." It stresses the ethos of *chiku* or "eating bitterness," because "sweetness" and happiness are the fruits of labor; they cannot be achieved without hard work and self-sacrifice. The Chinese state in both the Maoist and post-Mao eras has glorified the capacity to endure bitterness as a national virtue in order to mobilize working people to work hard, even as the purported goals of their labor changed over time from socialist production targets, to Cultural Revolution, and now economic development.[54] Within the family realm, working-class people and rural migrants often showed their willingness to endure bitterness and sacrifice for the sake of the family and especially for their children.[55] Enduring bitterness thus is not only endured as suffering but more importantly viewed as capital that these Chinese parents invest for their family's reproduction and intergenerational relationships.

Some Chinese parents may not have been effective baristas, but they played other significant and multi-faceted roles in the family's economy. The children who were excluded from the white-collar labor market and therefore continued in the family business relied on their parents' financial support, social networks, and other resources. The division of family labor was primarily determined by their language skills. Letai's mother who was able to communicate in Italian also worked as a barista. Both Letai's father and Uncle Gumin, whose Italian was less fluent, served as baristas only when necessary, but they performed all kinds of other-than-barista work that was essential for coffee bar management. Uncle Gumin's wife, who spoke little Italian, took on cooking, cleaning, and other domestic duties. In a coffee bar managed by a young married couple, their "retired" parents often helped take care of their grandchildren.

Chinese small entrepreneurs unanimously told me that the owner of the business was the whole family, regardless of whose name was on the registration documents.[56] I noticed, however, that it was the father who most often headed the family. Here, the term "family" usually refers to a patrilineal group, composed of immigrant parents, unmarried children, and married sons, along with their wives and their children. This model of family business ownership, which was predominant among Chinese immigrants from Southern Zhejiang, was grounded in a strong patriarchal family structure and kinship system, one that emphasized the continuation of the patrilineal line. The idea of "a business for each son" was an unspoken rule. Having a business or at least the ability to start up a *shiye* was widely considered a prerequisite for any young man who hoped to be competitive in the marriage market. To this end, parents commonly felt a responsibility to help their sons set up a business or to transfer the family enterprise to them. On top of being a crucial motivation, marriage was often a key strategy in pursuit of their entrepreneurial endeavors and economic aspirations. Chinese families from Southern Zhejiang typically preferred marriages with others from the same region for the sake of family solidarity and resource mobilization. A family's place of origin, its economic condition, and the potential children-in-law's work ethic and filial piety were often the main considerations for both sides of a potential marriage.

Strong kin-based social ties, mainly composed of what were called "relatives and friends," were moreover a boost to economic activities. A transnational network of kinship, in particular, often promised financial support that allowed easier access to start-up funding in the form of cash. "The idea is mutual help." An interlocutor who was managing a coffee bar with her husband and their eighteen-year-old son told me, "No one does business without borrowing money. You help me today, and I will help you one day in the future." This reciprocal credit system made it possible for many Chinese families to initiate a business. For instance, a Chinese couple in their early forties bought a coffee bar with financial support from the wife's sister, who was running a restaurant in Spain. Sometimes, when parents did not have an enterprise ready to pass on to a son who was getting married, or if they had younger unmarried children at home, the groom and his wife could still establish a small business by deploying the abundant cash they received as marriage gifts, collected from relatives and family friends from both sides, as in Uncle Gumin's daughter Ensi's case. The cash gifts that Letai's brother and his wife received from wedding guests not only paid for their wedding, but also contributed a major portion of the cost of a coffee bar that they bought afterwards.

Support and influence from social ties included, however, much more than merely financial help. As the last of six siblings to migrate to Italy, Linli and her husband first started out as market vendors before switching to the coffee bar business. Knowing that some of her siblings and Chinese friends were able to *zhuanqian* (make money) from this new popular business, Linli and her husband started asking around about opportunities and sometimes searched for coffee bars together with other would-be owners. Her siblings, other relatives and close friends who had already accumulated experience and knowledge in this business niche helped them get through the initial difficulties of finding a suitable coffee bar by evaluating the potential profitability of a prospective purchase and in other ways sharing their business knowledge. Ethnic resources and networks—the major social capital of these unskilled immigrants—once again played a crucial role in motivating and regulating their economic activities.[57] These reciprocal kin-based social networks eventually made possible the formation of a new ethnic occupational niche.

They Leave, We Fill In

"Have you ever met the *mafia cinese*?" I asked Stefano when he told me about its nefarious dealings. Stefano was an unemployed Italian worker in his early fifties and the father of two secondary-school students. We were in a Chinese-managed coffee bar where he took three to four glasses of white wine almost every afternoon. This became his new daily routine after the scooter factory where he had worked went bankrupt a few years earlier. He told me that he had applied for other jobs but never heard back from any of them. His family's income thus came from his unemployment benefits and his wife's salary from working in a daycare center. When I pressed him about whether he had ever actually encountered the supposed "Chinese mafia," Stefano replied firmly, "No, but I saw some Chinese going around in a car worth 50,000 euros, even 100,000 euros. They're for sure the *mafia cinese*. . . . They run casinos and prostitution. They exploit other Chinese." After a brief pause for a sip of wine, he added: "But most of the Chinese are *tranquilli* [calm, peaceful]. They probably work too much."

Stefano's comments took in the two most popular stereotypes regarding Chinese residents in Italy. For many Italians, Chinese people were either barbaric tools of capitalism—being workaholic and money-obsessed—or, alternatively, they were the victims of a vast co-ethnic criminal network, if they were not themselves the criminals. The perception that this work ethic applies to all Chinese is shaped and reinforced by native Italians' experience with the Chinese residents in their country. Most of the Chinese residents in Italy are immigrant workers, merchants, or other types of small entrepreneurs. Their storefront businesses are known for being "always open." They commonly maintain *orario continuato* or all-day schedules without lunch breaks, and many are open seven days a week. It is also unusual for coffee bars owned by Italians to take midday breaks. Yet, *orario continuato* is not a typical practice in Italy, as other small, Italian-run storefronts tend to take more daily and weekly breaks.[58]

Italian public discourses often cast this Chinese work ethic as an insurmountable cultural difference. *Noi italiani lavoriamo per vivere, mentre i cinesi vivono per lavorare.* "We Italians work in order to live, while the Chinese live in order to work." This saying, commonly heard in Italy, encapsulates the attitudes toward work and life that distinguish "deviant" Chinese from "we Italians" who embrace the ethos of idleness and enjoy leisure as both a condition and as the very meaning of life. This image of Italian life as a fundamentally leisurely existence prevails both in Italy and around the world. In its current form, it depicts a rather picturesque Italian idleness that effectively sells the country's image as a romantic vacation spot and tourist destination in a land of leisure inhabited by a pleasantly idle people. This construction of *italianità* that underlies the trope of *il dolce far niente*, "the sweet art of idleness," in fact runs deeper in the country's modern history than this current application.[59] Idleness and leisure were initially a

stereotype applied to Southern Italians in the early, newly unified
Italian state as being purportedly indolent and perpetually unemployed.[60] Thus, ironically, a stereotype first deployed against "idle"
Southern Italians has since morphed into a generalized *carattere
italiano* or "Italian character" to the extent that what was once a
national "vice" is now a glorified national virtue and an excuse for
excluding immigrants from some specific national backgrounds
because, unlike Italians, they "work too much."

My Chinese interlocutors also commonly shared the perception that "*laowai* [Italians] love pleasure" and that "Chinese are
more hardworking than *laowai*."[61] Many Chinese saw these different work attitudes as racialized cultural tropes, but some also
interpreted them as out-growths of class and the changing realities of a globalized labor market.[62] As Uncle Fumin's son Enbao
commented: "Who doesn't like holidays? *Laowai* have been here
for at least three generations. They have houses. They have social
benefits. They have a stable life. On the day off, they only need
to think about where to go for holidays." Although Enbao's comments blurred class differences among native Italians, he did make
the point that immigrants in Italy lead lives more precarious than
the lives of natives. Immigrant labor world-wide gravitates to "3D"
jobs (dirty, dangerous, and demeaning), very often in the shadow
economy, that are rejected by more established citizens, thereby
creating a segmented labor market.[63] The self-employed coffee bar
business in Italy, although not on the same low rung as a 3D job,
has also emerged as a new type of undesirable work that is abandoned and rejected by middle-class Italians. Yet, it offers foreign
laborers, including Chinese immigrants, what seems to them to
be an accessible opportunity that rewards them with economic
autonomy in their pursuit of a good life.

As we have seen, Chinese ownership of coffee bar businesses
primarily adopts a kinship mode of production. Domestic work,
childcare, reciprocity, and other non-economic practices, as well
as family values and social relations, are all articulated by means
of economic practices. This mode of production not only enables

both old and new migrant families to achieve economic autonomy, but also promotes the production of kin-based social relations. And this is in turn founded on a particular family model of
reciprocal and flexible kin labor. The Campagna family, the Sicilian couple, and the previous owner of Lisa's coffee bar, abandoned
their businesses not because they themselves found it too *faticoso*.
The problem was instead that their family formations had changed
due to aging, illness, or the children's transformed values and aspirations, which no longer matched the reciprocal kinship mode
of production that is optimal for the coffee bar business niche.
Thus, Chinese families who were located in structural positions
similar to those of previous Italian owners, many of them internal
migrants, replaced them to fill this niche.

Yet, the Chinese families' presence in this specific micro-business
shows a noticeable degree of historical contingency. The Chinese
families I encountered commonly considered their international
migration to be an active and persistent ongoing process of striving for a good life, defined not only as material returns, but also as
a way of preserving family unity and other social rewards. In this
process, these convivial bricoleurs actively made do with limited
capital and resources at hand, coped with adverse socioeconomic
circumstances, and actively participated in the forging of new economic pathways. Many of them tried their hands at more than one
business sector. A coffee bar owner might have worked as a market
vendor, restaurant owner, grocer, wholesaler, subcontracting workshop owner, or as multiple business owners. Few of them saw coffee
bar businesses as the end of the road in their entrepreneurial careers,
and many expressed to me a sense of uncertainty about the future.
This uncertainty is particularly associated with the demographic
nature and class composition of both the current Italian society and
Chinese communities there in a continuous process rather than social stasis. Coming-of-age children and grandchildren of Chinese
immigrants increasingly strive to climb up the social ladder through
education, while abandoning self-employment as a way of life, just
as many younger generations of native Italians have already done.

"In the end, it was they who sold all the *jiuba* to us. If we don't take them over, many would just close their businesses. *Laowai* wouldn't have so many places to drink coffee." This was Uncle Gumin's eldest daughter Ensi's response to the resentment and criticism of native Italians regarding Chinese ownership of coffee bars. Yet, as I will show in the next chapter, Chinese would-be coffee bar owners don't just "fill in," taking over just any coffee bar. They make their own calculations about what kind of coffee bar is a good match for their unique family composition and available labor.

3

Situating Space

DURING THE CHRISTMAS season of 2014, I went to visit my friend Giulia in a peripheral town just outside of Milan. Giulia and her brother were born and had grown up there, but by then only their parents were still living in the town, where they managed a small family-run artisanal *salumeria* (delicatessen). Giulia had moved abroad while her brother moved to Milan after graduating from college. Her parents told us that over the past few years four *bar cinesi* had opened in the town. All of them were *bar tradizionali* that had been there for decades. Giulia had never been to any of them, despite being aware of their existence. The next day, we decided to stop by one of the bars for breakfast. We had a 15-minute *passeggiata* (walk) along the zigzag lanes of the ancient town with its cobblestone streets and medieval architecture before arriving at the place, which was located in a residential area.[1]

A couple of elderly men were sitting in white plastic chairs by the sidewalk under an azure sign with a big white capital letter "T," indicating that tobacco products were also sold there. Two younger men who looked like immigrants from North Africa stood against the wall next to the glass door. Followed by the gazes of these men, Giulia and I, two women in our early thirties, entered the place, encountering even more male gazes. We were not the only women present, but the other two were working behind the bar counter. One was a young Chinese woman, the other an older white woman. With them was a young Chinese man. We later discovered that the two Chinese behind the counter were a couple and the new owners of the business, while the white woman was the previous Italian owner, who was now employed by the Chinese couple who had purchased her business.

Giulia and I ordered our cappuccinos and *brioche* croissants and decided to sit at a table in the corner so as to make ourselves less noticeable. Looking around the place, Giulia commented: "This isn't a nice place for women to stay. If it were not for your research, I would have been reluctant to come in." She then added, "Maybe I'd just come in to buy a pack of cigarettes, if needed when I passed by, and leave right away. I would not stick around." Worried that I might be misunderstanding her meaning, Giulia continued, "I don't mean that women don't go to a *bar*. We go to other ones which are not occupied by all these elderly men, where I can easily meet some friends." While Giulia was talking, an elderly man walked towards us. It was her retired uncle, who lived a few blocks away. Hearing that I was interested in coffee bars, he joined us at the table with a glass of white wine, while Giulia and I were finishing our breakfast. Giulia's uncle was an *uomo da bar* (literally "a man of the bar" or "a *bar* regular"). He liked this coffee bar and knew "everything" about it, since he had come here every day for many years, even before the Chinese couple bought it, to drink, meet his friends, talk, and buy lottery tickets. Later on the same day, Giulia's brother also told me that he too would not typically frequent that bar. Along with the same reasons that Giulia had given about it being unlikely that he would find his friends there, he emphasized: "It's not because it's Chinese now. The idea is that I don't like coffee bars with *macchinette* [slot machines] in general."

There are two aspects of this episode that I want to highlight because they reveal how native Italians perceive coffee bars. First, coffee bars are fundamental places of urban sociability that embody and imply particular social relations. Giulia and her brother did not frequent the same coffee bar as their retired uncle, but they both made it clear that just as in their uncle's case, coffee bars played the role of a *punto di incontro* or "meeting point" in their everyday urban lives. Second, as we can see here quite clearly, the social practice of drinking coffee in a particular coffee bar gives expression, by means of temporal distinctions and spatial segregations, to a customer's gender, generation, and social class. Space produces and is in turn produced by social relations.[2] Coffee bars are in principle open to everyone. One to 1.1 euros could buy an espresso in most of Bologna's coffee bars when I was doing fieldwork there in 2014 and 2015, but social actors with their own sets of identities exhibited different consumption patterns in their choice of the places they visited, the duration and the rhythm of their visits, and their loyalty to a particular place. With a cup of espresso, one can stand at the bar counter for five minutes or sit outside in the *al fresco* area for the entire afternoon. One can stand quietly at the bar without communicating with anyone or play cards with friends while initiating a debate on hot button political issues. All of these observations tell the story of an "embodied space," which Setha Low defines as "the location where human experience and consciousness takes on material and spatial form."[3] The sociality of such a space in turn expresses with its own logic the power dynamics between different social groups and reflects ongoing patterns of cultural change.

The *bar cinesi* is the local vernacular term for coffee bars owned and managed by Chinese people. The term seems to suggest that these bars are a new category within the vast spectrum of Italy's coffee bars. Yet, as I discussed in the previous chapter, Chinese owners are not in fact creating a new business niche, but rather filling an existing one. Most of the so-called *bar cinesi* that I visited in Bologna and elsewhere were "traditional bars" with an existing sociality that predated Chinese ownership and management. The new Chinese owners strive to preserve the existing sociality so as to maintain the regular clientele. So then, how exactly do Chinese entrepreneurs understand and situate themselves in their variegated socialities? What are their roles in the production of such a "traditional" social space and in the social construction of its spatial and cultural meanings?

To answer these questions, I will examine ethnographic descriptions of coffee-drinking and coffee bar culture in the history of Italy from the time when the early Venetian coffeehouses flourished in the seventeenth century. Over these four centuries, consumption patterns of this single commodity show a wide range of social and cultural shifts.[4] Most significantly, the history of coffee-drinking and coffee bars parallels the social transformation of Italy from a primarily agrarian economy to an industrialized nation.[5] Over time the commodity itself went from being an exotic beverage to a national icon that exemplifies a form of "banal nationalism," expressing Italian national identity at a level of everyday life.[6] Once an elite beverage, coffee became an ordinary, everyday drink for mass consumption. And in the same vein, the public institutions dedicated to coffee-drinking also shifted from elite clubs to public venues open to the everyday urban population. In this history, we can see productive forces, including technology, the state, capitalist industry, the social division of labor, as well as individual negotiation and resistance in the use of space and its construction of meaning.

During my fieldwork, I heard several contested if not contradictory narratives about coffee bar traditions in Italy. In these different versions, notions of both "tradition" and "modernity" take on different meanings in different contexts, often meanings of an ambivalent nature. Rather than being value neutral, these distinctions always imply a hierarchy of value. Yet, in all cases, the past is used for the purposes of the present, either for embracing supposed continuity with history or for celebrating a disconnection from history. The historical approach thus allows us to examine local populations' spatialized social relations and cultural practices that reflect and are also embedded in the larger contexts of political, economic, and social transformations.[7] My ethnographic findings show that Chinese-managed coffee bars and their sociality constitute a significant part of this social history rather than a cultural disruption within it.

Changing Traditions

Pietro, a friend of my second host family, is a native *bolognese* born in the late 1930s who worked as a local high school teacher before retiring. On one of the early days of my fieldwork in Bologna, I was at his farmhouse workshop watching him make *grappa* at home. While waiting for the distilled spirit to fill a glass container one drop after another, Pietro told me a version of the history of coffee bars in Italy that I had never heard before. "Until the 1960s, a *bar* was called an *osteria*." Pietro's words surprised me. "Not *caffè*?" I asked. In my understanding at that time, *osterie* (plural of *osteria*) are taverns with local specialties of food and wine. *Caffè*, the Italian word for "coffee," is commonly used in the names of the renowned *bar storici* or historic coffee bars in Italy. Caffè Florian in Venice (1720), Caffè Greco in Rome (1760), and Caffè Pedrocchi in Padova (1831) are some famous examples. These places are important historic and cultural sites where curious tourists eagerly seek to replicate the authentic Italian coffeehouse tradition. "Aside from the *bar storici*. There were, yes, two or three of that kind of *bar classici* in a city. But all the rest were *osterie*." Pietro recalled, "In the 50s, when I was still a young boy, wine, boiled eggs, sausages, and side snacks for wine were served. Then people started consuming coffee there, and then taking coffee more than wines. . . . And little by little, *osterie* were transformed into today's *bar*."

Later in my fieldwork, several other native *bolognesi* over seventy years old gave me the same version of local coffee bars' history, as well as their own stories of witnessing or experiencing that transformation. None of them traced the roots to the Venetian *caffè* of the late seventeenth century. The early Venetian *caffè* as well as many other early modern European coffeehouses were closely associated with the emergence of a new male bourgeois sociability that went along with the rise of a capitalist economy.[8] This new public social institution became an alternative space for political activity, where the rising bourgeois class could consolidate social power through open communication and informal gatherings.[9] The early *caffè* in Italy were crucial social spaces where new political and cultural ideas spread among the new bourgeoisie, revolutionaries, and intellectuals during the Enlightenment and the later Italian Risorgimento (the Italian unification movement). They were also key sites where the fascist regime promoted their imperial projects in East Africa during the interwar period.[10]

However, *caffè* were not yet social spaces for urban working-class men and were also out of reach for the many Italians who remained at that point rural dwellers, even if they were in principle open to people from all classes.[11] Coffee was not habitually consumed by the common people in early modern Europe, for like the sugar often used to sweeten the beverage, it was a luxury commodity imported from the European colonies.[12] Instead, the *osteria*, which has the basic meaning of a "place of hospitality," was, for much longer than the *caffè*, the major gathering place for male sociability in the urban areas of Northern and Central Italy. These were originally drinking establishments primarily serving wine, while food was optional.[13] Men of all social classes could go to an *osteria* to take a rest, have a chat, play cards, drink, and generally pass their leisure time with friends.[14]

Behind the emergence of the contemporary *bar* in Italy lies the social history of the mass consumption of espresso that began after the Second World War. Until then, early espresso machines were primarily confined to elite establishments due to their high cost, while coffee was also an expensive and heavily taxed imported commodity.[15] A new espresso machine with a more affordable price was finally developed through a series of technological innovations in the post-war period. The coffee made by these new semi-automatic appliances was advertised as *caffè crema* (cream coffee) due to a creamy skin of essential oils on the surface of the cup. It took very little time to produce individual cups of tiny amounts of this coffee, which allowed customers to quickly take a shot while standing at the bar counter without the need to pay an extra service fee.[16] A decline in the price of coffee beans in the global market further contributed to lowering the price of a cup, so that common people could afford it.[17] The new espresso machines were then widely introduced to both *caffè* and *osterie*. Drinking coffee while standing at the bar remains to this day one of the most characteristic features of Italian-style coffee consumption.

Coffee bars where cheap coffee was served over the bar counter with minimum service gained popularity among working-class people and migrant workers in the decades following the Second World War.[18] They became a "third place" that offered a form of community distinct from work or family.[19] Indeed, many of them operated close to workplaces. Sidney Mintz shows how tea with sugar, being a stimulant, entered the English working-class diet by providing cheap calories that also allowed them to work longer hours from the mid 1800s to the mid 1900s.[20] Coffee breaks with *un caffè al bar* (a coffee at the bar) in Italy similarly helped shape a new connection between coffee and industrial work. Both in the morning and in the afternoon, industrial workers could escape from long hours of working and enjoy their breaks with a cup of coffee. Numerous small coffee bars, serving a combination of espresso coffee, snacks, and alcoholic drinks, also appeared in new peripheral residential neighborhoods where migrant workers and working-class people commonly lived. Overcrowded home spaces pushed hundreds of thousands of new urban residents from Southern Italy and rural areas to gather in these spaces for socialization. They could pay the lowest possible price for *un caffè al bar*, which was often the cheapest commodity and served as the effective price for admission. Besides allowing them to enjoy an inexpensive beverage, these bars also afforded the working class an inexpensive place to pass the time. Many were named "Bar Sport" and became a gathering place and community center where these new urban populations could watch TV, listen to or watch soccer games, play cards, and conduct other social activities after work.

Coffee bars in Italy, like those in other Mediterranean societies, were not only social spaces for leisure and entertainment, but also important public institutions that provided informal contexts for everyday political engagement.[21] Customers of similar political views tended to congregate in the same establishment, where they could discuss politics and daily news and form communities. Each establishment gained its own reputation, as being a "communist bar," a "fascist bar," or a bar of some other political persuasion, depending on its clientele as well as on the owner's personality and inclinations. Bologna, which was called the "red" city, is home to many coffee bars with a history of involvement in leftist political activism and social movements. This was true not only of those bars that catered to the counter-cultural youths involved in the feminist and student movements of the 1960s and 70s, but also for some bars deeply rooted in the residential neighborhoods. Among them, the cooperative *circoli* were a particular type of politicized bar historically associated with Italian socialist movements going back to the early twentieth century. David Kertzer's ethnographic study of a *bolognese* working-class *quartiere*, or neighborhood, in the early seventies vividly depicted the critical role of the cooperative bars—the major locales for adult male socializing in the *quartiere*—in the local political struggles between the Catholic Church and the Italian Communist Party.[22] The local Party established its power base in the neighborhoods by identifying itself with these social centers, where both formal and informal political events took place.

Beginning in the late 1960s, female patronage of coffee bars gradually became socially acceptable. The feminist movements of that time advocated the liberation of Italian women from socio-spatial segregation in the domestic sphere.[23] Many women responded. They joined the industrial labor market, became more active participants in public life generally, and left the full-time domestic realm behind them. Increased female patronage of coffee bars also coincided with the emergent trend of breakfasting out of the home. The public-private divide was thus breached, and this in turn reshaped gendered practices in coffee bar consumption.[24] Eating a quick breakfast in a bar became a daily ritual for many of the post-war generation—both men and women—and the habit persists to this day, despite initial criticism in defense of eating at home as preserving "the value of a supposed family food tradition."[25]

Nevertheless, women in Italy have never engaged with coffee bars in the same way as men. The unwritten social rules of respectability still to a considerable extent restrict their access to the public realm.[26] Their sociability in coffee bars is different, in terms of both temporal and spatial segregation. The anthropologist Jane Cowan, who studied local *kafeteria* (coffee bars) in Northern Greece in the 1980s, argued that a gendered practice of coffee drinking both expressed and reproduced the gendered ordering of the customers' world, even as the traditional local gender ideology was being contested.[27] In Italy, men tend to linger in coffee bars, while women normally consume their drinks or make their purchases and then leave quickly. For the most part, women show up during breakfast time; far fewer order an alcoholic drink or play cards in the afternoon, especially when they have come in alone. The male dominance in these establishments, evident at a glance, further discourages women from entering and consuming, as my Italian friend Giulia commented on the *bar tabaccheria* where we had breakfast.

Since the 1980s, coffee bars have further transformed into multi-purpose businesses under the slogan *non solo caffè* (not only coffee). Most found that they had to include other products and services in order to survive. For example, the *bar latteria* also specializes in dairy products, the *bar gelateria* provides fresh ice cream, the *bar pasticceria* offers a variety of fresh pastries, and the *bar tabaccheria* sells tobacco products. Some focus on breakfast and light meals with a variety of sandwiches to meet wage workers' demands, especially in large cities where people cannot go home for lunch. Some bars target both daytime business with coffee as their central product and then offer evening entertainment with alcoholic beverages. Since the Great Recession of 2008, some bars have introduced *apericena* or *aperitivo buffet* (happy hour buffets) in the early evening. These have become particularly popular among young adults, as they need only pay a fixed and relatively modest price covering an *aperitivo* (aperitif) and a plate of food which, in many cases, is refillable. Some bars provide quite a variety of entertainments, including forms of gambling. Billiards was a popular game in the 1970s, but many pool tables have been replaced by slot machines since the early 2000s.

The incredible number of different types of Italian bars makes it impossible either to generalize about these social institutions or to describe them one by one. In addition, the country's sociocultural,

FIGURE 3.1. A typical scene from a peripheral neighborhood bar managed by Chinese families: an elderly pensioner reads local newspapers after the early morning rush. (Photograph by author)

FIGURE 3.2. A typical bar for passersby in Bologna. Bars like this usually provide more options in terms of food and drinks to cater to a larger flow of clientele than a neighborhood bar. The owner of this bar is also Chinese. (Photograph by author)

geographic and economic diversity has produced distinctive regional variations in its bar culture. Yet, I often heard local Italians use the terms *centro* and *periferia* (periphery) to not only locate a bar physically, but also as a spatial metaphor to imply the social class of a locality as well as its sociality. *Bar di quartiere* and *bar di passaggio* are also two terms that native Italians commonly use to describe a bar's sociality, although the distinctions are not clear in many cases. The former, literally meaning a "neigborhood bar," suggests a social center for a neighborhood community; the latter, literally a "bar of passage," denotes a place frequented by passersby and implies that it is not a community center. In the following sections, I will describe three coffee bars: one in the *centro*, one in the periphery, and also a third located between the *centro* and the periphery. All managed by Chinese families, they also exemplify three types of sociality in association with how the clientele use the space, as well as how they develop social relations within it. These coffee bars, like those managed by non-Chinese owners, are woven into the city's ever-changing social fabric. They are locales where populations considered both "desirable" and "undesirable" carry on their everyday urban lives.

A Bar in the Periphery

Some coffee bars in Italy are so embedded in the fabric of their local community that they are virtually invisible to tourists or to anyone who does not reside in the neighborhood from which the business draws the vast majority of its clientele. Such bars have no online presence and garner no reviews from Google or from websites like Trip Adviser or Yelp. This is the case with the bar that Lanlan's family has managed since 2011. Their business is a typical *bar di quartiere* located in Bologna's periphery, on the road to the airport. It is tucked away in the corner of a five-story red-brick apartment building in a dense residential area close to several manufacturing plants. From the outside, the bar looks no different from the other small storefronts that line the ground floor of this large non-descript building. The only hints that it is in fact a bar are two outdoor tables where several elderly men often sit with a cup of coffee or a glass of wine. There is not even the simple white sign with the blue lettering "bar" so often seen hanging above the entrances of other similarly minimalist coffee bars. For this establishment, no sign of any kind is necessary, as virtually all of its customers reside within a couple blocks of the business. I got to know the bar through the youngest sister of my second host Anna, a single Italian woman in her early fifties, a nurse, and a practicing Catholic, who rented an apartment in the building. Lanlan's family—she, her parents, and her two younger siblings—also lived in an apartment unit just upstairs from the family business, making them neighbors to Anna's sister, although the sister never frequented the bar.

My overwhelming first impression of this bar was that I had stepped into a time machine and was back in the Italy of the 1970s, a place that I knew only from Italian movies of the period. Indeed, I later learned from some elderly patrons that the bar had opened in the 1960s, when the apartment building was constructed, and that it was the first coffee bar in this peripheral working-class neighborhood. They also told me that the décor of the bar had hardly changed since its inauguration. Indeed, the oak-paneled walls and the aluminum glass display cases holding the breads, cold cuts, oranges, and other products all seemed like relics from a half-century past. At the entrance was a long bar counter where beverages and a very few food options like *brioche* croissants and *panini* sandwiches were served. Just behind the counter was a small peg letter board with some letters missing. It listed the various drinks on offer, but the prices shown were a year out of date. The price of a cup of coffee had since gone up from 1 to 1.1 euros. The entrance area had only one small table nestled in the farthest back corner, next to a refrigerator that held ice cream and a glass cabinet for packaged cookies and snacks. Some local newspapers—thumbed through by customers looking into the news of the day—were on the table, a standard feature of such neighborhood bars in Italy.

Walking past the entrance and the bar counter, one realized that the bar was larger on the inside than its exterior appearance would suggest. In fact, the main draw of this establishment were two separate rooms at the back. One was a spacious dining room holding six tables, which on any given afternoon was usually packed with dozens of pensioners, mostly men in their seventies or older, playing cards. Many of them had frequented this bar since their days as rowdy youngsters who would stop by for a drink and a game of billiards after long shifts in the nearby factories. A billiards table is no longer as popular in Italy's *bar di quartiere* or in other similar social centers as it was in the 1960s and 1970s. Yet, here in Lanlan's

FIGURE 3.3. An old peg letter board listing drinks and prices next to the espresso coffee machine in Lanlan's family-run bar. (Photograph by author)

FIGURE 3.4. Old and new games in Lanlan's family-run bar. For many older patrons, slot machines have replaced billiards as the game of choice. (Photograph by author)

family-managed bar it had survived. As in decades past, it sat in what might be described as a game room, the third and most spacious of the rooms in the bar. Overlooking the entire space was a dated CRT TV hanging from the corner of a ceiling. Its prominent position further harks back to those bygone days when private television ownership was still considered a luxury and neighbors brought their own stools or chairs to the bar to watch the weekly soccer game. However, I never saw the TV actually turned on. The five electronic slot machines that lined the back wall of the game room seemed to have suddenly intruded into this tableau vivant from the 1970s, as if to remind people time had indeed marched on into the new millennium.

When I was in the bar, I was usually able to occupy the one tall stool that stood at one end of the bar counter close to the entrance. Most of the customers would not stay at the bar counter for longer than it took to order food, consume a drink, pay their bill, or exchange a few words with Lanlan or whoever from her family was on shift. Instead, many gathered in the dining room or game room, or in the outdoor space. Thus, from my seat I could see the familiar faces come and go—older and younger, male and female, Italian and foreign. I witnessed some teenagers run into the bar while dribbling a football to ask for a free cup of water, some middle-aged people paying their bills from earlier in the day when they had forgotten their wallet at home, and some elderly men holding packs of medicine to take with a second glass of wine, perhaps more hesitantly than usual. I saw male immigrants enter in groups of two or three and grab several beers after work, Italian mothers and retired grandmas stop by for a coffee while pushing a baby stroller, and the elderly card winners enjoying coffee paid for by their fellow players who had lost the game. There was also the usual gossip, complaints, and neighborly spats one would expect in just about any hub of community socialization.

Lanlan's family-run business was not the only coffee bar in the neighborhood. A cooperative *circolo* and a Chinese-managed *bar tabaccheria* were both only a block away. Each of them has its own loyal patrons and each its own reputation among the residents of the neighborhood. The *circolo* had a more spacious bar frequented by many more pensioners. The *bar tabaccheria* that more immigrants patronized was notorious for the presence of heavy alcohol drinkers and drug users. Lanlan's family's bar as well as their clientele was much more *tranquillo* (quiet, calm, peaceful), according to some regulars with whom I talked. People with shared interests in sports or politics commonly congregate in the same establishment and form a place-based community.

Many regulars derived a strong sense of comfort and familiarity from this setting that had not really changed for decades. "The bar is always the same. Nothing has changed. It always has the same *clienti* [customers]," an Italian woman who looked to be in her six-ties told me. She had lived in the neighborhood since she was three years old but had moved to another area of the city several years ago. I met her on one of her regular visits to the coffee bar. I was surprised when she told me that it took her fifteen minutes to drive all the way to the bar just to spend another fifteen minutes there with a glass of sparkling wine before heading back. She explained to me emotionally: "But I have spent my life here." A retired wid-ower expressed similar sentiments: "This is not only Annalisa's family's bar. [Annalisa is Lanlan's Italian name]. It's also my bar. It's my second home." He had frequented the establishment for nearly fifty years since moving to the neighborhood when he got married in his twenties. He used to pass his leisure time there after work, but since retiring he now spends six to seven hours in the bar every day, having breakfast, drinking coffee and wine, reading newspa-pers, playing cards, or just sitting and doing nothing at all. Every now and then he brings tortellini or some other homemade food to the bar as a gift for Lanlan and her siblings. He is one of those Italian pensioners who typically arrive at their chosen bar every morning promptly at opening time. The neighborhood bar offers them a sense of attachment, belonging, and loyalty, a temporary escape from their otherwise lonely lives.

A Peripheral Bar in the Center

Bologna's *centro storico* is famous for its extensive porticoes which offer urban dwellers relief from both the blazing sun and sudden rainstorms. My barista teacher Letai's family-managed coffee bar is in the shadow of one of these historic porticoes. While still part of Bologna's urban center, it lays hidden in a quieter back street away from the throngs of shoppers and tourists. The city's well-preserved medieval buildings have undergone significant gentrification in the past several decades, but this street and its surrounding block seem to have largely ducked the numerous re-development projects, at least so far. The father of my first host described this historically working-class neighborhood as "the periphery of the *centro*."

The appearance of Letai's bar also reflects its liminal location. When I first visited the establishment in 2014, Letai's family had just renovated the bar after having purchased it six years earlier in 2008. The new interior featured granite counters with stainless steel counter-tops and granite tiles on both the floors and wall panels in the main space. A brand-new flat-screen TV hung on the wall broadcasting some old songs most of the time. The dining room, which featured three small tables and the game room filled with five slot machines were also freshly whitewashed. While clean and new, this renovated locale still looked like a generic bar. It was a far cry from the stylish décor one would see in the trendier coffee bars frequented by college students, young professionals, and tourists a few blocks away. For instance, instead of showing updated daily prices on a chalkboard or erasable menu board of the sort found in many chic bars, Letai's drinks menu was simply printed on an A4-sized piece of white paper fixed to the wall next to the liquor shelf.

Nevertheless, the renovations must surely have been a considerable improvement over the establishment that Letai originally bought. I had not seen the pre-renovation bar, but some of the older patrons seemed happy with the renovation, praising the new interior as much cleaner and brighter, while the old place was *molto triste* or "very sad" with poor lighting, moldy walls, and dirty floors. Several others, including the son of one of the previous Italian owners, described the previous iterations of the present-day coffee bar, such as where the furniture was placed and what kind of food was offered. Yet, even the oldest customer whom I met was unable to describe how the *bar*—or more properly the *osteria*, as it was then called—looked like in its first iteration, allegedly during the fascist period. In spite of the changes in merchandise, spatial arrangement, and management over the years, they agreed, however, that what had barely changed was the vibe of the place. Indeed, the bar is itself an integral part of a still living and vibrant community, albeit one experiencing Bologna's and urban Italy's wider social and economic transformations.

The offerings at Letai's establishment are similar to those at Lanlan's bar. The drink list covers the staple espresso-based coffees and a wide range of other beverages, both alcoholic and non-alcoholic, but sophisticated cocktails are not among them, even though the business is open until 11 pm. The food choices are also limited to a few types of *brioche* croissants and *panini* sandwiches displayed in a small glass cabinet on the top of the bar counter. Yet, Letai's coffee bar doubles as a *tabaccheria*, a licensed seller of tobacco products, and provides multiple options of *gratta e vinci* (scratch cards). It is also the place where one can pay bills, buy bus tickets, recharge mobile phones, buy postage stamps, and find a wide range of the sorts of merchandise and services that a typical convenience store would provide.

Standing behind the bar counter for several months, I was able to talk to some of the pensioners who had patronized the business for most their lives. They were human reminders of Bologna's urban history and the history of this particular coffee bar, and from them I gained some insights into the older pattern of *bolognese* civic life that was centered around establishments such as Letai's. Among the regular customers there was a wine dealer in his early seventies who lived in an apartment building across the street and played cards with his old friends in the dining room most afternoons. There was also a businessman in his late seventies who carried a walking stick and always ordered a glass of Chianti after card games; he told me stories of his trips to colonial Hong Kong before its 1997 handover to China. There was also a German language teacher in his eighties who used to live in the neighborhood and would ride a bike or take the bus to the bar for a *caffè bassissimo* or "extremely short coffee" every few days. Other regulars included middle-aged Italian workers, such as a dance club manager who stopped by before opening time, a carpenter who would close his open tab only occasionally, after his projects on commission were paid, and a security guard who worked at a garage down the block. Alongside these pensioners and neighborhood locals were younger immigrants, including a Bangladeshi man who ran a grocery store next door, a Moroccan construction worker who often bought a beer for a homeless man who could not afford anything except tap water, and a Cameroonian ex-soccer player who lived in a shared apartment upstairs in the same building.

Unlike the more family-friendly atmosphere at Lanlan's establishment, which emerged alongside the post-war development of large workers' tenements in Bologna's outskirts, Letai's establishment was a much more male-dominated social space. In the morning hours, some women would regularly have a quick espresso or cappuccino and a croissant for breakfast, but by the afternoon, the coffee bar served male customers almost exclusively. Typically, they would pass several hours drinking, talking, playing cards, or watching others play, smoking under the portico with a beer in hand, and gambling on the slot machines. In my time at Letai's coffee bar, I only noticed two women—both native Italians—who regularly passed time there in the afternoon and evening hours. One was a middle-aged clothing shop owner who often stopped by to quickly grab a glass of wine and a *panino* sandwich before making the commute back home in the nearby city of Ferrara. The other was a woman in her twenties who appeared perpetually inebriated and would often spend many hours playing slots and chatting with the male patrons. As a legacy of the bar's older role as a community center of sorts, there were also occasional visits by retired women who resided on the block after breakfast time. I witnessed a woman in her seventies walk up to the counter and place a fifty-cent coin on the counter as a service fee for Letai to call her a taxi. On another occasion, an elderly woman recollected her lost youth by showing Letai photos of herself on the beach when she was young.

Because of its more central location, Letai's bar also attracts a much more diverse clientele than bars in Bologna's periphery proper and the surrounding provincial towns. Like *bar di passaggio* in the city center, it receives many passersby and occasional customers of all ages who stop for a pack of cigarettes or a simple caffeinated beverage. Yet, younger Italians who still reside in the neighborhood are conspicuously missing from the regular clientele. Urbanites of that demographic almost never sit down or stay for more time than it takes to finish an espresso. Over the several months that I apprenticed in the bar, the only younger customers I served were a young apprentice chef in his early twenties from a nearby restaurant (who spent much time on slot machines) and a young couple in their late twenties who showed up to drink a dozen shots each day for an entire week and then disappeared completely without closing their last open tab. It is basically a combination of middle-aged to retired Italians and younger immigrants—virtually all men from working-class backgrounds—who, through their faithful patronage, uphold the traditional role of Letai's establishment as a neighborhood center for male sociability.

A Passersby Bar

There are of course many centrally located *bar di passaggio* in Bologna's *centro storico*, and these give off a very different vibe from the liminal spatiality of Letai's establishment or the peripheral sociality of Lanlan's bar. The bar—or more accurately *caffè*, as its actual name indicates—that Ailin and her husband have managed since 2011 is a typical *bar di passaggio*. Only five minutes walking distance from Letai's establishment, it is situated at the corner of one of the city's busiest avenues close to the train station. Several 3-star and 4-star hotels, some banks, shops, offices, and local markets fill out the locale, while crowds of tourists, shoppers, university students, and other pedestrians pass under the porticoes that cover all of its blocks. While it is by no means a luxurious bar or one of the trendiest bars in Bologna, it is nevertheless frequented by customers with more disposable income. While the price of a cup of coffee is about the same in all the bars, drinks and other offerings are not. In 2014, when a spritz at Letai's place cost 3.5 euros, it cost

5 euros at Ailin's establishment. The greater affluence of this coffee bar's clientele is also reflected in the fact that, unlike the previously mentioned bars which offered patrons outdoor seating as a matter of course, Ailin's establishment charges a small fee for the use of their *al fresco* tables.

The appearance of the establishment is also up-scale, in tune with up-to-date middle-class aesthetics. By the coffee bar's entrance is a large blackboard listing the daily specials and their prices, all meticulously updated each day. The interior that greets a customer is bright and open, thanks to large glass doors, two tall French windows, and the absence of interior partitions. The glass contrasts rather nicely with the polished wood trim of the bar counter and wall panels, which gives the sense of a classic décor, but with a clean and modern twist. Before lunch time, the long glass cabinet always holds abundant and varied food offerings that one can see even from outside the bar. The interior open space is filled with several small IKEA-style dark oak tables and leather chairs, while slot machines are nowhere in sight. Ailin told me that she herself does not like those gambling machines and it would also be "very bad" if her customers were to see them since they are mostly office workers who "wear suits and ties."

Ailin's coffee bar is open from 5:30 am to 8 pm almost every day, including public holidays. Alongside the well-presented coffee beverages, a wide selection of pastries, sourced from a local historical *pasticceria* or bakery, has attracted something of a devoted breakfast following. Alongside sweet offerings, there are also many options for *panini* sandwiches, salads, cold cut meats, and even some cold *primi piatti* or "first plates," such as pasta and rice. Early every morning, Ailin prepares full-blown meals for *pausa pranzo* or "lunch break," working together with a middle-aged white employee who is also an experienced barista and has worked in this same coffee bar since it was under the previous management. After breakfast, lunch becomes the focus. This is when the bar becomes especially crowded, with customers occupying all the tables, the inner space, and sometimes even queuing under the outside portico. When I happened to be nearby at lunch time, I too was happy to go to Ailin's place to grab a *focaccia* bread or a *panino* sandwich for a quick lunch, and this was not only for research purposes. Their food was genuinely good. The lunch-time peak usually requires four laborers—Ailin, her husband, and the previously mentioned white employee as baristas, and a younger white woman as the waitress. By late afternoon, when the glass cabinet is nearly emptied, there are also some customers who stop by for a spritz or wine, although *aperitivo* business is not their major focus.

The pace at Ailin's establishment is typical of a *bar di passaggio*, as is its sociality. While the food was appealing to me, I found this kind of sociality much more difficult when it came to connecting with customers and having conversations with them. I also worried about staying too long and taking up more than my share of the limited space during the busy hours. The brisk volume of business this bar attracts left even the baristas with little time for long conversations with me, other than around closing time. While many of the bar's clientele were what can be considered regular patrons who stopped by frequently throughout the week to buy a coffee or have breakfast before work, none of the regulars spent hours, let alone entire afternoons and evenings socializing in the bar as the regulars did in Lanlan's and Letai's establishments. Customers who did not enter together rarely socialized with one another, and loitering was not commonplace as it was in the two previously described coffee bars.

I also picked up a vague sense of alienation between the staff and customers at Ailin's coffee bar from the fact that both of the two owners and the two employees wore uniforms, which was not common in more marginal bars. Their neatly pressed white or black shirts and black pants seemed to separate them from the customers and served as another reminder that the establishment was first and foremost a service business rather than a community center. This is not to say that Ailin's staff were unfriendly or distanced themselves from their customers. On the contrary, they always had smiles on their faces and exchanged pleasantries with the customers. They also clearly recognized and knew by name some of the bar's regular patrons. The customers, regulars or not, would generally walk in for a quick pick-me-up, a fast breakfast or lunch, maybe a coffee with a bite to eat, or some other sort of brief break in their day, and then they would leave. They were passersby in the truest sense of the term. The coffee bar itself was never their destination, only a quick diversion. At Ailin's, card tables and groups of idle retired men were conspicuously absent, and so was the deep sense of community that was so apparent at Lanlan's and Letai's establishments.

A Declining Social Space

A 1922 poster advertising an Italian espresso coffee machine designed by the Italian futurist artist Leonetto Cappiello featured a man leaning out the door of a passing train to grab a cup of coffee from an early espresso machine. The poster declared that this new coffee machine, like the locomotive, symbolized speed, a Zeitgeist of the fascist era lauded by the futurists, and one that heralded a particular brand of Italian modernity. Indeed, the Italian word *espresso* means rapid and fast. When the new espresso—initially re-named *caffè crema*—became accessible for mass consumption in the 1960s, the industry further advertised it as being not only a new caffeinated beverage, but also representative of a modern lifestyle and urban culture. The cream on the top of espresso coffee was synonymous with good quality and luxury.[28]

Espresso has since shifted from a symbol of an Italian modernity speeding towards the future to its current status as an icon of Italian tradition. Yet, like many other traditions, this one that seems so venerable and timeless, is in fact of quite recent origin.[29] Through a series of industrial and commercial advertising campaigns in the Italian domestic market and beyond, "Made in Italy" products achieved global renown as sophisticated and well-made, while the Italians themselves became associated with good taste in food, design, and fashion.[30] The construction of Italy's coffee tradition was a crucial part of this process. The Italian coffee industry promoted espresso as symbolic of what was "Made in Italy," marketing an Italian lifestyle that combined tradition and modernity, while resisting American coffeehouse chains and the globalized fast food companies that were invading Italian cities during the 1990s.[31] While some large Italian roasting companies branded themselves as the defenders of Italian coffee culture, claiming a lineage that went back to the very first Venetian *caffè*, smaller companies emphasized their embeddedness in local society, their close connections with local culture, and their locally rooted authentic brand of Italian coffee tradition.

It is not always, however, a positive judgment on the glorious past of the Venetian *caffè* when an Italian uses the term *tradizionale* to describe a coffee bar. The word can also be a synonym for "old-fashioned," "outdated," or "lacking in ingenuity," in short, as incompatible with the new middle-class Italian aesthetics. Lanlan's and Letai's establishments are *bar tradizionali* of this sort, which have survived for several decades with no substantial updating. They increasingly serve pensioners and new immigrants, while struggling to please generations of white, middle-class Italian urbanites. The daughter of my second host Anna, a first-year college student, shared with me her ambivalent perceptions of coffee bars in Italy shortly after she returned from her gap year in Australia in 2014:

> I know this kind of *bar* is something typically Italian. It's *cultura italiana*. . . . When I go around, I know the bars are there and I feel more *tranquilla* [calm, secure]. I know where I can possibly have breakfast, stop for a break, have a coffee, eat a pastry, or chat with friends. . . . But I almost never go to a *bar*. . . . I usually have coffee at home. . . . The idea is that I don't frequent a *bar* every day. I don't spend much time there. I have other things to do. They are for the elderly. . . . Passing time in a *bar* means wasting time.

Another local *bolognese* friend, a professor of medicine in his early thirties, shared Anna's daughter's attitude towards bars: "When

I was a teenager, I met friends in *centro*, somewhere outdoors, in a *piazza*, in front of the library. . . . Sometimes we also met in a bar, but not in a bar for retirees. . . . Now we meet in the evening for a drink, at a night bar. . . . Maybe in *periferia*, the young guys still hang out there sometimes."

The "traditional bars," no longer considered a symbol of modernity, have gradually lost their function as centers for socializing among the younger generations of native Italians. Educated urban youths, regardless of their gender, typically pass very little, if any, of their social lives in the neighborhoods where they live. This generational difference is related to fundamental changes in what it means to be a neighbor. It also reflects what anthropologist Biao Xiang has termed "the displacement of the nearby."[32] Urban dwellers' sense of community and their use of time and space have been reshaped by the increased daily mobility enabled by systems of mass public and private transportation, as well as by digital technologies. In this process of delocalization, sociologist Anthony Giddens has suggested, social relations are "disembedded" or lifted out "from local contexts and [re-articulated] across indefinite tracts of time-space."[33] People no longer live their lives at the neighborhood level. This deprives the *bar di quartiere* of its traditional central role as the social focal point of community socializing. The cooperative *circoli* have undergone a similar transformation. Many of these previously politicized bars are now entertainment centers catering almost exclusively to pensioners.

Some "traditional bars" did make a successful transition, attracting groups of college students and other younger people by providing low-cost alcoholic drinks. But for the most part, white, educated, Italian youths now frequent their own preferred social spaces in historical town centers, university zones, and gentrified neighborhoods. The bulk of their patronage goes to the *bar di tendenza* or "trendy bars." They are drawn by the innovative and stylish architecture and creative décor of these locales, and by their vibrant atmosphere and chic background music. Notwithstanding many differences in the look and feel of individual "trendy bars," they commonly manifest their spatiality and temporality as an integrated space combining the functions of a breakfast bar in the morning, a quiet café for lunch, a coffee shop where college students and young professionals can quietly work with their laptops in the afternoons, and then take on the guise of a pleasant *aperitivo* bar before dinner time. Some of them also eventually turn into lively cocktail bars in the evening. They almost never offer gambling. Their operators are often good at promoting their businesses on social media, organizing social or cultural events, and keeping up to date on new market trends. "Trendy bars" are still relatively few compared to "traditional bars," but they are rapidly emerging as part of the process of urban gentrification.

In Italy generational differences often go hand-in-hand with class distinctions. The country changed radically over the second half of the twentieth century, transforming from a largely agricultural economy into one of the world's most dynamic industrial societies. Many families who benefited from this rapid economic growth also achieved social mobility. Indeed, class distinctions were always highly noticeable in Italy, especially among men from the older generations. My two middle-class Italian host families, as well as their close friends, male or female, retired or not, older or younger, all engaged with coffee bars in one way or another, but none of them claimed to be an *uomo da bar* (literally "a man of the *bar*" or "a *bar* regular"), like Giulia's uncle or the card players at Lanlan's and Letai's establishments. The retired high school teacher Pietro who showed me how to make *grappa* at home explained to me why he had never been an *uomo dal bar*:

> I have always had other, more interesting places to go. I am a frequent cinema goer; I have my own cultural clubs and many other things for my leisure time. . . . *Bar* are the kingdom of retired men, unemployed guys, deadbeats, immigrants, slot machine addicts, alcoholics, and those who have nothing better to do.

Pietro's statement conforms to Pierre Bourdieu's understanding of social space. As "an underlying structure of symbolic classifications," it is not only "a given that people enter into" but also that they are in turn "composed by them."[34] For Pietro and the previously mentioned younger Italians, the "traditional bars" serving as community centers in the working-class neighborhood are stigmatized as undesirable social spaces for undesirable populations. Immigrant workers, usually men, have become an important source of clientele in these "traditional bars," where many Italian male pensioners—many of them originally internal migrants—spend their days. These immigrant workers from North Africa, the Balkans, Eastern Europe, and South Asia are *extracomunitari* (non-EU immigrants) in the eyes of native Italians and *banhei* (literally "half blacks") for Chinese immigrants.[35] They have replaced the previous Italian internal migrant workers from rural areas and Southern Italy, and were recruited into the Italian economy as cheap, low-skilled labor. They have faced the same problems of cramped housing, limited social space, and social discrimination that Italy's internal migrants experienced in the 1960s. The "traditional bars" are one of the few places where they can spend relatively little money to enjoy a social space and thus have become their after-work social clubs. Instead of coffee, they mainly consume beer and other alcoholic drinks. These coffee bars where a new working class of urbanites displayed *una bella figura* (a good impression) in the decades following the Second World War have been reduced to marginalized social spaces primarily for socially marginalized people. Watching TV and socializing with neighbors and friends in a coffee bar is now no more than a collective memory of childhood for the older generations who grew up in the post-war period. It is, however, predominantly these "traditional bars" that many Chinese families found accessible and potentially profitable.

Searching for Sociality

A few months before I left Bologna in 2015, Uncle Gumin, whose family story was introduced in the previous chapter, started searching for another coffee bar to purchase. His eldest daughter had recently married, and the young couple decided to continue to work in the coffee bar niche. Uncle Gumin convinced them to take over the current business where Ensi had worked as the primary barista, so that the young couple would not take the risk involved in starting up a new bar or go through in the "painstaking" searching process. Uncle Gumin told me that he spent a year just trying to negotiate the sales price with the previous owner of their current business. I also knew from other Chinese interlocutors that it took from several months to two years from deciding to enter the business to actually buying an establishment. This was especially the case for the pioneering Chinese entrepreneurs, because online platforms for advertising business transactions were not yet well developed in the late 2000s, as they could only collect information from their personal networks or by entering an establishment to ask the owner outright if the business was on the market. The search process also involves repetitive visits to the prospective businesses, consultations with the buyer's experienced "relatives and friends," and negotiations over the purchase conditions before delegating a *commercialista* (accountant and business consultant) to go through the paperwork with the local bureaucracy to finalize the exchange of ownership. Uncle Gumin believed that he had much more experience and entrepreneurial sensitivity than his children and could better evaluate what would be a good match for the remaining family to manage.

I happened to know of two Chinese-managed coffee bars for sale and passed on the information to Uncle Gumin. One was Ailin's establishment, the other was Lanlan's bar. Ailin and her husband, both in their early forties, had decided to sell the business for family reasons rather than economic concerns. Ailin told me that they had always wanted to bring their three teenage children to Italy, but the business intruded into their family time and made childcare impossible for them. Indeed, in a centrally located *bar di passaggio* targeting middle-class urbanites like Ailin's establishment, there was no physical space appropriate for children. Ailin and her husband lived in a peripheral neighborhood where the rent was cheaper, and they commuted to work every day. This was in contrast to Lanlan's family's case, as one of the reasons that her parents initially purchased the establishment was that "the family could stay together." They rented an apartment just upstairs from the business. I also saw Lanlan's younger sister, a high school student, doing homework behind the bar counter and her eight-year-old brother reading in the dining room, helping to clean tables, or playing pool with some teenage neighbors. Managing that establishment was a part of community life, and the boundary between the domestic and the public space was blurred. Yet, Lanlan's parents wanted to sell the establishment as the income they gained from it had decreased considerably and no longer met their expectations, especially now that a new *sala giochi* (arcade) that centered on slot machines had opened just a few blocks away and poached much of their gambling business.

Uncle Gumin did not want to buy either of the two coffee bars. He was clearly aware of the location of the establishments as well as of their different business models and socialities. Ailin's business was too expensive, and the risk was too high. Moreover, he knew that a business in the city center targeting middle-class urbanites, younger consumers, and passersby would have a less stable clientele. He feared that their customers would be "much more difficult to deal with, as they're more demanding and they aren't attached to one place." Thus, he did not even bother to visit it. By contrast, Lanlan's family-managed bar in the urban periphery was more appealing to him. However, he quickly lost interest after visiting due to the coffee bar's "poor" location and "unpromising" business potential. He commented:

It's a *laoren jiuba* [bar for the elderly]. Those elderly men won't leave if your skills are not perfect. They won't leave because of the change of management. . . . Their friends are all here. Many have been here for their whole lives. . . . It's also relatively cheaper, so the risk is low. . . . This type of *jiuba* can be a good start-up business for some [Chinese] families. . . . They don't have experience in this business but want to have a try. . . . But it's not good enough for my family.

In Uncle Gumin's mind, an ideal coffee bar would be somewhere between a *bar di quartiere* and a *bar di passaggio*. It would have a stable clientele of neighborhood residents as well as a good many occasional customers who would enter and make purchases. Thus, he sought out locations with a degree of foot traffic or which doubled as a tobacco shop. Indeed, his family's first coffee bar had been just such an establishment, as was Letai's and most of the Chinese-managed bars I encountered during 2014 and 2015.

Revenue from slot machines was another key criterion that Uncle Gumin and many other potential Chinese coffee bar owners sought. Unlike the selling of coffee, mixed beverages, or sandwiches, slot machines do not require any preparation work from staff and little if any maintenance or upkeep beyond the electricity needed to power them. The slots company from which the coffee bar owners rent the machines sends local representatives to collect the coins regularly and take charge of maintenance. Considering that coffee bars usually stay open long hours, it is especially helpful to include a labor-free and skill-free side business. "It can at least cover some expenses like the rent for us," Uncle Gumin's son Enbao once commented. Indeed, the slots have gradually become a new staple feature for coffee bars in Italy since 2003 when they were first allowed in these establishments. The fancier and trendier coffee bars targeting people from higher social classes usually exclude gambling, but slots are almost ubiquitous in "traditional bars" that depend on a less affluent demographic. Such coffee bars are also known as *bar popolare*, people's bars, implying that the business caters to the "masses" from a lower social status. Originally intended to bolster state tax revenue from small-scale gambling, slots have become one of the most reliable sources of income for the Italian state, proving highly resistant to economic recessions. By 2016, there was one slot machine for every 142 residents in Italy, the highest per capita percentage in Europe.[36] They

FIGURE 3.5. A display of winning Italian *gratta e vinci* cards hanging above the bar counter. This is another popular gambling game. (Photograph by author)

also constitute a considerable portion of a coffee bar's income and are thus crucial to surviving in an uncertain economy, especially for a business like a coffee bar that typically runs on a meagre profit margin.

That said, not all of Chinese-owned coffee bars have slot machines. The painstaking search for a "good" coffee bar to manage involved evaluating the family's financial ability, the number of effective family laborers, their language competence, and the sociality of the coffee bars themselves. Some Chinese families with greater economic capital bought more expensive and classy coffee bars mainly targeting middle-class urbanites, as in Ailin's case. These owners tended to hire white baristas to work for them, while partially or completely hiding their own presence so as to become practically invisible in their own coffee bars. Other Chinese families with more cultural capital bought coffee bars targeting native Italian youths, but such families were often young, second-generation couples who were born or primarily raised in Italy. Indeed, Ailin's establishment was sold after only several months on the market to another Chinese family with more capital and with an adult daughter who had grown up in Italy. Lanlan's establishment with its declining business has not found a purchaser after many years. Uncle Gumin ended up buying a storefront property on a main street outside of the historical center. There had been a "traditional bar" on that location, but it had closed down two years before. Uncle Gumin hired a Chinese decoration team to renovate the space and opened a new "traditional bar." With the knowledge his family had accumulated from their first business, he and his two unmarried children—both of whom were raised in Italy—have turned the place into a family-friendly social hub serving both neighbors and passersby, creating the impression that the original bar had never closed in the first place.

Matching Class, Situating Space

"Can you tell *i cinesi* [the Chinese] to remove the slot machines?!" I was at a house party organized by an Italian writer. An Italian woman in her fifties holding a glass of wine interjected this question casually when I was introducing my research to another guest. Her comment reflects the popular public perception that links Chinese ownership of coffee bars with the unsavory proliferation of slot machines throughout Italy. Indeed, elderly men, immigrants, and slots are the three features native Italians most readily identify with *bar cinesi*. The truth, however, is that *bar cinesi* are not and have never been homogeneous. They include a wide range of business types. Alongside increasing internal class differences and the greater socio-economic mobility of Chinese in Italy, an increasing number of Chinese-managed coffee bars now target middle-class urbanites. Even among the "traditional bars" some are family-friendly and gender-balanced, others are male-dominated and serve to a larger extent as drinking spaces. The type of coffee bar that a Chinese family manages reflects the owner's family's placement in Italy's class hierarchy.

Meanwhile, the stereotypes and labels attached to *bar cinesi* are by no means limited to Chinese-managed coffee bars, but are commonly employed more generally to "traditional bars," regardless of the owners' ethnic or national backgrounds. Many of these coffee bars, which once were community centers, have become "outdated" and marginal social spaces associated with an undesirable way of life that has been abandoned by younger-generation Italians who embrace new de-localized lifestyles, values, and consumption patterns. In this context of delocalization, many "traditional bars," as well as other elements of the neighborhood economy, are experiencing a shift of ownership from locally established residents to new immigrants. In this context, small gambling services have become a survival strategy that both established and newer business owners can deploy. Gambling is however incompatible with middle-class understandings of morality, civic responsibility, and respectability. The slot machines thus further reinforce spatialized consumption patterns marked by class distinctions. From a class perspective, the sociality of these "outdated" localities has remained relatively unchanged since the beginning of the mass consumption of espresso coffee in the 1960s. The main patrons who use the space as a community center have always been working-class people. What has changed is the makeup of that working class, which in Italy is increasingly composed of immigrants.

Their class-bound sociality has thus allowed many Chinese immigrant families to survive economic uncertainty. These convivial bricoleurs make do with what resources they have at hand to run either "traditional bars" serving marginalized urbanites or trendier coffee bars that sometimes host social or cultural events when they have more cultural capital. In many cases, it is actually the existing sociality of these *bar tradizionali* that is particularly attractive to Chinese immigrant families seeking to make a living through self-employment. Through their willingness to work long hours and exploit flexible family labor, they have enabled an otherwise declining social space to survive. In this sense, Chinese baristas are far from being the "cultural invaders" threatening Italian culture that nationalist and anti-immigrant discourses often portray, but rather seem to have become guardians of an older way of life centering on neighborhood community life that serves populations from working-class backgrounds.

One afternoon, I met a Bologna-based urban sociologist for a chat in a newly opened coffee bar that he suggested as our meeting point. It was located a few blocks outside of the loop that encloses the *centro storico* in a working-class, multi-ethnic neighborhood undergoing rapid commercial gentrification. This was a "trendy bar," configured as a combination of coffeehouse, café, and cocktail bar. People could go there for breakfast, a simple lunch, *aperitivo* in the late afternoon, cocktails or wine in the evening, and, quite often, musical events at night. I found out afterwards that the opening of the coffee bar was big news among intellectuals and young professionals and had been covered widely by the local newspapers and discussed excitedly on social media. An Italian food and restaurant website described its environment in this way:

> The environment is in line with the vintage taste that is all the rage, but at the same time the atmosphere is authentic, aesthetically refined, but not artificial. The renovation work brought to light the original tile, insignia and brickwork, and also incorporated new furniture, partly from thrift shops and partly created expressly for the bar (such as a marble table that leans on an old sewing machine).[37]

Using expressions such as "vintage taste that is all the rage," and "partly from thrift shops and partly created expressly," this review applauds the "authenticity" and "originality" of this coffee bar as it ingeniously uses "tradition" to create the kind of "modernity" that "Made in Italy" embodies. As the sociology professor also pointed out, "This isn't the kind of *bar* that can be opened by just anyone. It's the *bar* of the future. This kind of *bar* will be mainstream in the future, while the *bar tradizionali* will die out within twenty years."

One night, I went back to that trendy bar with some friends for a drink. When we were leaving at around 10:30 pm, half an hour from its posted closing time, the place was still crowded with young adults with several sitting on the floor against the French windows. I walked to the closest bus station three minutes away on foot. While waiting for the bus back home, I noticed on the other side of the street a "traditional bar" that was still open. It was a Chinese-managed coffee bar that I had often frequented for my research. There were two men sitting in the *al fresco* area with a couple of beers on the table in front of them. Their presence made the brightly lit spacious coffee bar behind them look even more desolate. At that moment, I recalled the sociology professor's "dying-out" prediction. Ironically, it is these purportedly moribund lower-class social institutions that have served many Chinese bricoleurs in their pursuit of a good life. Unlike the managers of many other small Chinese businesses, Chinese bar owners have striven to maintain the pre-existing sociality of these social institutions rather than to deploy, as a selling point, some sort of exotic Chinese-ness that meets the customers' Orientalist preconceptions. In the next two chapters, I will discuss how it is that newly self-employed Chinese baristas go about preserving the traditional sociality of their bars so as to safeguard this threatened social institution.

Intermezzo

COFFEE BREAK

IT IS AN ORDINARY AFTERNOON. Several regular *clienti* are whiling away their time at Uncle Gumin's establishment, intent on their coffee, beer, or slot machines, while occasionally a few passersby come and go for a coffee or just to enjoy a few minutes of rest. As usual, I am sitting next to Gigi, the Italian construction worker in his fifties, and observing and talking with the people around us.

Uncle Gumin, known to his *clienti* as Luca, is behind the bar counter, taking care of the business by himself. His eldest daughter, Ensi, has already finished her shift and has returned home. His second daughter, Enhua, and his son, Enbao, have gone off to attend the graduation ceremony of a close Chinese friend who grew up with them in Bologna. Whenever his children have other activities, Uncle Gumin steps in as a substitute barista.

Uncle Gumin looks exhausted. He had been working at the coffee bar without rest after spending the entire morning selling goods in a local street market. In spite of his weariness, he tries to keep up his smile in front of the customers. Only during the intervals between serving his *clienti* does he take a seat on a high stool behind the cash register, sip from a large mug of draught beer, and pass the time with his smartphone or simply hunched over the counter. Ironically, even though he owns a coffee bar and makes coffee every day, he does not like drinking coffee. It is a beer that gives him a much-needed pick-me-up.

As usual, I take the opportunity presented by one of these intervals to chat with him. Our conversations are primarily in Mandarin Chinese, but when *clienti* are nearby, we shift to Italian. Sometimes the regulars also join in our conversations. He is an excellent barista in the eyes of his regular patrons, praised for his proficient coffee-making skills and responsive service. According to Gigi, Uncle Gumin is the best coffee maker in the family, better than any of his three children. "I can't speak Italian as well as my children," he has explained to me, "so I have to make good coffees. I really practiced a lot. I'm happy that my *keren* (guests, customers) like it."

Everything was routine that day until an unkempt man in a dark jacket and jeans who looked to be in his forties interrupted the peaceful atmosphere. The man walked in, sneaking glances from side to side. His unstable gait came to a halt in front of the cash register where he propped himself up with his arms and leaned over the bar counter. "*Bagno c'è? Bagno!* [Is there a bathroom? Bathroom!]," the man muttered. His Italian had a strong foreign accent, but I was not able to pin-point his nationality. After hesitating for a few seconds, Uncle Gumin replied in Italian, "Go straight and turn left." Although the bathroom is supposed to be reserved for paying customers only, Uncle Gumin indicated its location to the man. I never once saw him refuse a request for use of the bathroom, even from passersby who did not buy anything. He once explained his business philosophy to me with a Chinese saying: *Jinmen doushi ke.* "Everyone entering the door is a guest." *Ke* or *keren* in Chinese refers to both a guest and a client or customer. While he did not decline the man's request, suspicion was written all over his face.

The man walked toward the bathroom, but then suddenly veered off, opening the barrier gate to enter the area reserved for baristas. Uncle Gumin's eyes were following his movements and he rapidly ran toward the man and tried to stop him. "*Cosa vuoi?!* [What do you want?!]" he asked in a defensive voice. The man pointed at Uncle Gumin's pants and then his own pants, saying in broken Italian, "Pants, pants, same, same!" Then the man approached Uncle Gumin and grabbed him by his legs. Uncle Gumin tried to stop him and, after tussling for a few seconds, he demanded that the man leave the establishment.

Everyone in the bar, several customers and myself, stopped what we were doing and watched the scene unfold. Everything happened so quickly that no one could really follow exactly what was happening. Even Uncle Gumin was at a loss to figure out just what transpired. When the strange man left the coffee bar, everyone started asking Uncle Gumin if he was OK and if anything was missing.

"Nothing happened. Just a drunk man!" Even while he spoke, Uncle Gumin checked his pants pockets. He suddenly turned pale with shock. "My wallet!" he cried out. As he ran out the door he shouted to me and some of his regular patrons in Italian, "Watch my *bar*!" Everyone encouraged him, yelling, "Go, go!!!"

A young Bangladeshi man named Raffel, a regular at the bar, and his friend left the slot machines behind and rushed out the door. As Uncle Gumin turned right, they turned left in an attempt to intercept the thief. The other *clienti*, including Gigi and a retired man whom Uncle Gumin's children call Nonno Pino (Grandfather Pino), all rushed to the entrance and craned their necks to see what was going on outside.

Uncle Gumin didn't make us wait for too long. After a few minutes, I saw him and the two Bangladeshi helpers coming back triumphantly. All three men's faces were soaked with sweat.

"Got it!" Uncle Gumin panted.

"*Bravo*, Luca!" His *keren* cheered almost in chorus.

Uncle Gumin got back to his seat, while Raffel and his friend returned to the slot machines. While playing his game, Raffel began vividly describing the incident: "Fortunately, I was sitting here, close to the door. I saw the guy's face. . . . We found him in a back alley. He was so scared, hiding himself under a car. But Luca dragged him out and slugged him!" Raffel imitated Luca's action, punching his fist in the air and went on: "And then that bum gave him the wallet back right away! . . . I never thought Luca was that kind of guy!" Making another fist, the short Bangladeshi signaled his respect for Uncle Gumin. Others echo him with applause and shouts of "Bravo, Luca! Bravo!"

"How much was in the wallet?" I asked, in Italian to make sure that everyone was included in the conversation. "Two or three hundred, not so much." Uncle Gumin answered. Gigi looked at him sympathetically and said: "That's 300 coffees he's made!" "True!" Nonno Pino echoed, "An entire day's work!"

Raffel was about to leave. He stood up, put five euros on the bar counter, and declared, "I'm paying for the two beers I ordered earlier." Uncle Gumin shook his head, waving his right hand up and down with his fingertips together and upright. This is *mano a borsa*, "hand purse," a gesture frequently used in Italy, roughly meaning, "Come on! What are you talking about?" "Two beers, my treat!" he said to Raffel. The Bangladeshi man didn't insist. He took back the money. "*Grazie*, Luca! *Ciao ciao!* [Thanks, Luca! Bye bye!]" He left with a big smile on his face.

The other patrons who had witnessed the whole drama talked endlessly about what had happened and shared the breaking news with newcomers who had missed out on the incident. They spoke with great relish of Uncle Gumin's bravery and manliness. This Chinese man, a husband, a father, and the head of his family was now, suddenly, something of a hero in this coffee bar community.

4

Reproducing Taste

FROM THE FIRST day of my fieldwork in Bologna, I sought opportunities to learn barista skills so as to gain an insider's perspective into the lives of Chinese baristas. This plan, however, was delayed when I broke my right arm in a bicycle accident in September 2014. For the following three months, I was the "girl in the cast" and a "vulnerable observer," to echo Ruth Behar's classic work on reflexive anthropology.[1] I spent the time navigating my way among several Chinese-managed coffee bars and building trust relationships with my interlocutors. I got to know Letai and his family-run coffee bar in the "periphery of the *centro*" during that period through his father, who was a leader at the Chinese Evangelical Christian Church of Bologna. Letai joined his parents in Italy when he was fifteen years old. He was an experienced barista, having worked in his family's coffee bar since his parents bought it in 2008. I often heard customers compliment his professional skills. Letai also proudly told me that he had trained at least five or six Chinese at his establishment, including Meili's son, whom I knew in person. All of them eventually ended up managing their own family-run coffee bars. In mid-December, when my right arm was finally liberated from its cast, I too became Letai's student, an informal apprentice barista and unpaid worker at his establishment.

Upon hearing that I was learning coffee-making from a Chinese barista, my physiotherapist abruptly paused in the middle of treating my arm. This middle-aged man, who had lived in Bologna for nearly twenty years, but originally came from Calabria, a southern region of Italy, made a "hand purse" gesture and looked at me with suspicion in his eyes. He asked me in a strong southern accent, "Are you serious? From a Chinese?" He slowly shook his head. His skepticism was typical of the reactions of native Italians who heard about what I was about to do. Espresso coffee is a commodity integral to the notion of *italianità*. Many Italians have a strong and patriotic conviction as to the excellence of *caffè italiano*, which they associate more generally with the exclusively Italian cultural competence that goes into its production. With this perception in mind, native Italians often have a kind of knee jerk reaction at the thought of sampling coffee made by someone from another ethnic group or *cultura*.

In addition, a barista in the Italian context must not only know how to make caffeinated beverages, but must also possess other technical skills such as mixing drinks and making sandwiches. Indeed, the term *barista* in Italian refers to someone working in a *bar*, no matter if it is a daytime bar focusing on coffee drinking or a night bar focusing on mixed drinks and other alcoholic beverages.[2] This is different from its meaning in the English context, where it is used to describe a specialized profession in which a person's job involves preparing and serving different types of coffee, principally espresso-based. Borrowed from Italian only in the 1980s, the word *barista* in English is itself part of the wider effort to construct a global Italian coffee culture. In Italy's "traditional bars" for mass consumption, self-employed baristas play an all-in-one role, taking care of everything related to their business. Apart from manual skills, they also require knowledge related to spatial arrangements, the creation of ambience, the development of a sometimes extensive menu, and the purchasing needed to maintain stocks, as well as the social skills for serving and interacting with diverse customers. They have to keep up the quality of the food and beverages and see to the aesthetics of the space, since after all the coffee bar itself, as a space, is a commodity. How do Chinese baristas—these supposed cultural outsiders—then acquire all these labor skills adequate to produce an authentic, aesthetically pleasing place with coffee that tastes good enough to satisfy local Italians who vigilantly police its cultural legitimacy? What bridges the knowledge gap between the *italianità* of its taste and the foreignness of the labor that produces it?

Letai and his parents have never been coffee drinkers. "Going to a *bar*" was never a cultural practice in their everyday lives, and they had no knowledge of coffee bar management up to the point when they decided to enter this business. Despite this, Letai's family was not intimidated. They did not see the coffee bar business as inaccessible to them. Far from it, "doing *jiuba* [bar] business is easy," they thought. This was a common perception among Chinese baristas whom I encountered in Bologna. While they agreed that coffee consumption and coffee bar frequenting belonged to the Italian, or *laowai*'s, culture, they did not connect barista skills with *italianità*. For them, coffee bar management required rather simple labor skills, which could be acquired through practice and had little to do with the barista's own tastes, lifestyle, or ethnic identity. Chinese baristas' perceptions of coffee bar management thus echo Marxist theories of the alienation between production and consumption in capitalist economies, even though these Chinese baristas were themselves the owners of their own modest means of production and labored on their own behalf. In this context, taste becomes a commodity and a consumable good. It is produced by immigrant laborers and consumed, mainly, by local consumers. These classical theories of labor and capital, however, are inadequate to explain how these immigrant laborers from different cultural backgrounds were able to produce and reproduce the taste of so quintessentially a cultural expression as Italian espresso.

Letai's learning process in becoming an experienced barista provides us some clues. He had spent three months at a relative's coffee bar learning basic coffee-making skills and getting a general idea of coffee bar management before starting work in his own family business. "Once I knew how to make a *caffè* and a cappuccino, I was able to manage my own business," Letai claimed. As to drinks-making and other knowledge and skills, he emphasized the impor-tance of on-the-job training in his family's own business, where he then passed his skills on to his parents and his brother. "The *keren* [guests, customers] are different in each *bar*," he said. "They will tell you what they want and how they want it." As I will explain in greater detail in this chapter, Letai's understanding of barista skills as practice-based, site-specific knowledge is in line with what one might call the infrastructure of learning in Italy's coffee bar indus-try, which includes understanding the typologies of the business as well as its existing sociality, and the nature of the barista's work as manual labor, all of which together make the reproduction of taste possible. As what I term "fill-in laborers" in an existing establish-ment, these Chinese bricoleurs purchase from the previous owner the entire package of the established coffee bar community they are now taking on. Crucially, both taste and clientele are included in the package. They know that reproducing the previous taste of the establishment's commodities rather than producing a new taste is the best strategy for business success.

This chapter is also a reflection of my own experience as an apprentice barista learning through practice-based workplace training. I benefited from four Chinese families, as well as from their coffee bars. Thus, I was able to compare their manual skills and understandings of taste-making. Letai was my main barista teacher. I worked with him roughly three times a week from mid-December 2014 to mid-April 2015, each time working for three to four hours during his afternoon shift. Letai's mother worked the morning shift together with a Chinese employee, so there was not enough space for me to stay behind the bar counter then. I also received occasional opportunities to practice coffee-brewing at Lanlan's establishment, but only when there were no or only a few customers around. Linli's sister, Meili, and her husband al-lowed me to experience intensive coffee-making on a busy morn-ing when a third laborer was needed, in addition to providing me with many other pieces of advice and chances to practice. Linli,

instead, started learning barista skills after I did before managing
her own coffee bar. We had many discussions about barista skills,
the spatial arrangement of the coffee bar, and other business strategies at the newly purchased coffee bar that she and her husband
managed and where they successfully preserved, unchanged, an
established taste community.

Taste Community

I met Linli for the first time in her older sister Meili's coffee bar,
where I regularly visited. She and her husband had just purchased
a coffee bar in a peripheral town twenty minutes by bus from Bologna's *centro*. While waiting for the long bureaucratic process to
confirm the change of ownership, she visited her sister's establishment in the afternoons to learn coffee bar management. After
about a month of frequent visits, she stopped going. Meili told
me that her sister had by now learned the basic skills for coffee
making and feared staying longer would risk being fined by the
police, as she did not have a work contract with Meili's business
and thus might easily be mistaken as someone working *in nero* or
"undeclared."

I saw Linli again about two months later in her own establishment, which had opened ten days earlier. However, it took me
some time to find the place. After getting off the bus, I found myself facing the main *piazza* of the town hall. Linli had told me that
her bar was next to the *piazza*, but as I looked, I saw at least five
or six coffee bars. There was no way to tell which was the bar that
Linli and her husband had just bought. The exterior appearance of
a coffee bar generally gives no clue as to the owners' ethnic background. Unlike many other kinds of Chinese businesses in Italy,
bars display no eye-catching "exotic" Chinese goods, and there are
no Chinese characters, red lanterns, or other typical signs of Chinese ownership. I also saw nothing to indicate new management,
no balloons, colored streamers, or inaugural signs. All of the coffee
bars were fully integrated into the neighborhood environment and

seemed to have been there for years. I finally found Linli's place by taking a closer look at the baristas behind each bar counter one by one.

The inside space of Linli's bar looked minimalist, but was neat and tidy. Two refrigerators full of beer and other drinks stood by the door on the left, while several types of croissants were displayed in a glass cabinet to the right of the entrance. The cash register was at the curved intersection between the glass cabinet and the bar counter, hidden behind two small candy stands. Various bottles of alcoholic beverages stood on the shelves of the cupboard, while glasses were lined up neatly by size and shape. An espresso machine occupied the left side of the bar counter. All of the coffee cups carried the same logo of a local coffee roasting company that I had seen in many other coffee bars in Bologna. A television hanging on the wall in front of the entrance was broadcasting old music videos in black and white. Five slot machines and one coin-changing machine were lined up against the left wall far back in the space, while the central area was filled with several small square tables, just like those in front of the bar counter close to the entrance.

Linli told me that the spatial arrangement remained just as it was before they purchased the bar. They had spent a week whitewashing the walls, replacing old, dusty window curtains and shabby chairs and giving the whole place a good cleaning. The interior design style and the positions of all of the furniture, equipment, and items, however, remained unchanged. Even the landscape photographs on the wall and the two warning signs that read "*Vietato fumare* [No smoking]" were still in place. Linli explained that they had made no changes for economic reasons as well as other considerations:

> This *jiuba* already has stable *keren*. We bought it also for this reason. Our *keren* are familiar with the previous environment here. They might not be used to big changes. . . . Also, we don't have experience in this business. We aren't sure how to change

it in a way that our *keren* like. . . . Maybe in the future we can renovate it, when we are more certain about it.

Linli was aware that she and her husband were not equipped to evaluate coffee bar environments, as they had neither previous familiarity with this specific cultural experience of everyday urban life in Italy nor prior experience in the management of such spaces. What they could do was preserve the existing ambience so as to keep the bar's regular patrons satisfied. Indeed, none of the Chinese owners I know even made new sign boards for their new businesses. Many of them told me that there was no sense in branding the business with a new sign, as most of the customers were regulars. Because of this, some Chinese-managed coffee bars have as many as three names at the same time: the official registered name, the name displayed outside of the coffee bar, and the popular name. Uncle Gumin's coffee bar was popularly known as *Bar da Luca* (Luca's coffee bar) among his regular patrons, even though a large sign reading "Bar Lucia," the previous owner's name, hung above the entrance, and the officially registered name "Bar Gumin" was printed on the receipts.

Coffee bars are a constructed social institution for everyday urban consumption, where not only products are sold, but the space itself is also consumed. The layout, interior décor, signs, music, smell, and all of the spatial elements speak of a taste and a style and have a meaning. As we saw in the previous chapter, even though virtually everyone engages with coffee bars in their daily life in one way or another, different people go to and segregate in different coffee bars, where the taste, the style, and the ambience conform to their comfort and preferences, which in turn are almost always marks of class distinctions. Everyday tastes are a product of social differentiation based on power and social status. As Pierre Bourdieu has suggested, taste is a social weapon in the defense of social hierarchies, excluding outsiders who do not, or supposedly do not have access to the cultural capital of a given social group.[3] As such, coffee bars, as a space centered

FIGURE 4.1. Inside a coffee bar in a residential neighborhood. The new Chinese owner told me that they maintained the interior décor and spatial arrangement of this taste community unchanged. (Photograph by author)

on the production and consumption of taste, reify the underlying tensions and power dynamics within Italian society. The taste that is "proper" to a particular social group can legitimate its spatial segregation in a particular coffee bar. If its food, drinks, or even ambience change and no longer fit with a customer's taste, that customer may no longer enjoy going there. The new Chinese owners, supposed cultural outsiders, thus feel limited power to determine the taste of their own establishments, as a certain taste community is firmly in place.

Nevertheless, it is this very disempowerment of decision making that paradoxically has allowed these Chinese fill-in entrepreneurs and laborers, who have little relevant experience or knowledge, to gain access to this established taste community and achieve their own economic ends. Purchasing an existing establishment, rather than opening a new one, simplifies the process. The bar comes with a ready-made interior décor, left-over equipment and products, a list of regular suppliers, and essentially anything else one might need, not the least being the regular customers. The only change is to the ownership and management. Continuing to use the same suppliers is especially convenient for the new, inexperienced owners. Every coffee bar has its own specific suppliers for coffee, pastries, wine, soft drinks, slot machines, and even candies. The suppliers usually deliver the products directly to the coffee bar and the new owner can simply plug into the existing pipeline to keep the business going.

Among all the products, coffee is of course the most important to a bar's reputation. Each coffee bar typically has its own distinctive coffee brand, as well as flavor, and this constitutes a crucial part of its taste community. Maintaining the same coffee brand and the same supplier thus become prerequisites for reliably reproducing the taste of the coffee as both fixed and unique. To change the supplier or type of blend without a good reason would be a risky move. The consistent blend of a specific coffee brand is often more important than what the market decides is a quality product, which often comes at a higher price. The price of a commodity is set by the global capitalist market and by institutions through their regulatory and qualification practices, which are largely hidden from ordinary consumers.[4] In contrast, consumers' perceptions of a quality product derive from a subjective expression of social approval that cannot be reduced to a number or a price.

In a Chinese-managed neighborhood bar, many consumers are regular patrons who have grown used to one specific flavor of coffee. They usually pay little attention to which brand of coffee is being served or how the blend is composed. Their concern is that the taste is the one they are used to. Changing coffee brands or categories within the same brand risks negative feedback from regular patrons. For instance, in the early days of managing the bar, Linli's sister, Meili, once tried to change to a more expensive brand of coffee beans to please the customers; she quickly changed back to the former brand when regulars complained about the new taste. This knowledge, accumulated through Meili's unsuccessful attempt, was transmitted to Linli and her husband, so that they continued using exactly the same roasted and blended beans as the former owner had in order to keep the same taste of coffee for their customers. Lanlan's parents, whose family business was introduced in the previous chapter, once attempted to use a less expensive quality of coffee beans from the same roaster to save on costs, but in the end, they too gave up. Lanlan's mother told me: "Those old men have the habit of drinking this quality. If we change it, they can taste the difference. We don't want to hear complaints from them."

It would be fair to say that Chinese baristas possess little or no cultural legitimacy in the production of taste. They have economic power over their business ownership, but rather limited power in making decisions concerning taste-making. On the contrary, it is their regular Italian patrons who hold cultural power over taste. It is they who police cultural legitimacy and determine whether the taste of the coffee and the ambiance of the coffee bar are authentic. Such power dynamics in taste-making echo postcolonial scholars' arguments about authenticity, carrying cultural, racial, sociopolitical connotations in both colonial settings and those of global capitalism.[5] Native consumers use their own locally distinctive benchmarks to evaluate particular commodities, while producers are required to showcase particular local and cultural characteristics to match the demands and expectations of the consumer market.[6] Chinese baristas are aware of their disempowered position in constructing the taste community, and they make proactive use of this disempowerment to meet their economic ends. They are also conscious of their limited cultural competency and the limits of their labor skills. Their business strategy is primarily directed to maintaining the status quo. Taste-making is thus a collective process of reproducing an authentic taste for a particular coffee bar community.

Industrial Taste

Coffee and espresso are practically synonymous in Italy, as the mass-consumption coffee sold there is virtually all espresso-based, rather than drip coffee or any of the other styles.[7] In Italian, *caffè* assumes *caffè espresso*. Some Chinese baristas in Italy among the first-generation immigrants I met did not even know that *espresso* is another word for *caffè*. Only tourists or foreigners who are unfamiliar with this social convention would use the word *espresso*. In this sense, if each coffee bar is a local-level taste community, Italy can be considered a national-level taste community. There is throughout the country socially accepted conformity concerning the meanings of coffee at a bar, that is expressed in a shared collective taste, in spite of a certain range of geographical diversity.

"*Un caffè, per favore* [A coffee, please]!" When a customer spoke these words, I would simply follow my barista teacher Letai's instructions and imitate his operations step by step: remove the portafilter from the machine, empty the old coffee grounds from it, hold the portafilter below the coffee grinder and pull the handle of the grinder to fill it with freshly ground coffee, tamp the coffee grounds firmly into the portafilter for uniform consistency, attach the portafilter to the coffee machine, and then press the appropriate button to start up the machine. As long as I followed these instructions methodically, a decent cup of espresso would be ready in several seconds. It was almost impossible to fail. Letai, as well as other Chinese baristas with whom I am familiar, all told me that the espresso machine and the grinder were both pre-set. The roaster would deliver ready-to-use coffee beans directly to the coffee bars, so that the baristas need not worry about anything except running the machines. Throughout my entire apprenticeship, no theoretical knowledge about espresso making was passed on to me, the mechanical functions of the espresso machines remained mysterious, as did the composition and the place of origin of the coffee beans used and how they were roasted and blended. Coffee's global commodity chain was certainly never discussed, nor was there any mention of Italian coffee's East African colonial legacy.[8] None of my Chinese barista teachers were even aware of these issues. Their ignorance of specialized knowledge about coffee, however, did not affect the operational aspect of the production of a good cup of coffee in a coffee bar. I received many compliments from customers about the espresso that I made, beginning on the first day of my apprentice training. And I also shared with other Chinese baristas the feeling that making espresso is very easy.

Rather than the baristas' labor skills, the taste of a cup of espresso is ultimately something that is regulated by the industry infrastructure. Italy's coffee industry essentially prescribes the preparation process for espresso by focusing on the four elements critical to the results, the "four M's" as they are called: *macchina* (machine), *miscela* (blend), *macinazione* (grinding), and *mano* (hand).[9] Sometimes there is also a fifth M, *manutenzione* (maintenance).[10] Of these four or five M's, only the *mano* is closely associated with baristas' manual skills. A barista only needs to tamp the coffee grounds into the portafilter, and then the semi-automatic machine will automatically force pressurized water directly from the boiler and through the coffee. It is a highly standardized process that does not allow for much creativity. Italian coffee roasters also play a crucial role in regulating the taste of a cup of espresso, and this too makes it easier for unskilled laborers to enter the business. Most coffee bars employ ready-to-use roasted and blended coffee beans purchased from the roasters. They are the ones who decide which kind of coffee beans to use and how to blend them. In the end, then, it is quite unnecessary for baristas to equip themselves with knowledge of the entire coffee production process from planting to consumption.

These coffee roasters, mostly locally based, establish close ties with coffee bars, offering a set of services alongside the packages of roasted and blended coffee beans they sell. Many are themselves small-scale companies that sell their coffee beans throughout the city or region in which they are located. They often subdivide the local market into smaller sales regions, and salespeople are sent to take care of each region, so that they can engage directly with coffee bar owners, provide services, carry out machine maintenance, and resolve problems as soon as they arise. They also commonly provide a free espresso machine, a coffee grinder, a glass and cup washer, an ice machine, and branded items, such as cups. Thus, the bar owners usually do not need to equip themselves with knowledge about what would be a proper coffee machine or grinder; the coffee roasters will take care of this, as well as other details. In some cases, coffee roasters even provide financial assistance to new clients who have just opened or purchased a new business in return for an exclusive contract supplying their coffee beans. Letai's family was one such client. Among all of the services that coffee roasting companies provide, technical support and barista training are perhaps the most crucial to new coffee bar owners and baristas who lack experience in coffee-making. The salespeople from coffee roasters commonly teach their clients how to use the espresso machines, which show some variations in how they operate. They also provide technical support. Chinese baristas often told me that when they had any problem related to the espresso machine or coffee-brewing, they would contact the coffee supplier's salesperson in charge of the geographical area where their coffee bars were located. Similar services are also available from other suppliers and collaborators, such as slot machine companies.

The teaching of barista skills is indeed a crucial part of the Italian coffee industry's marketing strategy. Since the 1980s, coffee roasters, espresso machine companies, and the FIPE have offered baristas training in the "correct use of the machine," and in addition have organized cultural events and educational tours for local students in their factories.[11] The idea is to deliver "authentic" Italian culture. They consider baristas ambassadors of Italian coffee culture and thus a keystone in their campaign to make coffee "Made in Italy" a global brand. In the eyes of the public, it is after all the baristas who brew the coffee.

Baristas working in a place for mass-market coffee consumption in Italy act as the final technicians in the coffee-making process. They do not necessarily acquire an understanding of coffee blending or of the global commodity chain of coffee, nor are they equipped with a depth of knowledge of the coffee industry or how this commodity fits into global markets. What they need and develop is technical production knowledge of a highly standardized commodity beverage, which they acquire by focusing on technical coffee-brewing through the operation of the espresso machine. Similar to other industrial aspects of food production, coffee production is characterized by extensive mechanization and the de-skilling of labor.[12] A colonially rooted product can itself be an ongoing economic, imperial, or post-imperial project in the global capitalist mass-market, in which quality has been standardized and objectified, beginning at the earliest stage of its cultivation.[13] Standardized industrial production is what has made the mass consumption of coffee commodity possible. This is in sharp contrast to specialty coffee—a class-conditioned pattern of high-quality consumption—that has been on the rise in the United States since the late twentieth century. In the latter context, baristas with specialized professional skills play an indispensable role in the production of quality coffee taste, as well as in the class-based imagination of consumption.[14]

Unskilled labor can benefit from this mass production system in that a new worker can acquire all needed technical knowledge through practice-based training with experienced baristas. Indeed, on-the-job training is the primary way in which many baristas in Italy, not necessarily Chinese, learn labor skills. My first host's daughter, and my second host's niece, both college students, worked as part-time baristas in Italian-run coffee bars. They had no prior experience, but learned barista skills at work from more experienced baristas without attending any barista school or courses.

They both told me that it was not a difficult job and that anyone could do it with a few days of practice. This pattern holds not only for "traditional bars." In a trendy bar I visited, an Italian barista who was also one of four partners in the business, confessed that only one of them had gone to a barista school, and he then taught the skills to the other three through on-the-job training.

This kind of practice-based learning is also facilitated and legitimized by the Italian legal infrastructure and its regulations, which further lower the bar for access to this business niche. Although the legal representative of the business is required to obtain a professional certificate in order to start up the business, no particular professional certificate of barista skills is required for the management of the business. Moreover, the certificate is a general license for food service businesses and is not specifically geared toward coffee bar management.[15] Individuals with two years of formal working experience in food service within the last five years can also be exempted from the certificate examination. When a business is sold to a new owner, the previous owner often stays over for a couple of weeks to a month to teach barista skills and pass on management tips to the new owners. Sometimes this transition period is even written into the purchasing contract.

For Chinese coffee bar owners, reciprocal social and ethnic networks further facilitate on-the-job training. While it is not uncommon to see Chinese owners keep one or two of the previous skilled Italian baristas after taking over the business, many Chinese families will instead send one family member to a friend or a relative's coffee bar for a couple of months to learn basic barista skills before starting up their own businesses (as was the case with Letai and his apprentices). Other Chinese families send one of their members, usually an adult child, to formally work as an employee at a Chinese-owned coffee bar for a couple of months or longer. When the family starts managing its own business, that family member then teaches the others, as Letai taught his parents and his brother. Hiring a skilled Chinese barista is another alternative. Sometimes, an inexperienced new owner will hire some friends or relatives to work for them during the brief start-up period in order to learn the necessary skills.

Sensory Taste

On the first day that I became an apprentice barista, Letai brought out a liter container of milk from the refrigerator, placed it in front of me, and said, "This is your job and your exercise! Making *caffè* is easy, but cappuccino needs a lot of practice." Chinese baristas commonly think that cappuccino-making is the most critical labor skill that they must acquire if they are ever to manage a "traditional bar." Among the common types of coffee beverages, a cappuccino is certainly the most technically complicated. By learning how to make a cappuccino, the baristas also acquire the skills of making both espresso and macchiato, and together these three are the most common coffee beverages served in a typical Italian coffee bar.[16] A cup of cappuccino stands as an artisanal item, individually made by each barista. There is an art to it that is different from the standardized production process for a cup of espresso, or for *brioche* croissants made from ready-to-bake dough sent by the bakery suppliers every morning, different also from *panini* sandwiches made from ready-to-use ingredients, or packaged food commodities. It requires the barista not only to follow the machine operation step by step, but also to embody sensory skills through repetitive practice. In fact, cappuccino-making was the main manual skill that I learned from Letai and, throughout the entire learning process, I spent most of my time trying to improve my cappuccino and to stabilize its quality.

The first step in cappuccino-making is to prepare a shot of espresso. The preparation is no different from making a standard shot of espresso, except for the cup that is used. Cappuccino requires a larger cup, while espresso is served in a standard small cup, both usually ceramic. While the machine is dripping espresso into the cappuccino cup, the barista begins the second step of milk frothing. This is the most challenging part for a fresh apprentice.

The goal was to make milk foam with smooth, tiny bubbles. Letai described a good foam in this way: "It should look like cream, very smooth and consistent. All of the bubbles should be equally tiny with no large ones." However, no one told me how many hot, smooth, and tiny milk bubbles there should be. There was no quantitative standard that I could follow. This step depends greatly on experience and on rather subjective sensations. In the first days of learning, every time that I frothed the milk foam, I would show it to Letai and some regular patrons for feedback. My first three cups were total failures, the milk froth was all wrong. When I showed one regular, he teased me, saying "You're good at making foamless cappuccino!" Letai encouraged me to practice more until I could "get a *ganjue* [feel] for it by yourself."

To "get a *ganjue* for it by yourself" was the general instruction that I received from Letai and other Chinese baristas who allowed me to practice my cappuccino techniques at their establishments. The operation procedures were generally the same and quite simple, aside from some small variations in the machines used: fill a stainless-steel frothing pitcher with refrigerated milk, turn on the steam briefly to clean the steam wand, turn off the steam, insert the steam wand into the pitcher, turn on the steam again to heat and swirl the milk, turn off the steam when the milk is hot, and then remove the steam wand. The difficult part was figuring out where exactly to position the steam wand in the milk and when to stop the steam. I noticed that each barista had personalized tricks for making milk foam. The Chinese baristas commonly told me to use my senses to hear, feel, and see the process of frothing the milk. Some specific instructions include: "Watch the milk. When you see too many bubbles, insert the steam wand deeper into the milk!" "Listen to the sound of the frothing! When the sound gets deeper, it's ready!" "Put your hand against the outside of the pitcher and feel the temperature. When the pitcher gets uncomfortably hot, it's ready!"

To "get a *ganjue* for it by yourself" is a knowledge-production process in which sensory perception is mobilized as a form of labor.[17] Anthropologist Cristina Grasseni pointed out that vision, while also connected to other senses, is a sensory practice that needs "educating and training in a relationship of apprenticeship and within an ecology of practice."[18] She emphasized that this seemingly informal, personal and subjective sensibility has its disciplined and disciplining aspects embedded in mediating devices, contexts, and routines. By this means an insensitive novice is transformed into a sensitive expert with embodied sensory knowledge. As an apprentice, my body did not initially perceive in a meaningful way the sensations of sight, sound, and touch involved in the mechanical process of milk frothing. It took me some time to understand what was meant when someone said the sound was "deep," when the pitcher was too hot, when there were too many bubbles, and so on.

Despite some Eureka moments and much repetitive practice, I was never able to achieve a stable technique. Letai told me that it usually took one or two months of morning shifts to become proficient, since most of the customers take cappuccino in the morning. Indeed, Linli who started learning barista skills later than me quickly became much more skilled, as she had started her own business where she worked in the mornings. As Bruno Latour argues, being sensually affected is related to learning. Acquiring a sensitive body is "a progressive enterprise that produces at once a sensory medium and a sensitive world."[19] He gives the example of a tester in France's perfume industry who, through training sessions, "learned to have a nose that allowed her to inhabit a richly differentiated odoriferous world."[20] Similarly, it is through repetitive practice and bodily experience that the baristas have learned to have sensitive eyes, ears, and hands that combine to detect even minor sensory differences in their procedures.

The last step in making a cappuccino is to combine the milk with the espresso. All of the Chinese baristas I met could make one or more latte art designs, although they were also aware that the decoration of a cappuccino was not a widespread practice in Italy's coffee bars. Even so, I often saw them make quite nice de-

FIGURE 4.2. My first "successful" cappuccino with a heart-shaped latte art design. It received the approval of my barista teacher and compliments from some of the regular patrons who witnessed my efforts.

signs on each cappuccino for their customers. Linli's sister, Meili, explained to me her philosophy behind latte art: "The *keren* will be happy to see the nice design, and then they'll come back to our *jiuba*." Decorated cappuccino thus constitutes a part of her business strategy of good service. Chinese baristas, especially the first-generation immigrants whose Italian is less fluent, particularly emphasize the aesthetic aspect of the cappuccino they serve. These immigrants are often highly aware of their Chinese identity as *stranieri* (foreigners) and cultural outsiders in Italy. They commonly believe that they must make more of an effort and provide better service than their Italian counterparts so as to compensate for their disadvantages in terms of language competency and ethnic identity. However, in contrast to their desire to be acknowledged by Italian customers, good service is not provided to "bad" customers, a term they often use to identify certain immigrant groups. More details about service will be discussed in the next chapter.

While for the customers, a good coffee is based on its taste, for many Chinese baristas, a good coffee is about more: a good appearance and the sound, touch, and sensation of the process of coffee-making. A good shot of espresso should have a thick layer of golden-brown coffee *crema*, and a good cup of cappuccino should have even milk foam, with smooth, consistent, tiny milk bubbles and a nice latte art design. While they can readily recognize the quality of a cup of espresso or cappuccino by its appearance, many Chinese baristas do not have the ability to tell whether a cup of coffee is good or not by tasting it. They are often skilled coffee makers, but not necessarily sensitive coffee tasters. Some of them, such as Meili's husband, did drink coffee every morning and claimed to have the ability to taste the variations. As he told me, "You can tell the difference if you drink more." This would be another example of acquiring by experience a sensory skill and embodied knowledge, similar to "getting a *ganjue* for it by yourself." Some Chinese baristas, such as Uncle Gumin's son Enbao, do drink coffee occasionally, but they often claim to be unable to tell the difference in taste between a "good" cappuccino and a "bad" one. Others, such as Linli and Uncle Gumin, are not coffee drinkers at all and have never liked the taste of coffee. For these Chinese baristas, coffees are good for looking at, but not for tasting. For them, coffee-making is artisanal work and an aesthetic art, rather than an experience within a cultivated drinking culture. It has become an embodied habitus for them of a different sort from that of drinking. It is their embodied sensations, combined with their technical knowledge, that produces the good taste of a cup of coffee for the consumers, though not necessarily for themselves, the producers. In this sense, it is the alienable nature of taste that has allowed these sensory laborers, supposed cultural outsiders, to produce authentic taste that is recognized by the native consumers who regulate its cultural legitimacy.

Subjective Taste

Many Chinese baristas with whom I talked emphasized the importance of site-specific on-the-job training, but considered barista training courses impractical. A formal barista training course, such as vocational schools or industrial associations offer, is often at the very bottom of their list of choices for acquiring barista skills. Lisa, one of the first Chinese coffee bar owners in Bologna, was the only Chinese I encountered who had gained her technical skills through formal education at a secondary vocational school in restaurant and hotel management. Another young Chinese woman whom I talked to had enrolled in a similar secondary vocational school but dropped out after only one year when her father bought a coffee bar. She complained to me about the school: "I stayed there for a whole year, but they only taught me some theories. There was no practice at all in the first year. I learned everything later on in our own *jiuba*, not in school." Similar commentary came from Uncle Gumin's son, Enbao, who had attended a barista training course where he learned how to make cocktails rather than coffee. He regretted spending money on this useless course that was not helpful for his family's business: "I've already forgotten almost everything, since I have no chance to practice. It isn't useful in our *bar*. Our *clienti* don't drink cocktails."

The local knowledge that baristas gain on the job includes an understanding of the different consumption patterns of populations of varying race, ethnicity, class, and gender. Letai told me that only after managing his own business did he learn that *laowai*, which is how he refers to native Italians, rarely drink cappuccino after lunch, in contrast to some *banhei* or "brown" immigrants, who would order a cappuccino in the afternoon. He also learned that elderly male *laowai* more often order wine, while *banhei* immigrants drink more beers, and female *laowai* more commonly show up in the morning for breakfast, while some male *laowai* drink alcohol in the morning. Another Chinese barista, whose coffee bar was frequented by many Muslim immigrants from North Africa, learned that every year in the spring there is a month (Ramadan) in which many of his customers do not drink or eat during the daytime.

Since Chinese coffee bar owners interact primarily with their regular patrons, learning their individual preferences is useful local knowledge that can only be learned through everyday encounters. The judgment of taste is never a priori. It depends on subjective experience. Taste preference as everyday practices is not only shaped by structures like social and economic class, but also embraces ambient contingencies, contexts, and aspirations.[21] Each customer chooses a food or beverage and then judges the taste and quality of what the barista serves based on their subjective preferences. For instance, espresso-based coffee has an industry-regulated taste, but at the same time it is also a customer-contingent product in Italy. There is no universal standard for a "good" cup of coffee. Each customer makes a judgment based on their own likes and dislikes in terms of strength, serving size, added ingredients, heat level, cup material, and so forth.[22] I once encountered a customer who judged my freshly made espresso as not good enough because, according to him, it wasn't hot. I was shocked when I heard his comment, since I had followed the instructions step by step and could not understand how a freshly machine-made coffee could not be hot. Then Letai told me that the customer in question preferred boiling hot coffee, and so I had to use the hottest cup in the bar, the one that had been sitting closest to the radiator outlet.

Chinese baristas make a point of memorizing each "good" customer's preferences as soon as possible, because this enables them to deliver what the customer wants before they have even requested it. *Come al solito!* or "As usual!" is a phrase that I often heard from regular customers while taking orders. Some of the familiar faces would simply say "Leo knows!" Leo, which was Letai's Italian name, often reminded me of the special preferences of each individual, saying things like: "Don't put a spoon on the dish. Daniele doesn't add sugar to coffee!" "Add vodka to the coffee.

This is Franco's habit!" "Make the milk foam hotter than usual. Francesca likes a hot cappuccino!" "Add a few drops of prosecco to Massimo's liqueur. That is his special drink!" A good memory thus makes for good service, instilling patrons with a sense of community. This was what persuaded the father of my first host Melissa and his wife to became regulars at a Chinese-managed coffee bar close to their new apartment. Melissa's father told me, "The first time, the barista asked us what we wanted to drink. But, the second time, when she saw us entering, she said in a Chinese accent, 'A very hot cappuccino and a macchiato, right?' She had already remembered! Just one time was enough! Since then, we've always gone to that bar."

Chinese baristas not only learn to know the subjective tastes of their customers, but also receive many useful comments from them and feedback on their skills and manners. The customers are thus among the most important learning resources during on-the-job training. Letai told me that he received tremendous tips from an Italian *keren* who had been a barista for over thirty years before retiring, but he added that he had also benefited from many other *keren* who had never worked in the business, because "they have much more experience than us, because they have frequented *jiuba* for years, some even for their whole lives." When I was learning barista skills at Letai's coffee bar, I too received many useful suggestions from regular patrons, including nuanced instructions on which cups match which drinks and how to place the cup and teaspoon on the coffee dish properly. When I didn't know where a bottle was, they would always kindly remind me: "The yellow bottle on your left!" "The second bottle from the right!" Regular patrons may have witnessed a change of management several times in the same establishment, so they tended to be kind and patient with new baristas who were still learning the skills of the trade.

Sometimes a Chinese identity can be an advantage for inexperienced baristas. The regular customers were usually patient with me, carefully explaining which drinks they wanted and how I should serve them, while assuring me that, with time, I would know what to do. As a non-smoker, I also had initial difficulties in recognizing brands and types of cigarettes. The bewildering names of cigarettes brands confused me. How was I to know, for example, that Camel Blue cigarettes are sometimes called Camel Lights? One more problem was that many cigarettes were not Italian brands, so when a customer said the name in an Italianized way, I was unable to understand the word. The Italian pronunciation of "Lucky Strikes" was particularly troublesome for me. Nevertheless, the customers—both regular and occasional—were invariably patient with me, pointing out their desired cigarettes' position or searching for them together with me. In this way, I not only got to know the names and appearances of different cigarettes, but also the Italian ways of referring to them. I cannot explain with certainty why customers were so kind and patient with me, but one possible explanation is that as I am Chinese, they concluded that my ignorance was perfectly understandable. An Italian barista might be criticized for not knowing the names of drinks and cigarettes or how to mix certain common drinks. This was a kind of "discrimination" that actually benefited Chinese baristas. Being served by a cultural outsider could also in turn benefit customers with unusual personal tastes, sparing them the embarrassment they might otherwise experience. A *bolognese* friend of mine in his early thirties told me that he did not need to worry about being judged by Chinese baristas and he could ask them to mix a drink however he wanted it. Partly because of their lack of cultural baggage, many Chinese baristas had an easy-going philosophy of coffee bar management: "As long as the customers like it!" Rather than acting as cultural judges, they self-defined as service laborers.

The site-specific local knowledge that the Chinese baristas learned from their *keren*, however, was not necessarily "correct" or recognized by the larger market. In other words, Chinese baristas—especially those who did not read Italian—might learn mistakes from their customers. While some such misconceptions could eventually be corrected during the learning process, others might persist and negatively impact the baristas' efforts to expand their clientele. They might, for example, be able to satisfy the demands of regular *keren*, but not those of a passerby or of the general public more broadly. A Chinese woman in her early thirties, who had moved to Italy only three months earlier to reunite with her husband and mother-in-law, recounted an episode during her working shift:

> A *laowai* asked for a prosecco this afternoon. . . . When I was serving him, he insisted it was not prosecco. But how could that be possible?! It was the same "prosecco" that I served to my *keren* every day!

When she showed me the bottle, I saw that it was indeed just a normal sparkling white wine, while a prosecco is a particular sparkling white wine named after the *terroir* where it is produced. It seems impossible that the woman could make this mistake as the word *prosecco* is always printed on bottles of prosecco. However, it is also understandable, as the alcohol drinkers in her family-run business were primarily immigrants from North Africa. They may well have faced a similar situation to that of the Chinese woman, who had just arrived in Italy, could not read Italian, and had little knowledge of Italian wines. More common is what occurred when I went to some Chinese-managed coffee bars with my Italian university friends. We ordered mixed cocktails, but what the Chinese baristas made were different from our understanding and expectations. I have also heard native Italian youths complaining of Chinese baristas that "They only know how to make coffee, but nothing else!" These negative experiences discouraged them from frequenting such establishments. They further puzzled the youths as to how Chinese people would be able to manage a bar if they do not have sufficient knowledge of a wide range of commodities served in these businesses.

Many Chinese baristas are aware of their knowledge limitations. In the trendier and fancier coffee bars that target middle-class urbanites, Chinese owners more commonly hire white baristas who have more experience and cultural capital in taste-making and can meet their customers' expectations. Ailin's coffee bar in the city center is that kind of place. By contrast, the business strategy more commonly adopted in neighborhood bars is for Chinese baristas to learn the skills that are useful for serving their regular customers. Most Chinese baristas I know have learned how to make spritz, which is a popular form of cocktail in Italy, commonly served as an aperitif.[23] Many also know how to make a signature mixed drink that is exclusive to the coffee bar they manage, having learned it from the previous barista or owner. Yet, few of them are familiar with typical night bar cocktails, such as mojitos or margaritas, and cocktail-shaking techniques are usually not a part of their skills set. Very often, they only need to open bottled beer, pour wine or other drinks, or put several ingredients into a glass and mix them well with no need for special shaking techniques.

Several Chinese baristas confessed that they were interested in knowledge and skills useful for serving their regular customers and cared less about losing one or two passersby. I once brought with me lecture notes on bartending techniques from Enbao. Letai expressed his indifference to the recipes, as those cocktails were not drinks that his regular *keren* would order. "It's ok if we can't please some passersby," he told me, "since the regular *keren* are the major customers that we target!" Letai's words confirmed that what many Chinese baristas are most concerned with learning is site-specific local knowledge that enables them to maintain a coffee bar taste community. The larger range of the customers outside of their taste community is often beyond both their reach and their interest. For similar reasons, most of the Chinese entrepreneurs purchased coffee bars that focus on drinking, rather than providing the sophisticated *aperitivo buffet* that might attract younger middle-class urbanites.

The reproduction of local taste, however, does not mean that the Chinese baristas are simply slavish copycats imitating predecessors' coffee bar management without agency. In her study of mass reproductions of European-style hand-painted art in a South China shanty town in the 2000s, Winnie Wong shows that the artisans producing those reproductions also gave expression to their individual and creative selves in practicing skills and bodily knowledge, regardless of their sense of detachment from their painting as a manual job.[24] Chinese baristas also brought in some new tastes occasionally, although these were never allowed to overshadow the existing tastes for fear that they might damage the taste community. They were usually presented as sample foods and withdrawn immediately if their customers proved unappreciative. For example, sweetened garlic and multiple flavors of pumpkin seeds that Lanlan's father had brought from China were at one time offered as free snacks to their customers. Sweetened garlic soon disappeared as the customers were not enthusiastic. But whenever Lanlan's father came back from China he brought more pumpkin seeds for the customers who liked them "a lot." Meili also told me that her family often bought discounted salami and wine from the wholesale supermarket, but they would then ask their regular customers if the quality and the taste were good enough before they bought them again. I also saw a Chinese-managed coffee bar in an office zone provide Cantonese fried rice, while another one served sushi lunch sets. A Chinese barista who had previously worked in a Chinese restaurant offered free home-made *jiaozi* (Chinese dumplings) to her customers as a Christmas gift, and sometimes her regular customers would order from her freshly made *jiaozi* to bring home. To a degree, Chinese baristas and their regular customers are thus co-producers of the taste community.

The Locality of Taste

A filmmaker from a small town of around 5,000 residents in Liguria told me that it was practically a "*scandalo* [scandal]" when the *bar centrale* (central bar) in her hometown was taken over by a Chinese family. However, even while the townspeople showed their general distrust at the new ownership, the business survived.

This is a vivid illustration confirming the seeming paradox that while Chinese-run bars commonly evoke skepticism, distrust, and cynicism, they nonetheless have spread rapidly. A vast gap, meanwhile, has been observed between the negative comments made in public discourses and the positive or neutral reactions expressed by regular patrons as to Chinese baristas' competence when it comes to their labor skills. Those who are rarely—or refuse to become—*clienti* of Chinese businesses, the relatively wealthy and young for example, often criticize Chinese-managed coffee bars as too *popolare* (working-class) or *vecchio* (old, out-dated), in serious need of renovation and limited in their product offerings. The regular customers, very often retired working-class men and immigrant workers who may not have other options when it comes to where they spend their daily leisure time and are essentially stuck with the Chinese-managed coffee bars, have instead shown tolerance and patience with Chinese baristas as they gradually acquire necessary labor skills. These customers in fact actively participate in the reproduction of the taste to which they are accustomed by transmitting local knowledge to the new Chinese generation of baristas.

Co-production is a form of knowledge production that both embeds and is embedded in global and local institutions, social identities, and cultural representations during the dynamic interaction between technology and society.[25] As co-producers, Chinese baristas provide manual and sensory labor as a mode of production in the standardized capitalist mass-market, while their regular customers provide the experience of consumption as specific local knowledge for taste reproduction within the industry-regulated context of an established taste community. This taste production is thus an intersubjective process, echoing Daniel Miller's argument that consumers are not passive choosers, but rather play an active role as shapers of commodities.[26] His ethnographic study of the localization of Coca Cola in Trinidad also highlights the importance of local knowledge and locality in transnational food producers' business practices. In the case of Chinese Espresso, locality also plays a crucial role in Chinese taste production, or more accurately, reproduction. Here I do not use "locality" or "the local" simply as a geographic concept that implies a place with a homogeneous culture, as opposed to its counterpart "the global." Rather, I see locality as social practice and experience "characterized by social relations and interdependencies among those using a particular space."[27] In anthropologist Arjun Appadurai's words, locality is "primarily relational and contextual rather than scalar or spatial."[28]

Chinese baristas' subjective efforts at reproducing taste also entails reproducing locality. The locally rooted commodity chain of coffee production, the coffee bar as a local space, and the site-specific community of regular patrons together constitute a locality of taste. The association of taste with place is by no means new. The French concept of *terroir*, often translated as the "taste of place," is a good example of the use of a naturalized taste, both in cuisine and in agriculture, to define a place, shape the practices of production and consumption, and develop and sometimes market a local, regional, or national identity.[29] The taste and smells of public and social spaces, such as coffee shops and farmers' markets, often constitute the sensory sociality of place-making.[30] The taste and other sensory aspects of food can also serve as collective memory, for example by attaching immigrants to a particular place in the course of their identity-making process.[31] Chinese baristas' reproduction of taste further suggests that the impact operates in both directions. Taste affects place-making, shaping a sense of place, a *terroir*, or locality. Meanwhile, the locality itself can also be constitutive of taste. In other words, taste and locality are mutually constructive in the process of producing and reproducing a local commodity culture. Commodity consumption has its own "social life."[32] It can be "used as fences or bridges" for social purposes.[33] That is, the locality attached to the taste-making of a specific commodity has the potential to bridge the knowledge gap between the local taste and immigrant labor, thus helping to embed immigrant labor in local economic structures and social relations.

Taste is thus not only an artifact of consumption or of production, but also an artifact of sociality. Coffee bars are established workplaces for Chinese baristas, but at the same time they are also an established community institution that provides their customers with a sociality for their own. This sociality includes, most importantly, the human characters and qualities of the place that are conducive to a pleasurable experience of both taste and place. This is vital for reframing a new relationship between taste, its producers, and its consumers. One of the major reasons that many Chinese-managed coffee bars were able to retain their previous clientele is the effort that the new owners put into preserving the social and cultural nature of their coffee bar. Keeping its sociality intact allowed these immigrant laborers, who were short on cultural capital, to be first transplanted to the taste community and then incorporated into it as they learned and equipped themselves with not only embodied sensory skills but also local knowledge for taste reproduction. These laborers became rooted in its material and social environment and participated in the process of place-making within a given mode of production.

Throughout this process, Chinese convivial bricoleurs have actively benefited from their workplace as a community institution with both ethnic and non-ethnic resources that are within their reach, while they have also been motivated to achieve a certain conviviality with their customers. Meanwhile, by transmitting local knowledge to the new baristas, the regular patrons, whose social lives were often restricted to these places could also maintain their taste experience and benefit from the conviviality of the place. Yet, to achieve this conviviality, the baristas in Italy took on the additional role of being emotional laborers, socializing on a daily basis with a wide variety of customers, ranging from occasional passersby to regular patrons. Sociability is thus another key factor crucial to the success of their businesses. I demonstrated earlier that providing good service is a part of Chinese baristas' business strategy, which can be achieved in a variety of ways as for example by upgrading the aesthetic taste of cappuccino. But how is it that Chinese baristas, supposed cultural outsiders, have been to demonstrate their sociability in interactions with the customers from diverse social and cultural backgrounds? In the following chapter, I shift my focus from Chinese baristas' labor skills to their social skills.

5

Performing Sociability

I ONCE MET a middle-aged magazine editor at an Italian friend's house party. He claimed to have never entered a coffee bar managed by Chinese people, even though there was one just below his office. This Italian man had two concerns. The place looked very *popolare* or working-class from the outside, just as other typical *bar cinesi* did in his eyes. Also, he felt it a little *strano* (strange) to see a coffee bar managed by *stranieri* (foreigners), since coffee bars are quintessentially Italian. Then, he told me, he decided to go in one day out of curiosity. The place was as he had imagined just so-so, but the service was *ottimo* (excellent). "The Chinese lady was very *cordiale* [warm, friendly], smiled a lot, and was very *educata* [well-mannered]." Since then, every time he passed by, the Chinese woman would greet him. He did not know if this kind of *cortesia* or "politeness" belonged to Chinese culture, but he was sure that it was integral to *la cultura italiana* (Italian culture).

This is quite an unusual story. A middle-class Italian man became a patron of a working-class coffee bar after a convivial "fleeting" encounter with a Chinese service worker.[1] At the same party, where I was the only non-white intellectual, no other guests professed to have ever frequented a *bar cinese*. Their reasons included inadequate beverage lists, undesirable customers, and an unpleasant atmosphere with slot machines. Back in 2015, Chinese-managed coffee bars targeting middle-class urbanites in Bologna were still rather few. However, feedback about good service in terms of the *accoglienza* or "welcoming feeling" received from Chinese baristas was a fairly common compliment that I heard. Native Italians were often impressed by Chinese baristas' extraordinary cordiality, especially that of Chinese women, regardless of their manual skills or the ambience of the coffee bar space. Such positive perceptions and recognition of the barista's sociability seem decidedly inconsistent with native Italians' general feeling of social and cultural distance from Chinese immigrants, whom they supposed were unassimilable cultural aliens.

Baristas are interactive service workers. They perform not only manual but also "emotional labor," as they need to manage their "heart" in addition to merely managing their "hands" to provide good service.[2] They thus engage in emotional and bodily performances in a way that conforms to the societal norms or "feeling rules" expected by their customers.[3] In the previous chapter, I investigated how and why Chinese fill-in labor was able to bridge the knowledge gap so as to produce and reproduce a good tasting coffee, acknowledged as such by both Italian and immigrant customers. My focus in this chapter will thus shift to what it is that closes the supposed cultural gap of sociability between Chinese baristas and their local customers from diverse racial and ethnic backgrounds. In other words, how is it that these Chinese immigrants, who are supposed to possess intrinsic and insurmountable cultural differences from their customers, able to manage a convivial coffee bar space in which their sociability is accepted, recognized, and even appreciated by diverse local populations?

The Italian coffee industry often describes baristas as a crucial component of the particular Italian coffee culture that is associated with urban civility and modernity. A guide for baristas in the late 1970s emphasized that a good barista needs to have a *natura umana* (human feelings and emotions).[4] They require adequate psychological sensitivity to act as a good listener who can keep in strict confidence the private life stories shared with them by their customers. A prestigious Venetian barista also declared in the 1980s that *buona volontà e gentilezza*, "good will and kindness," were the essential qualities of a barista, because "a coffee bar was re-spectable only when a barista was respectable."[5] Such understanding echoes the Italian expression *fare bella figura* or "make a good impression." It requires people to be aware of their appearance and image in order to be respected while simultaneously showing respect for others. *Fare bella figura* is thus in line with sociologist Erving Goffman's notion of "face," which he defines as "an image of self, delineated in terms of approved social attributes."[6]

Such descriptions of the generic requirements that make for a good barista, one who is successful at emotional labor, however, have not taken into consideration the various social contexts or "stages" in which baristas' performance is situated.[7] There are many types of coffee bars in Italy, each with their own sociality marked by class, gender, race and ethnicity, as well as by other social distinctions. In a centrally located *bar di passaggio* that targets passersby, baristas do not form a close relationship with their shifting customer base. When the setting is a peripheral *bar di quartiere* embedded in neighborhood life, however, the baristas themselves constitute an essential component of the coffee bar community. The self-employed owners and their families often live in the same building as their business or at least nearby. Their economic life and their social life are highly interconnected. Not merely a laborer, a barista in such a social space is also an acquaintance, a neighbor, a friend, in short, a person who has developed personal connections with other members of the community.

Most Chinese families I knew purchased this kind of neighborhood bar, frequented, at least partially, by regular customers who live or work in the same neighborhood and form a specific coffee bar community. Diverse racial and ethnic groups converge, meet, and interact with one another in these convivial establishments where power dynamics are highly asymmetrical. Though acting as business owners, Chinese baristas, perceived cultural outsiders, possess little to no cultural legitimacy in this setting. It is instead their native Italian customers who have the power to determine the cultural legitimacy of the place, in terms of both the taste and the service. Multi-racial and multi-ethnic non-Chinese immigrants, including those from North Africa, Eastern Europe, and South Asia, also possess a certain degree of power. These more recent local populations, usually immigrant workers, often constitute an important customer base and make up a considerable portion of many Chinese-managed coffee bars' income, especially through alcohol sales. Under such power dynamics, Chinese baristas are doubly motivated to perform their sociability; first, to maintain the existing coffee bar sociality, but also in order themselves to be included in the coffee bar community.

The ethnographic stories that I tell in this chapter cover various social situations in which Chinese baristas interact with their customers in different types of bars. I follow anthropologist Michael Herzfeld's "social poetics" approach, which treats social interaction as rhetorical encounters in which social agency operates in the creation of social relations.[8] Sociability as a performative effect of social interaction consists in "the art or play form of association," driven by "amiability, breeding, cordiality, and attractiveness of all kinds."[9] It is a central aspect of sociality, which presents as a complex value-shaped social and relational dynamic.[10] Chinese baristas actively perform sociability in the form of cordiality and hospitality as a strategic resource to "extend opportunities or consolidate power" for the construction of convivial sociality in their pursuit of economic ends.[11] The magazine editor was transformed by this strategy from being suspicious of Chinese management to becoming a regular customer, who even developed an interpersonal relationship of sociability with the Chinese woman. Yet, as I will show in this chapter, hospitality is not the only form of sociability that Chinese baristas deploy to construct a convivial coffee bar space. Social interactions are never gender, class, racially, or ethnically neutral. All these positionalities intersect with one another to form a social relationship of power in which sociability is performed and experienced.[12]

Speech Community

Not only did Linli and her husband decide not to give a new name to their newly bought coffee bar, they also decided to take Italian names for themselves. Linli started thinking about her need for a new name while she was still learning barista skills at her sister's place. She asked me to suggest a "good" name. I gave her several options, but she eventually chose "Angela," a name suggested by a regular customer, a retired man who lived next door and claimed to have frequented the establishment every day since the 1950s when it was still an *osteria*. This decision was consistent with Linli's business philosophy: "As long as the customers like it." Indeed, most of the Chinese baristas whom I knew—both self-employed and hired labor—used their Italian name at work. Some children of Chinese immigrants born in Italy already had an Italian name listed as their official name and used it in their everyday lives. Others who went to Italian schools would take an Italian name alongside their Chinese name and use it when they interacted with non-Chinese people. Yet, many Chinese residents—including first-generation Chinese immigrants and some 1.5 generation Chinese residents who had relatively few interactions with Italians—had only a Chinese name prior to becoming a barista. When they needed to pick an Italian name and were uncertain about which name to choose, they often asked for suggestions from their customers.

For Chinese baristas, the use of an Italian name was an effective social strategy that enabled them to fit themselves more efficiently into the established coffee bar community. Personal names can both identify individuals and classify people into groups.[13] They often imply social relations. A "proper" name might even be necessary if one was to be included in a certain social setting.[14] While a passerby would not ask for the barista's name, a regular customer who lived around the coffee bar community usually called the barista by name, and vice versa. My Chinese interlocutors commonly claimed that having an Italian name was a matter of "convenience" in dealing with their regular patrons, avoiding the need to teach and repeat to them Chinese names that would be "hard to say and to remember." For the same reason, while coming up with an Italian name for work purposes, Chinese bricoleurs also tended to choose a name that would be "easy to say and to remember." They took a name that did not incorporate the rolling "r" sound, as this is difficult to pronounce for native Chinese speakers. I often encountered Chinese men with names like "Matteo," "Stefano," or "Luigi," and women named "Lucia" or "Sofia," while other common Italian names such as "Carlo" or "Piero" for men and "Barbara" or "Aurora" for women were not popular.

Chinese baristas are also commonly sensitive to the language they used in different situations, Italian is often the *lingua franca* in coffee bars in Bologna. I noticed that in a coffee bar primarily targeting middle-class passersby, the Chinese baristas avoided speaking Chinese almost entirely, or at least used it in a restricted way. The coffee bar that Linli's sister, Meili, and her family manages was such an establishment. Once I was interviewing Meili while she was making a sandwich. A white man in a light blazer walked in. Meili suddenly lowered her voice and whispered to me, "Some *keren* don't like us speaking in Chinese. Wait a moment until he leaves." She then spoke loudly in Italian to the man who was now walking away: "Paolo, *tutto bene* [is everything good]?" Indeed, Meili often spoke Italian with her husband and son in their coffee bar, reserving Chinese for times when there were no customers around. Or, if she did speak Chinese, she kept her voice very low. This self-discipline of language use served to maintain an Italian-speaking environment in which she and her family could also be included.

Such language restrictions were less rigid in the more peripheral bars that targeted a population of regular customers. My barista teacher Letai usually spoke Mandarin Chinese with me, even when customers were around. When I asked him if we should switch to Italian, he told me that it was not a problem as these customers were so established that they would not be offended.

That said, sometimes he would also suspend our conversation in Chinese and exchange some words in Italian with Italian patrons or include them in our conversations when questions or common topics came up. However, I also noticed that Letai and many other Chinese baristas did not pay particular attention to which language to use in front of immigrant customers. Letai told me that it was not a problem, since these immigrants often came in small groups and socialized with one another speaking a language unintelligible to the baristas. While this was certainly true in some cases, I also learned that some of these immigrants were viewed as undesirable or less desirable customers, with whom Letai was unwilling to talk and whom he did not value enough to show his hospitality.

Unlike Italian, the local *bolognese* dialect did not seem to be a prerequisite even for managing a *bar di quartiere* in residential areas. Bologna is a city of internal migrants where Italian is the *lingua franca* among urban dwellers. Nevertheless, speaking *bolognese* certainly earned bonus points in the eyes of some local *bolognesi*. Uncle Gumin's son, Enbao, who had grown up in Bologna from the age of five, could speak one or two sentences in the dialect. He sometimes used these to interact with his *bolognese* customers "for pleasure" and to "make *clienti* happy." In places where regionalism and localism are stronger, the ability to speak the local dialect brings even more benefits to the business.[15] A university professor from the Veneto region told me that there were two Chinese coffee bars close to her father's home in a *paesino* or small town. Her father went to only one of them every day. When she asked him why, he told her that it was because the barista at the one he frequented could speak their local Venetian dialect. The professor told me also that the barista in fact could only speak one sentence of greeting in the Venetian dialect, but this was enough to influence the decisions of some local people like her father. Similarly, anthropologists often learn a few expressions in the local language with just the right intonation as a strategy to gain greater access to the community that they intend to study.[16] A speech community is about more than shared language. It is also a place within which identity, ideology, and agency are actualized.[17] Through their linguistic strategies, Chinese baristas showed that they valued communication and thus meaningful participation in the local speech community. As a result, they were accepted by local customers as part of the community.

Service with a Smile

Voi cinesi mangiate il riso, quindi avete sempre un bel sorriso. "You Chinese eat rice, so you always have a nice smile." A retired Italian man who always ordered his special Campari soda with a splash of prosecco at around 4:30 pm used this expression to share with me his appreciation of Linli's family's new management of the bar. With a simple rhyme between *riso* (rice) and *sorriso* (smile), an ordinary human facial expression was essentialized as an attribute of exotic "Chinese-ness." I also heard from many other native Italians that they appreciated the Chinese baristas' *sorriso* (smile) and *gentilezza* (kindness), which they often associated with a sort of *cortesia orientale* (Oriental courtesy). This was also a common perception of the Chinese management of restaurants and other service businesses.

The *accoglienza* or hospitality, which is part and parcel of many Italians' Orientalized image of *i cinesi*, is part of what Chinese baristas understand as a "good service." It serves then as a social strategy that furthers their economic goals. Ailin, who manages a centrally located coffee bar targeting middle-class urbanites, once said, "I know the basic logic. If you treat the *keren* very well and always have a smile on your face, they will come back to your place." She and her husband are highly aware of their image as Others, strangers, and cultural outsiders in Italy. While working as baristas themselves, they addressed this social aspect of their business by hiring white baristas to obscure the Chinese-ness of their management. By contrast, many other Chinese owners are self-employed laborers who strive diligently to demonstrate their own cultural and social competence in conforming to social convention. They commonly believe that they must make more effort and provide better service than Italian baristas. As Uncle Gumin emphasized to me, "We have to do a better job than *laowai* [Italians]. They say we can't make good coffee, so we study hard to make it perfectly. We always receive them with a smile, we're polite to them, we provide good service, and we make everything good so they can have nothing to complain about." Service with a smile thus becomes a social strategy that Uncle Gumin and many other Chinese baristas employ to compensate for what they see as the defects inherent in the Chinese management of coffee bars. A smile is one way in which they attempt to convey the message that they are sociable and hospitable, so as to achieve social recognition.

Hui shuo hui xiao or "the ability to talk and to smile," in Linli's words, is how my Chinese interlocutors characterized the qualities that a barista must have. They believed that smiling and talking were good social skills that would convey their hospitality and sociability to their customers. For this reason, they strived to impart these elements of good service, regardless of the different social settings of different coffee bars. Here, talking or verbal communication was not limited to instrumental talk about a commercial transaction, but also included pleasantries and "gratuitous speech," such as words of greeting and small talk.[18] When they initiated a conversation, they commonly choose topics relevant to their customers' everyday lives—the weather, family, health, holidays, sports. I also quite often heard female Chinese baristas compliment their female customers' dress, makeup, new hairstyle, or nail polish, both in establishments that targeted middle-class passersby and in *bar di quartiere* that neighbors and regulars frequented.

This linguistic strategy conforms to societal expectations. The exchange of salutations and small talk is a crucial part of Italian politeness, a way to *fare bella figura*, and an explicit expression of *italianità*.[19] These verbal communications constituted, as we have seen, an indispensable part of their economic practice. Di Wu's ethnographic study of affective encounters between Chinese migrants and local Zambians shows how speech can be mobilized as effective capital in workplace and business negotiations.[20] Linguistic anthropologist Jillian Cavanaugh's study on heritage food producers in a northern Italian town also notes that proper conversations benefited economic practice.[21] She uses the concept of "economic sociability" to analyze the interactions between people and goods in the process of production and circulation and argued that talk among producers and their customers creates meaning and value as "both a social act and an economic practice."[22] Rachael Black's ethnographic study of an Italian local market also demonstrates that shoppers were willing to pay for the vendors' sociability, even if it was clearly motivated by monetary gain.[23] Much like local markets, Italy's coffee bars double as an everyday social space. Customers, especially regular ones, visit them in order to socialize with people, including the baristas. As the father of my first host Melissa told me, "A barista does not only sell coffees, but also talks with people."

Chinese coffee bar owners often rely on the labor of family members who can, at the very least, handle daily conversations in Italian. Sometimes, of course, not everyone in the family possesses adequate linguistic competence to initiate topical conversations. Those whose Italian was limited would put extra emphasis on service with a smile and polite words. Letai's father told me his philosophy: "If you can't speak Italian very well, but you have a nice smile, are nice to the *keren*, always say *ciao* [hi or bye], *grazie* [thanks], and *prego* [please] to them, they'll be very happy too." When they cannot understand what customers say, they often pretend to listen to their words carefully with a smile on their face. Linli told me her understanding of such sociability: "Some *keren* just need someone to talk to. It's fine if you can't understand all of their words. Just show your attention and keep a smile on your face." Chinese baristas thus deploy "goodwill and kindness" and a willingness to be a good listener as compensation for their language deficiencies.

Linguistic politeness, however, is also a learned skill. Misunderstandings are unavoidable. Lanlan told me a story about a friend of
hers, also a barista who had migrated to Italy in her teenage years.
In one of the very early days of her management, an Italian customer had entered to exchange some small bills. After greetings,
Lanlan's friend simply asked "Cosa vuoi?" meaning "What do you
want?" While this was for her a sincere question, the customer was
offended and replied in an irritated tone, "Cosa vuoi?!" Lanlan's
friend was very confused and thought the customer was just rude;
she didn't realize that her question could be viewed as expressing
annoyance in some contexts. She managed to understand his request and gave him the small bills anyway, albeit reluctantly. She
only learned afterwards by asking her Chinese friends that a more
polite way to ask the question in Italian would be "Come posso
servirle?" (How may I serve you?) in the formal form or "Come
posso servirti?" in its informal form.

While Lanlan's friend's story was a case of unintentional impoliteness that was redressed soon afterwards, impoliteness can also
be an intentional choice. Indeed, Chinese baristas' hospitality is a
situational performance rather than a universal dogma governing
their coffee bar management. Undesirable "bad" customers rarely
receive hospitality and service with a smile. As Linli's sister, Meili,
said, "Not only are the *keren* choosing which coffee bar to go, but
we're also choosing which *keren* we want. We don't want those
bad *keren* to stay at our place, because good *keren* won't come in
if they see the bad ones are in here." No smile, no greeting, and
unresponsive service are the common strategies that Chinese
baristas deploy to weed out unwanted customers. Therefore, the
performance of "goodwill and kindness" is far from the "Oriental" cultural attribute that many native Italians imagine it to be. A
counterexample of such cultural essentialization was presented
in Derek Sheridan's ethnographic study of Chinese small entrepreneurs in Tanzania, where the Chinese were famous for not
greeting either Tanzanians or each other.[24] Sheridan argued that

the ethics of greeting and the experience of interpersonal relationships are preceded and shaped by global material inequalities.

Neighborly Hospitality

Uncle Gumin's first coffee bar is known by its customers for its
family-like vibe. It is a "traditional bar" outside of one of Bologna's
medieval city gates that serves a multi-ethnic working-class *quartiere* undergoing rapid gentrification. Located amid dense residential buildings, it is close to a bus stop, a small supermarket, several
banks and restaurants, as well as a number of white-collar office
buildings. The business caters mostly to those who live or work
nearby and come to eat breakfast and/or to grab a sandwich for
lunch, take a coffee, or drink a beer. I got to know this establishment through the introduction of a middle-aged official in Bologna's local government. After interviewing him one late summer
afternoon of 2014, he brought me to Uncle Gumin's, one of his
favorite Chinese-managed coffee bars close to his office.

A young Chinese man behind the bar counter wearing a casual
blue and white striped t-shirt greeted us after serving a customer
who bought a *gratta e vinci* (scratch card). The official called the
young man "Daniele," briefly introduced me and my research to
him, and then left. I was a bit worried at that moment due to an
unpleasant experience that had happened a few days earlier when
a sister of my second host Anna brought me to a Chinese-managed
coffee bar close to her office. I was almost kicked out by the Chinese owner—a fiftyish Chinese man—right after she introduced
me to him and kindly left to give us space to talk in Chinese. It
seemed to me that the introduction, through a native Italian,
might have been what caused the bar owner to suspect that I was
possibly a commercial spy or an investigative journalist. Nothing
like that happened to me, fortunately, with either Daniele, whom
I later learned had the Chinese name Enbao, or with his family
members in our subsequent encounters. They were always patient

and friendly toward me, and their establishment quickly became a key site of my fieldwork.

As I spent more time there, a retired man named Pino caught my attention. I saw him every time I was there, and he went in and out of the bar as if it were his own home. He had breakfast and drank coffees and drinks there regularly. Sometimes he would also play the slot machines for a while or buy a *gratta e vinci* to try his luck. Sometimes he just entered to have a look around without buying anything. He was not talkative, and I never had more conversations with him than an occasional smile or greeting. Instead, he preferred to exchange some words with Uncle Gumin's family or with some other friends or acquaintances. Uncle Gumin's three children all called Pino *nonno* (grandfather). I often saw him take out the garbage and clean the tables in the dining room when Uncle Gumin's family was too busy to do it. Like a real grandfather, he would also scold the three siblings when they did not place the bottles in the correct recycling bin. I got to know from Uncle Gumin's family that Pino was a retired man living alone in the same building where Uncle Gumin's establishment was located. His only daughter lived elsewhere and rarely came to visit him. They also told me that Pino refused to accept any gifts, including the daily left-over pastries or free drinks that they occasionally offered to regular customers.

Uncle Gumin and his three children all considered Pino to be a difficult *keren*, while nevertheless appreciating the kindness with which he treated them. In their eyes, Pino was moody and too easily hurt or offended. Uncle Gumin told me about one of his unpleasant experiences with Pino: "Once he got angry because I didn't say hello to him. He thought I didn't greet him on purpose. But, it wasn't true. I was busy with other *keren* at that moment. I didn't see him entering. I said I was sorry, but he couldn't forgive me. He ended up leaving my place with an unhappy face." Enbao's sister, Enhua, once shared with me her interpretation of what she termed Pino's "childishness." "I guess he's jealous," she said. "Once, he saw us talking for a long time with another *keren*, and he started quarrelling with that *keren*. For the next couple of days, whenever he saw that *keren* in our place, he wouldn't enter." Despite the complaints, Uncle Gumin's family had carefully learned how to get along with Pino and satisfy his emotional needs. They tried to avoid leaving him alone and made sure to greet and talk with him. In the many times that I visited, at least, I never saw Pino get upset.

While service with a smile is the most prevalent social strategy, Chinese baristas often intentionally seek out local knowledge for tailored social interactions with their regular patrons. They are aware of each patron's distinct tastes, personality, temperament, preferences, and hobbies. They know who is irritable, who is easygoing, who is always too serious to joke with, and which customers do not have good relations with one another. Such local knowledge allows them to interact with each customer in an effective way and also contributes to shaping and reinforcing their perceptions of essentialized cultural differences. After telling me about Nonno Pino who got angry at him, Uncle Gumin commented: "*Laowai* are not like us Chinese. They can get upset and lose their temper suddenly over just a tiny reason. . . . But they don't bottle up their emotions. . . . After a few days, they come back again as if nothing happened." Uncle Gumin's interactions with Pino thus reinforced his perception of Italians or *laowai* as temperamental.

Chinese baristas also demonstrate neighborly hospitality and family-like friendliness to their patrons through gift-giving. In Letai's words, it is *gei dian xiao pianyi* or "giving petty gains." Such petty gains might be an occasional free drink, a couple of unsold sandwiches at closing time, extra wine poured into someone's glass, abundant free snacks, or a small Christmas gift. Indeed, Uncle Gumin's family prepares Christmas gifts for their regulars every year. For Christmas 2014, they ordered 200 Christmas candles as presents. Once, an Italian couple was at Uncle Gumin's place with their newborn child for breakfast. When they tried to pay the bill, Enbao gave them a big smile and said in a very soft voice, "Can I treat you to breakfast this time? It's my best wishes for the baby!" The couple did not seem to expect this and thanked Enbao for his kindness. They had previously been only occasional customers at Uncle Gumin's coffee bar, but after that they showed up much more frequently for breakfast, and a more personal relationship was built up between the two families. Gift-giving can often put the gift receiver under a moral obligation, since the giver's seemingly voluntary gift has the intention of forming an attachment with the gift receiver, who is then expected or even obligated to repay the gift.[25] Through gift-giving, as well as other everyday activities of greetings and politeness, Chinese baristas strive to create *ganqing* (good feelings) with their customers and then to further build up and reinforce their *guanxi* (social relationship) with them. As is also common practice in post-Mao China, they particularly deploy the subjective and emotional aspects of *guanxi* production in the interests of a mutually beneficial relationship.[26]

A more intimate and reciprocal relationship of trust as well as a sense of community are thus constructed and reinforced between Chinese baristas and their patrons. Not only gift givers, Chinese baristas and their families also become gift receivers. Uncle Gumin's family often received small souvenirs and postcards from their patrons after they came back from a holiday. An elderly man often brought delicious pasta or desserts to Lanlan and her siblings, and a middle-aged customer accompanied her to practice driving before her license exam. A retired insurance agent walked a Chinese barista's dog every afternoon while she was back in China for a month. These people are no longer strangers, but valued acquaintances, neighbors, and even friends. Gigi, the construction worker in his fifties, told me of his appreciation for Uncle Gumin's family and the way they managed their business. He said "I watch people. I don't care where they come from." In their everyday interpersonal interactions, ethnicity and national identity have thus retreated to a less critical position. Some Chinese families and their patrons, especially those lonely elderly customers who do not have close kin living with them, have also constructed a kind of fictive kinship, as in Nonno Pino's case. In the process, Chinese baristas become more comfortable in showing their moods and personalities in the presence of the regulars. A regular customer once banteringly commented on two Chinese brothers' different patterns working on morning shift: "When they open the door, one always looks angry, the other always looks sleepy." His comment shows that the two brothers are no longer alienated service workers but embedded in a neighborly relationship in which human emotions can be revealed and shared.

Yet, as with hospitable "service with a smile," not all the customers receive such neighborly treatment. A sign declaring *Non si fa credito* or "No credit" hung on the wall behind the bar counter at Meili's establishment, although they commonly ran open tabs for regular customers with whom they had established a relationship of trust. My barista teacher Letai refused to pour more alcoholic drinks for a young Italian couple who became extremely loud after several shots. Another Chinese owner managing a marginal coffee bar posted a sign reading *Guasto* (broken) on the bathroom door, although the bathroom was still in service for "good" customers. She told me that it was to stop some "bad guys" using drugs in the bathroom. Sometimes, Chinese baristas even forced troublemakers or those who did not pay on time out of the coffee bars with offensive words or even physical violence. Lanlan told me how her father protected the business and the family in the early days of their neighborhood bar: "When we first bought the business, some very bad *keren* often showed up at night. Once, two drunk guys even smashed our windows. . . . You know my dad is very smiley, but he can also be very ferocious. He guarded the door and didn't let those guys enter. Once they even ended up fighting! Fortunately, those bad guys didn't show up anymore." By performing differential sociability, Chinese baristas seek to self-police the kinds of customers and thereby construct a moral space conforming to their own and to their "good" customers' expectations.

Playful Sociability

One winter afternoon I went to Letai's establishment in the periphery of the *centro* for my regular barista training session. Upon arrival, I saw that the entrance door had been removed, and I heard the noise of an electric saw coming from the dining room, which was being used as a repair shop. Indoors it was frigid as the heat was off due to the repair work. I quickly put on an apron and stood behind the bar counter where Letai's mother, whom I called Auntie Xiaowei, was also working. She hadn't left after her morning shift, as Letai had to supervise the repair work. Auntie Xiaowei was still on the job even though she had come down with a fever and had a severe cough. She was wearing a heavy down coat with two scarfs loosely wrapped around her neck, yet she could not stop coughing in front of everyone in the bar. She was not wearing a mask, something unheard of in 2014. The regulars in the bar did not seem to be disturbed at all by either the noise or Auntie Xiaowei's cough. In the following hours, a few North Africans came in, stood at the bar counter or sat at the tables drinking beers and talking to one another, just as usual; three elderly men who normally played cards in the dining room moved their table to the narrow aisle of the slot machine room. Occasional passerby customers were much fewer than usual, however. Some entered the place but immediately left. At some point, an Italian patron, a carpenter in his fifties, came in while Auntie Xiaowei was coughing. He was not bothered at all, but laughed at her, saying: "Ciao Sofia [Auntie Xiaowei's Italian name]! ... Look at you! You look like a *zingara* [Gypsy woman]!"[27] From across the bar counter, Auntie Xiaowei grabbed him by the shirt and playfully slapped his face. This didn't bother the man in the least. He just turned to me, shook his head and joked, "Sofia is too *forte* [strong, fierce]!" After finishing his usual coffee, he looked into the makeshift workroom to watch how the Chinese repair team was working.

At around 5 pm, an Italian pensioner came up to the bar counter for his usual post-card game glass of wine. Auntie Xiaowei served him, but poured much less than Letai usually offered. He complained, telling her, "Sofia, you gave me too little wine!" This angered Auntie Xiaowei, who pointed her finger at him and answered back in her broken Italian (with no changes in tense, no complete sentences and peculiar pronunciation): "Not little. Giacomo, you didn't pay for the tea yet. You are *furbo* [sly]! You are rich, you have a lot of money, but you don't want to pay! *Furbo, furbo* you are!" Then she left the bar counter for the slot machine room because someone else was calling her name. Giacomo did not seem offended. He sipped the wine with a smile and then said, "I really enjoy it when Sofia gets angry." Two pensioners who had been playing cards with him earlier burst into laughter.

Unlike the family-like vibe that is typical for family-friendly *bar di quartiere* like Uncle Gumin's establishment, Letai's bar exudes a decidedly masculine bravado. In masculine social circles of this kind, the social atmosphere is different, a teasing kind of sociability predominates. An Italian security guard working at the parking garage nearby routinely directed remarkably loud and comical greetings to Letai every time he entered. Some days he boomed out a comparatively civil "*Ciao, Matteo numero uno* (Hey, number-one Matteo [Letai's Italian name]!)" Other days it was "*Ciao, Vaffanculo* (Hey, fucker)!" It seemed to me that his choice of between the two versions was random. Sometimes Letai simply ignored him, other times he would shout back a profanity or pretend to pick a fight with him in jest. While Chinese baristas commonly tell me that service with a smile is fundamental to coffee bar management, it is clearly not a universal rule applied in all circumstances. Sociability is not necessarily communicated through politeness. Joking, teasing, banter, touch, and feigned fighting are common forms of interpersonal interactions, especially among men.[28] I was shocked in the beginning when I saw such frivolous behavior, so far from my understanding of "good" service. Letai told me that he had his own philosophy for interacting with his *keren*:

We can't be careless with the products we serve. Everything has to be good. We need to be polite to new *keren*, but with these *shuke* [familiar customers, regular customers,] it doesn't matter. . . . We know each other very well. . . . You only need to make some jokes with them sometimes and they will adore you.

Indeed, the customers who were yelled at or made fun of didn't seem to take it personally. They assured me that Letai and his family were very *simpatici* (nice) to them, and they seemed to enjoy the friendly horseplay. A playful sociability, which is most often mutual, thus becomes part of what makes the atmosphere enjoyable. It helps to build affection and friendship between Chinese baristas and some of their regular customers.

The playing, however, is often specifically gendered. As a young woman, over my four months of barista training I never developed such a playful friendship with any of the customers at Letai's place. I always tried to be polite, to smile and greet every customer, and no one ever shouted at me. It was not rare, however, to see middle-aged Chinese mothers engage in friendly or even flirtatious banter with their patrons. Sometimes, it was even the women who would initiate flirting. Once, when I visited a coffee bar managed mostly by a mother and her unmarried daughter, a retired man banteringly commented: "The daughter is very nice, but the mother isn't. She likes commanding people. It makes her happy." When she overheard this, the mother pretended to be angry, telling him: "Vaffan [Screw you] . . . !" But all the while she had a smile on her face and covered the left side of her mouth with her right hand and indicate that she was whispering and not publicly shaming him. The man was not offended at all, he just laughed. After he finished drinking, he deliberately put his glass upside down on the bar counter, letting some liquid spill over the counter that had been cleaned just a moment before. The Chinese woman just stared at him and went on cleaning. The man suddenly put his hand on the counter, pretending to try to catch her hand, but she swiftly pulled it away, so that the man only grabbed the dishcloth. They both laughed. The mother then told me that this man was a good *keren* who "is funny, nice to us and likes making jokes."

Many Chinese male baristas emphasize the importance of a joking relationship with their patrons. They believe that humor can bring in good business. Uncle Gumin makes humorous jokes and offers free drinks to his patrons from time to time. On a day when it rained heavily, he laughed at a regular customer who had rushed into his bar without an umbrella and then went about making him a warm coffee. "Good!" he told him, "today you don't need to take a shower at home, since you've already had it. You can save a bit money!" Another time, a patron was leaving after a shorter stay than usual, and Uncle Gumin commented: "Are you leaving? Oh no. I will be left alone here!" Then he made a sad face. The customer laughed and said he would come back the next day. While I was often amazed by his communication skills and sense of humor, Uncle Gumin continued to regret not being able to speak better Italian, as "otherwise my business could be even better, because *laowai* like it." Humor proves especially effective when it comes to solidifying relations in male sociability, where the skillful deployment of edgy jokes can foster closeness.[29]

While Chinese femininity can in itself be an effective social strategy, male baristas must be more proactive in their interactions with customers, making use of humor, playful gestures, generosity, and other social competencies that go with a masculine image. These forms of male sociability are enacted in all types of coffee bars, not just in male-dominated social spaces, such as Letai's locale. The short time while food is in preparation and being served creates a space for these little social dramas, which not only demonstrate male sociability but constitute a form of entertainment that can create value for the business. At a coffee bar managed by two Chinese brothers, the young men often give bottle-flipping displays as they prepare drinks. And, since many of their customers are soccer fans, they also are always prepared to talk about the latest soccer news and to show excitement or disappointment at the local team's performance. Meili's husband is a master at this. He often looks like an actor in a theater when talking with his customers. His hands, arms, and face are all expressive. His voice actually becomes operatic, much lower and stronger than the way he would talk with his family or me or to other Chinese. Overall, Chinese male baristas tend to show more generosity with small extras than female baristas do, treating customers to a drink, for example, to show manly hospitality.

Gender and Sociability

The widow Liu initially struck me as a "legendary" Chinese woman. She was the only Chinese barista I knew who used her Chinese family name rather than taking an Italian name at work. I heard many stories about her from her elder son and daughter-in-law, as well as from several retired Italian men who had frequented her coffee bar for years. Since her daughter-in-law had rejoined the family in Bologna a few months earlier, she only occasionally came to the bar to socialize with patrons. Of the Chinese coffee bar owners I met, she was one of the earliest, having entered the coffee bar business niche in the early 2000s. She started her establishment after she married an Italian barista. When they divorced, she purchased his portion of the business. One by one, her two sons rejoined her from China in the following years, and they managed the establishment together. When the younger son married, he started a new coffee bar business in another neighborhood. Her elder son told me that their business still relied on her, because most of their regular customers were her old friends.

I finally met Liu in person a week after my first visit to her coffee bar. When I entered, I saw a Chinese woman in her late fifties sitting at a table with two Italian elderly men, each with a glass of wine in front of him. She had long black hair and was wearing heavy makeup. A long, tight-fitting green dress outlined her figure. Her daughter-in-law, wearing a gaudy V-neck shirt cut quite low and a mini skirt, was standing behind the counter, and she confirmed to me that this was Liu. While I was still hesitating over how to approach her, Liu called me over to sit next to her. With no further introduction, she asked me who I was. She poured a glass of wine for me and proposed a toast to the two Italian pensioners in fluent Italian, though with a strong accent: "Now you have new company!" While she was saying this, the two men scanned me up and down from head to toe. Their male gazes made me uncomfortable, but I decided to stay but to keep my physical distance from them. Over the next two hours, except for the time when she left to take care of other customers, Liu kept a running narration about her lifetime of struggles, her two marriages, and her migrant adventures. She often touched one or the other of the two men on their arms and sometimes leaned in to whisper to them. The two were good listeners, responding with sympathy and respect for this Chinese woman.

This intentional deployment of female sexuality at Liu's establishment created an atmosphere evocative of a hostess club in East Asia.[30] The vibe was very different from that of Uncle Gumin's family-friendly coffee bar, which was just five minutes away across the *piazza* that separated them. Although there was no actual sex work at Liu's place, flirting was common and conspicuous between some customers and Liu, Liu's daughter-in-law, and two hired baristas—a twentyish Russian woman and a fiftyish undocumented Chinese woman. Liu's son, the only male barista on the premises, was clearly aware of these interactions involving his wife and his mother, but tacitly consented. In his understanding, "*Jiuba* rely on women." Once he also resignedly added, "Female baristas are like *sanpei* [the pejorative word in Chinese for nightclub hostess]." Every time I went to their place, they would ask me to stay longer and chat more with their *keren*, because as Liu's wife said, "If you talk with them, they will drink more."

An atmosphere of this sort is exceptional among the Chinese-managed coffee bars that I experienced. Indeed, most of my Chinese interlocutors did not agree with Liu's son's understanding of baristas as similar to nightclub hostesses. Businesses like Liu's often become stigmatized and the objects of gossip and criticism in the Chinese community. Linli's sister, Meili, whose family manages a family-friendly coffee bar targeting middle-class urbanites, particularly criticized those Chinese owners who used female sexuality as a business strategy. According to her, it is "immoral" and "harmful to family integrity." She also emphasized that her family-managed coffee bar was a decent and moral establishment where there was no place for dirty words, foul jokes, or inappropriate behavior. She gave me an example to illustrate the moral rectitude of her family's business: A new customer made a dirty joke and was quickly stopped by his friend who was a regular customer at her place. "This was not that kind of place," the friend said. I never saw Meili engage in any sexual banter with male customers, but I also could not verify the story she told me. Yet, Meili's words make clear how much she valued and how carefully she sought to protect the moral reputation of her family business, as dictated by her understanding of middle-class respectability. Similarly, Aiyue and her husband, whose middle-class coffee bar was centrally located in Bologna's *centro*, used the Chinese word *zhenggui* or "regular, formal" to describe their establishment and to distinguish it from "irregular and informal" businesses where female sexuality is used as a business strategy.

Yet, all of my Chinese interlocutors agreed that gender identity is a key factor in their business's performance. They commonly believe that like restaurants and other service industries, "good" service in a coffee bar is provided in part through performing gender.[31] Uncle Gumin's son, Enbao, explained to me his view of gendered roles in the business: "If it were only me, our business would go under. If it were only my two sisters, it wouldn't be a problem. This isn't because the *clienti* want anything from my sisters. It's just pleasant for a single or older man to chat with a young girl." Some others further conflated the attributes of service work with natural femininity. As Meili's husband commented, "The women are more painstaking than men. One euro per coffee, little by little—it's too womanly!" For him, women were more suited to service work because it involved repetitive manual tasks and could only produce small sums of money, a little at a time, while men were supposed to manage on a larger scale and to think about big numbers. Nonetheless, women play so important and effective a role in these family-managed businesses that having effective female labor is widely considered no small advantage. Daughters, mothers, and wives with a degree of language competence often become the main workers in the business, while their fathers and husbands only "help out" as security guards, drivers, and stockers. Some who speak good Italian also served as baristas, but more often a man worked alongside a female barista in the afternoons when alcoholic beverages are typically consumed, or alone in the periods when there are fewer customers.

When they need extra baristas, Chinese owners favor women. Aiyue and her husband hired two of them—one from Romania and the other from Albania—for their "regular" business to obscure their Chinese ownership. Aiyue was very satisfied with their choice: "It's better to hire female workers than males. Have you seen the two workers we hired? One is good at working, the other is good at smiling!" Liu's son hired a "sexy" Russian woman and he credited her presence with doubling his business income. It is debatable whether this was the result of her sex appeal or her greater language competence and barista experience—perhaps both were factors, but Liu's son's observation that "some customers even brought her roses" suggests that sexiness had at least a little to do with it. Sometimes my Chinese interlocutors also posted or re-tweeted hiring ads posted on WeChat, the most popular Chinese social media platform, that suggest a similar line of thought. One example: "A *jiuba* in Bologna is looking for a barista, preferably a woman. Board and lodging are included. Italian is required. Bar experience is not a requirement." The owner clearly considered gender identity a more important qualification than manual skills.

As a young woman fluent in Italian, I was also considered an ideal employee by some Chinese owners—regardless of the sociality of their place—who expressed their willingness to hire me to work for them. Some immediately asked for my phone number when they heard that I knew the basic manual skills of coffee-making. They believed I could at least "help" them out as a part-time barista in emergency situations when they were short on labor.

The shortage of Chinese female labor is another reason why some Chinese owners subordinate language skills to gender identity. In one case, a Chinese owner hired a young Chinese man and a young Chinese woman to work the afternoon shift. While the young man had labor skills and also spoke good Italian, the Chinese woman, 18-years-old Fangfang, had been in Italy for only one year, could barely communicate in Italian, and her skills were limited to making espresso. Moreover, she was neither a friend nor a relative of the coffee bar owner. Nevertheless, she was hired. Her boss, a Chinese man in his forties, explained his thinking to me: "It's better if they already know how to do the barista job, and it's better if they can speak Italian well. But sometimes you just need them to stand there. Some *keren* come in to buy a coffee or a drink just to get a closer look at our barista."

Chinese owners' perceptions of the gendered nature of the barista job are in line with the sex segregation that prevails in a wide range of service work, particularly in positions that call for direct interaction with clients.[32] The FIPE's 2014 annual report documented that six out of ten workers in Italy's coffee bars were women.[33] Male workers were long dominant in service industries in Italy, but beginning in the 1960s female workers increasingly entered the labor market, and they have since considerably feminized the sector. The father of my first host Melissa, a retired *bolognese* land surveyor, told me that female baristas who are not family members of the owner have become even more common since the 1980s when *bar di passaggio* targeting passersby became popular in Bologna.

This gendered strategy in labor use is in keeping with many customers' preference. Melissa's father explained to me: "Of course, both men and women can work in coffee bars. But, it's always pleasant to have a woman working there, since most of the *clienti* are men." My own experiences confirmed his words.

When I was learning barista skills at Letai's place, several customers voiced their preference for me over Letai, even though he was the much more experienced of us. A retired man said, "Since the *signorina* [young lady, miss] is here, may I ask her to make a coffee for me?" He always asked me to brew his cup of coffee and chatted with me. In another coffee bar, where the baristas were two Chinese brothers, a patron in his forties suggested the owner hire me, because "this *bar* needs a woman." He said, "If you work here, business will double!" The man did not mention my language competence. The first reason that came to his mind was my female identity.

The gender preferences of Italian customers seem somehow magnified in a Chinese-managed establishment. This is a result of the way the performance of gender draws upon and even reinforces existing gendered stereotypes, cultural expectations, and racialized representations.[34] An Italian woman in her fifties, who also worked as a self-employed barista, told me, "Oriental femininity is fascinating. You Oriental women are very sweet. You talk slowly, with a soft voice, and your body shape is very different from ours. . . . My father is very interested in Oriental femininity. . . . It's not just the men. It's pleasant for the women, too." Her words highlighted a stereotypical racialized image of Chinese women as a more submissive, docile, and feminine than Westerners. I also heard several Italians, both men and women, remark that they found Chinese women more sociable than Chinese men and for that reason preferred Chinese female baristas over males. In this context, Chinese convivial bricoleurs are strategically using a racial imaginary to engineer gendered labor in their own favor.

Performing gender, however, is sometimes accompanied by unwelcome flirting and gender harassment. Even Meili, who emphasized that her establishment was decent and moral, admitted that this gendered aspect of social interactions was something that female baristas had to face every day. I noticed also that Chinese female baristas performed gender and reacted to gendered interactions in different ways according to their age, generation, marital status, education backgrounds, and language skills, as well as with a view to the sociality of the place where they worked. I mentioned earlier that some married Chinese female baristas engaged in friendly or even flirtatious banter with some of their regular patrons. However, this was usually not the case for unmarried Chinese women. Several young female baristas confided to me their discomfort when faced with flirting, and some viewed it even more negatively as a form of harassment.[35] All the while, though, they often believed it to be a part of the business that could not be avoided, so they made what adjustment they could to this nuisance. Emotional labor requires workers to "induce or suppress feeling in order to sustain the outward countenance that produces the proper state of mind in others."[36] These personal compromises, acceptable in the particular convivial setting of their workplace, would not, however, be made outside of it. They maintained strict boundaries when it came to their gendered interactions with male customers. As Letai's sister-in-law once told me in quite a determined way: "As long as they're at my *jiuba*, they're my *keren*, but outside of it, we don't need to compromise ourselves." I rarely heard of a Chinese female barista socializing outside of work with a male customer.

When I was learning barista skills at Letai's establishment, flirting and friendly sex-related banter by male customers was quite frequent. Dirty jokes, unpleasant gazes, or malicious "accidental" touches were also issues that I needed to deal with. I usually ignored those gazes and never engaged in sexual banter with any customers. I pretended that I did not hear or understand their foul words and merely smiled back. I also made efforts to stay out of the way of lascivious hands, always dressing modestly to avoid verbal (or non-verbal) appraisals. Such self-surveillance and evasive strategies would likely be criticized by some feminists, and in truth I also questioned myself on how I should have reacted to such behaviors, even though I knew full well that these encounters were material to my research. Strategically managing the boundaries of intimacy, as well as feelings of embarrassment or respect, are a part of relationship construction.[37] The evasive strategies I came up with were much the same as those deployed by many other young Chinese female baristas. Once I saw a North African man flirt with eighteen-year-old Fangfang, but she just stood there with a smile. When the customer left, Fangfang sighed and told me, "At the beginning, I really couldn't understand what they were saying, so I just smiled at them. Now I can sometimes understand what they say, but I just ignore it, whether I understand it or not." Chinese identity, along with the supposed lack of linguistic skills had thus become a good excuse and a strategy that both of us used to refuse unwanted communication and to dodge awkward and embarrassing harassment.

The Spatial Politics of Sociability

When I crossed the almost "sacred" wooden gate that separated the working zone from the customer area at Letai's establishment, I found myself immediately immersed in a new species of social interactions with the customers. My staying in the bar for hours on end as a young Chinese woman was no longer odd or out of place amid this predominantly male sociality. Nearly all the regulars, whether they had spoken to me before or not, began greeting me and talking to me, and with time some began sharing with me their stories. While acquiring labor skills, I also learned how to interact with the customers as individuals, each with their own personality and social identity. The relationships I formed with the customers were different now from the ones I had experienced in all the other Chinese-managed coffee bars I had visited. I found myself being gradually included in the coffee bar's community.

Like labor skills, Chinese baristas' social skills are also an inter-subjective learning process on how to construct a convivial social space and community. In this process, Chinese convivial brico-leurs seek to conform to social conventions of politeness and hos-pitality, match customers' gendered preferences and expectations, and establish a reciprocal, neighborly, and even playful friendship with the regular patrons. All the while they are bombarded with cultural essentialism, stereotypes, and misunderstandings, as well as subject to broad structural inequalities in terms of race, culture, class, and gender. Yet, they also learned to deploy certain apparent differences and disadvantages strategically in their favor. A convivial, heterogeneous social space is thus produced through "the awkward, unequal, unstable, and creative qualities of interconnections across differences," which anthropologist Anna Tsing has metaphorically called "friction."[38]

Yet, no matter how Chinese baristas try to perform their sociability, it does not always work. When sociability breaks down, Chinese baristas seek to overcome their unease, to find a way to neutralize the negative consequences, and to become more effectively sociable. Those who do not speak Italian very well display politeness to compensate for their language deficiencies, young women deploy Chinese identity and their supposed lack of language skills to refuse unwanted interaction and avoid embarrassment, and some men perform masculinity to compensate for their gender disadvantage. In dealing with Nonno Pino and other Italian customers' temperament, Uncle Gumin confessed: "In the beginning, I didn't know how to react, but then I learned to just accept their unstable moods. . . . I smile, greet, and talk to them as usual, no matter what happens between us." Service with a smile again served as a strategy to deal with unexpected tensions, and the local knowledge that he accumulated over the years enabled him to actively manage these tensions.

Chinese convivial bricoleurs are acutely aware of the distinct sociality of their establishment, which is expressed through race, class, and gender distinctions. How sociability is performed is thus dependent on the type of sociality that characterizes a place. I noted earlier that the family-style atmosphere in Uncle Gumin's establishment is in striking contrast with Letai's coffee bar's atmosphere of male sociability. These two families, as it turns out, not only shared similar migration backgrounds, but were even distant relatives from the same rural hinterland of Southern Zhejiang province. Yet Uncle Gumin's son Enbao recalled his visit to Leitai's coffee bar as if it were an experience of another world:

> Some guys were smoking and playing the slot machines in the small room. . . . Letai shouted distantly from behind the bar counter in a playful way, "No smoking inside!"[39] He wasn't angry, just really loud. . . . He repeated this several times. Then one of them shouted back, "'I lost a lot of money.'" In this case, if he were my *cliente* here, I would say, 'I'm so sorry.' But Letai replied loudly, "I don't care!" . . . I mean, it doesn't matter to make such jokes with those thick-skinned people. But, at our place we can't do that. We have to make every *cliente* happy, otherwise they'll leave.

The socialities of the bars differ widely, as we have seen, but the core strategy of establishing personal connections with regular customers and building a sense of community is the same for all Chinese baristas, no matter the sociality of their establishment. A study on Korean-run nail salons in New York City in the late 1990s also illustrated reciprocal and even affectionate relations between Korean workers and both white and black customers through service interactions in the face of pervasive racial and class divisions.[40] In the convivial social space that Chinese baristas manage, we likewise see emotions, friendship, care, and ultimately a kind of social solidarity that goes beyond the transactional nature of business exchange. Letai once told me of his moral struggles when a patron would come to him to change bills into coins after losing hundreds of euros on the slot machines: "I'm a businessman. Of course, I wish to earn more. But every time I see them lose money again, I feel very bad. I always try to persuade them to play less and hope they get something back from the games. It's true that they're my *keren*, but they're also my friends!" In this case, economic exchange again facilitates social interaction and creates a space for sociability.[41]

Yet, such kinds of personal connections and the sense of community within the coffee bar stand in contrast to the private lives of baristas and patrons outside that space. When I asked Chinese baristas if they sometimes socialized with their customers outside their bars, the answer was nearly always negative. Chinese bricoleurs' sociability thus shows itself to be spatial in nature. As I will discuss in the next chapter, their construction of such a convivial social space is a dynamic process that runs in tandem with their contested racialization and with the rise of their ethnic consciousness.

6

Contesting Racialization

LATE IN THE AFTERNOON on August 8, 2019, a man rushed into a Chinese-managed coffee bar in Italy and stabbed the barista multiple times. The victim, a 24-year-old Chinese woman, was pronounced dead at the scene of the crime. The murderer, an undocumented immigrant from Morocco in his thirties, a *banhei* (literally "half black") in Chinese immigrants' racialized vocabulary, had been a regular customer of the establishment where he took the life of the young woman. That bar, which had been owned by a Chinese family since 2009, was located in a peripheral *quartiere* (neighborhood) of the city of Reggio Emilia, 45 miles from Bologna. I did not personally know the victim, but several of my Chinese friends and interlocutors did.

The murder triggered widespread emotional outbursts and intense discussion among Chinese residents in Italy. In the days that followed the murder, the feed on my WeChat, a Chinese social media platform, was flooded with posts about the tragedy and the victim, yet few of my Italian interlocutors seemed to have heard about the case.[1] While mourning their compatriot, some Chinese interlocutors lashed out at Moroccan and Maghreb immigrants at large, people whom they describe as *banhei*. This tragedy seemed to have confirmed their association of *banhei* as a racialized group synonymous with danger and crime, whose activities have contributed to Italy's deteriorating social climate and public safety in general, as well as the security of Chinese residents in particular.

Others addressed their disappointment to the Italian state and questioned whether and to what extent the state would protect their interests and security. Widespread Chinese perceptions that the Italian police were incompetent, that the judicial system was overly lenient, and that government regulation of undocumented immigration and crime was ineffective magnified their anxieties. Ironically, many Chinese immigrants used to be undocumented themselves, especially those of the murder victim's parents' generation, who had joined the Italian labor market in search of economic prosperity between the 1980s and early 2000s.

Chinese residents' united grief at a fellow Chinese victim's death, their anger towards *banhei* immigrants, and their overall disappointment in Italian society grew out of their racial perceptions as well as from their pronounced ethnic consciousness in Italy. *Banhei, laowai* (literally foreigners, here meaning white Italians) and *heiren* (black people) were the principal terms in the racialized vocabulary that Chinese residents in Italy deployed to make sense of the hierarchical racial reality in which they lived. Even the children of Chinese immigrants who spoke limited Chinese, like Enbao, are commonly aware of these terms, although their definitions and boundaries are often blurred and shifting. In this chapter, I will examine the ways in which Chinese diasporic subjects produced this racialized vocabulary and how it connected to racism and to racial formations in a host society of the Global North where the Chinese themselves are subject to racialization. In particular, I try to answer the question, how do Chinese baristas contest and form new racialized understandings in their everyday business management and social interactions with "superdiverse" populations, to use Steven Vertovec's term, from various racial, ethnic, national, class, and other social backgrounds?[2] And how do these racial perceptions impact their construction of a convivial community within and beyond the coffee bar space?

The concept of race overlaps with other concepts such as nationality, ethnicity, and social class. It serves as a convenient social category that provides "a way of making sense of the world," of constructing hierarchies and establishing boundaries between Us and Others.[3] Immigrant populations in the world are widely constructed as racialized Others who come from geographical areas beyond ethno-national borders and supposedly possess intrinsic and insurmountable cultural differences.[4] These racial formations, as defined by Michael Omi and Howard Winant, are "the sociohistorical process by which racial categories are created, lived out, transformed, and destroyed."[5] While racialization justifies inequality, oppression, and exploitation, it can also become a way of resisting oppressive racial institutions and practices. Racialized subjects also have their own racial formations "from below," which they employ to negotiate and resist inequity and to re-organize and redistribute resources through contested racialization for their own benefit.[6]

The transnational contexts in which immigrant subjects form their ideas about race as well as their own identities shape my analysis of Chinese baristas' everyday racial perceptions and identity formation. Migration studies from a range of locations have shed light on this process and described its dynamics, citing culture, economics, social class, and geopolitics as instrumental factors. Tiffany Joseph's study of Brazilian immigrants to the United States shows that immigrants initially rely on the racial ideology that they acquired in their place of origin to understand and interpret race in their host society, a process that in turn reconstructs and gives new meaning to race.[7] Wendy Roth's case study of Latinos in the United States also suggests that the understanding of race is an aspect of culture that can be transformed by migration.[8] In the US context too, Aihwa Ong shows that the racial formation of Cambodian refugees in terms of cultural citizenship is a dual process during which refugees self-fashion identity while also being made citizens through various cultural and institutional encounters.[9] Andrea Louie's study of Chinese Americans' identity formation reveals that Chinese-ness, as a "dynamic formation," was simultaneously produced on local, state, and transnational levels.[10] In the Italian context, a recent historical study of Chinese residents in Rome also emphasized the reciprocal impacts of both global and local ideas about place, culture, and societies in shaping their identification process on multiple scales.[11]

"*Jiuba* have become a high-risk business for us Chinese now," Jiayi texted me shortly after the tragic murder. He was a university student in 2014, one of my key interlocutors and a close friend in Bologna. Although he had never worked as a barista, Jiayi told me that his parents wanted to close their shoemaking workshop and purchase a coffee bar for the family to manage. To be fair, this tragedy is an exceptional case, the first and only instance of the murder of a Chinese barista. Most of the time, Chinese-managed coffee bars, just like coffee bars managed by native Italians, seem to be places where people come and go and meet and interact with baristas every day. Such conviviality is commonplace even for bars located in relatively high-crime neighborhoods. As we have seen, this was achieved through the co-production of taste and place by Chinese baristas, in collaboration with their customers, for their own economic or social purposes. These convivial bricoleurs have learned to build relationships and a sense of community with a clientele from diverse racial and ethnic backgrounds through everyday social interactions.

Yet, the tragedy reawakened Chinese immigrants' anxieties about their insecure and vulnerable position in Italy. The apparent conviviality that Chinese baristas strive to construct stands in sharp contrast with their lingering sense of precariousness, an unease that does not come only from insecurity over the supposed cultural illegitimacy that should disqualify them from operating the quintessentially Italian businesses that they own. Many also feel themselves to be vulnerable bodies exposed to unknown and unpredictable violence, crime, and conflicts. While the murder was an exception, small crimes on coffee bar management are commonplace. Several Chinese-owned coffee bars that I came to know had been direct victims of theft and robberies targeting the cashier and slot machines containing large amounts of euro coins, and they knew of many more cases as these were widely reported in Italy's Chinese media.[12] Meanwhile, several Chinese interlocutors also claimed to face more surprise inspections and various forms of discrimination from the Italian state and local bureaucracy than their Italian counterparts.

Jiayi and many other Chinese residents in Italy thus felt trapped in lives brimming with insecurity, uncertainty, and vulnerability, regardless of the economic prosperity that they may have achieved. This sense of precariousness derives not only from job insecurity, but is reflective of an increasingly common existential state and condition of uncertainty shared by people throughout late-capitalist societies.[13] Yet, precarity is a condition differentially distributed according to class, citizenship, race, and other social backgrounds that impact access to resources.[14] Precarity and privilege are not, however, necessarily mutually exclusive. Some immigrant subjects can also play out their relative privilege within predicaments of precarity and struggle against structural uncertainties.[15] In my ethnographic account, Chinese baristas are economically privileged but socially vulnerable. Their contested racialization offers ways of understanding how these convivial bricoleurs manage obstacles while constructing spatial conviviality.

Laowai and Whiteness

I met Jiayi for the first time at Uncle Gumin's coffee bar when I stopped by to say hello to the family. Enbao was on his shift. The two young men knew each other from the Chinese Evangelical Christian Church of Bologna and had attended the same youth fellowship. I took the opportunity to introduce myself and my project to Jiayi. To break the ice, I asked him if he had ever heard of the alleged *mafia cinese*. This young Chinese man, the child of immigrants and a college student who had lived in Italy since the age of eleven, replied with a sarcastic laugh. Enbao also gently shook his head while continuing to clean the bar counter as he listened in on our conversation. He commented in Italian mixed with some relevant Chinese terms, "*Laowai* are like this.

It's because they have the mafia themselves. When they can't understand something, they say it's the mafia. They say we Chinese are *mafia*. They say *banhei* are *mafia* as well. We're all *mafia* in their eyes." Enbao's words showed an awareness and discontent over racialized discourses concerning Chinese and other immigrants in Italy. After a short silence, Jiayi brought up his own perceptions of Italy as a xenophobic country where Chinese people continued to confront a lot of racism. On this occasion, he didn't go into much detail about his personal experiences, but in our many subsequent conversations he shared quite a few private stories of his traumas and struggles living in a predominantly white society.

My Chinese interlocutors in Italy commonly refer to native Italians as *laowai*.[16] Although its literal meaning is "foreigner," studies of the use of the term in China have confirmed that it is used to refer to white foreigners more than to any other racial and ethnic group and incorporates an Occidentalist imaginary of Western modernity, wealth, and civility.[17] This is consistent with my own understanding of the term when I was growing up in China. The conflation of whiteness, Westernness, and foreignness is a historical construction that derived from China's interactions with Western colonial powers in the late nineteenth and early twentieth centuries.[18] It was later applied to foreign experts from the Soviet Union and Eastern Europe in the socialist period, and more recently has been used to refer to Western investors and managers in the post-Mao era. In the Italian context, the interchangeable use of the terms *yidali ren* (Italians) and *laowai* suggests that Italians represent the white Westerners in my Chinese interlocutors' racial perceptions. No distinction is made between northern Italians and southern Italians in this racial vocabulary. The North-South divide and the racialization of southerners in Italy's racial discourses does not seem to have made a clear impact on their racialized perceptions of Italians. Yet, several Chinese residents who had years of lived experiences in Italy mentioned to me that they were aware of the discrimination that southerners encountered in Northern Italy.

All my Chinese interlocutors had a strong sense of otherness in Italy. They all had their own stories or stories from their families or friends about everyday forms of racism they experienced, while not denying that some *laowai* were nice to them. These racist encounters range from institutional discrimination in the form of residency and citizenship policies, to more banal racism in everyday life, such as being bullied in school or receiving verbal insults on a bus. As a Chinese and a *straniera* (foreigner), I also confronted cliched questions about *i cinesi* or "the Chinese," as well as verbal harassment or even insults within and beyond the coffee bar space from Italians of all social classes, sometimes in friendly and joking tones, but also in a more aggressive sense. Like many of my Chinese interlocutors, I felt uncomfortable when the term *i cinesi* was used as a racially charged label to describe the entire Chinese population, with its implication that these people are uniformly mysterious, have an inexplicable culture, and are suspicious for their alleged illegality.

First-generation Chinese immigrants share a clear understanding that Italy is not their home as this land is *"laowai* territory," as Uncle Gumin once put it. This sense of social exclusion is independent of their economic status and how long they have lived in the country. After living in Bologna for more than twenty years, Uncle Gumin told me that he was aware of how *laowai* have changed their perceptions of Chinese people. "In the 1990s, *laowai* saw us Chinese as beggars, but now everyone knows that China is rich, and we Chinese are rich. They have become jealous." Like many other Chinese interlocutors of mine, he was proud of the economic mobility that his family and numerous other Chinese immigrants had achieved, but he had mixed feelings about this transformed image, as it made him feel even more socially vulnerable.

The prejudice, racialization, and social exclusion that Chinese residents encounter and perceive in one form or another remains a lived experience shared by both the first-generation Chinese immigrants and their children. Those who were born or raised in

Italy and speak the same language and drink the same espresso coffee as their Italian age-mates, often employ the Italian word *razzismo* when complaining about the discrimination and marginalization that they experience. Uncle Gumin's eldest daughter Ensi, who migrated to Italy at the age of ten, wrote the word *razzisti* (racists) on a napkin when our conversation turned to the topic of how she thought Chinese people were treated. We were speaking in Mandarin Chinese, but she found this Italian word best suited to describe her thoughts. She did not say it aloud for fear that it would draw attention from her Italian customers. I prompted her to tell me how she knew they were racist. She replied confidently: "It's so obvious. For example, some *laowai* were about to enter our coffee bar, but they left when they saw Chinese standing behind the bar counter. I could tell by looking at their facial expressions. Some even speak out loud so that you hear the reason why they're leaving, that it's because the bar is managed by *i cinesi*."

Ensi's experience is one of many shared observations that Chinese baristas regard as evidence of pervasive anti-Chinese racism in their everyday racial encounters. A young Chinese man in his twenties who managed a peripheral bar with his younger brother became somewhat emotional when he commented mostly in Chinese on his similar experiences: "Those *laowai* think we're Chinese, so surely our products are not good. They like using some exceptional cases to generalize about all us Chinese. They think we're all the same. . . . They have a strong sense of superiority. They think they're better than us. If this isn't *razzismo*, what is it?" I do not think avoiding Chinese management is necessarily a product of racism, as there are other reasons, including distrust of the supposed cultural outsiders' labor skills, the *popolare* or working-class ambience, slot machines, the presence of undesirable customers, and so forth. Yet, anti-Chinese racism seems to be a blanket accusation levelled by some Chinese at all encounters that they view as negative, whether they are in fact racist or not.

Many Chinese baristas who were born or had grown up in Italy, for example, told me about their perceptions of otherness in their everyday interactions within the coffee bar space. During Hong Kong's Umbrella Movement in 2014, Enbao complained to me in Italian, saying, "These days my *clienti* keep on asking me what happened in Hong Kong. It seems to me that I should know everything about China. I've lived in Italy just like them for so many years. I've only been to China once. I don't even have any idea where Hong Kong is located exactly." Race thus infuses merchant-customer relations in diverse ways and can polarize the simplest social interactions.[19] Chinese baristas often connect everyday happenings as well as unintentional offenses to their social marginalization in Italian society at large. For Enbao, native Italians repeatedly reminded him of his Chinese identity and of how much he was "out of place" in this country. Meanwhile, he admires the multiculturalism in the United States. He once said, "You can always see people of different racial backgrounds shown in American TV commercials. The Italian ads only include white Italians. No blacks, no Chinese. We're ignored by them." Regardless of how much he romanticized racial realities in the United States, Enbao's words revealed his frustration at being marginalized and even ignored by the society that he considers as home.

Encounters deemed racist and perceptions of anti-Chinese prejudice aside, everyday coffee bar management also has reshaped Chinese baristas' racialized perceptions of *laowai*. Lanlan, who migrated to Italy at the age of twelve, confessed to me that prior to emigration, she thought *laowai* must be rich and nice. This imaginary, however, shattered after she saw and experienced the diversity among *laowai*. She discovered that "not all *laowai* are rich" and "not all are good people." Several Chinese baristas I talked to also shared their earlier positive expectations and imaginary of a developed Europe with only respectable white Westerners. They gave up all such illusions once they got involved in the coffee bar business. A civilized, developed, and affluent Western country with only well-educated and respectable white Westerners turned out to be an Occidentalist fantasy. While some racial stereotypes were deconstructed, others were reinforced. New stereotypes were constructed through "racial learning" in their everyday social, cultural, and institutional encounters.[20] These old and new stereotypes and perceptions now constitute their new localized racial formations of whiteness as in sharp contrast with "us" Chinese, and this draws new racial boundaries.

On the basis of what they had learned from white customers, several Chinese owners, first-generation immigrants, commented on *laowai* as being *furbo* (cunning, sly.) A *furbo* person in a pejorative sense is dishonest and tends to use tricks and shortcuts to serve their own interests while manipulating others. "Some customers say we Chinese are *furbo*. They say it to our faces!" Lanlan's mother told me discontentedly, "But, I want to say, they are much more *furbo* than us! . . . Some drink and then leave without paying. Some even steal!" In this case, white customers accusing the Chinese owner for being *furbo* in their business practices, and then the Chinese owner using the same term as a counter-criticism aimed at native Italians. Uncle Gumin also told me about encounters with *laowai*'s deceptive tactics to increase the purchase price when selling their businesses. Several other Chinese owners told me that they discovered their hired *laowai* workers stealing at work. For Meili's husband, however, "The Italian government is the most *furbo*." He said, "They're the same as robbers! They say they charge a high tax on slot machines because gambling isn't good, but they like it. They make a lot of money from slot machines! . . . We work very hard and take care of our business, while all they need to do is to collect the money, and then all that money is wasted by those working in the government!" The analogy between the Italian state and robbers highlights Chinese entrepreneurs' distrust of the Italian state. In their understanding, the state impedes their economic accumulation while not providing reciprocal services.

"*Laowai* love pleasure" is another widespread stereotype. It stands in sharp contrast to the work ethic that self-employed Chinese immigrants feel is a prerequisite to making a living. Many of my Chinese interlocutors hold ambivalent feelings on this issue.

On the one hand, they admire native Italians for not working as much as Chinese immigrants and enjoying a more laidback lifestyle. This new racialized stereotype can be seen as part of a revised Occidentalist imaginary linked to a desirable middle-class lifestyle. On the other hand, they do blame *laowai*'s lax work ethic, as well as their supposedly innate laziness and sloppiness, as responsible for Italy's economic stagnation. In contrast, it is in their view the innate hardworking virtue of the Chinese people that has brought them family wealth and economic prosperity, as well as China's rapidly growing economic power in the world.

The notion that "*Laowai* are perverted" is another popular stereotype among Chinese immigrants in Italy. Sexual misbehavior and gendered interactions that Chinese baristas witness, experience, or hear about have reinforced such gender-specific racial stigmatization. As we saw in the previous chapter, unwanted flirting and gender harassment are common in everyday coffee bar management. A Chinese woman working as a barista would be hard-pressed to avoid such annoyances, including unwanted courtship from some customers. The social reality of Italy's more liberal sexual mores and pluralistic family structures that Chinese baristas have learned about from their customers seem to have confirmed their negative stereotypes of *laowai*'s callousness regarding marriage and family. They contrast this with the traditional value of family integrity espoused by recent Chinese immigrants, who see this also as a prerequisite for a family business and its economic prosperity. Consequently, while gendered sociability is commonly employed as a business strategy, interracial relationships and marriages are strongly discouraged by Chinese immigrant families, no matter if they are Christians who are more rigidly against pre-marital sexual relationships or not. The only case of a serious interracial relationship that I knew of was a Chinese young woman in her twenties from a non-Christian family who dated a middle-aged divorced Italian man. Her parents were so upset that they sold their bar and the entire family moved to another city.

Structural inequalities, in this case, race and class, once again intersect and impact social interactions between Chinese baristas and their host society.[21] Most Chinese-managed coffee bars are class-bound social spaces. Understandably, Chinese baristas readily generalize their perceptions of the specific social class that patronizes their bar as representative of all *laowai* as a racial group, since in many cases their *laowai* customers are the few native Italians whom they interact with on a daily basis. Improper sexual behavior, poor manners, the excessive consumption of alcohol, addiction to gambling, and other perceived misbehaviors all run counter to Chinese baristas' family values, work ethics, and their perceptions of modernity in one way or another. As Lanlan commented: "How would a good person spend so much time in our *jiuba* without doing anything else. They spend so much money on drinking and gambling without thinking about their family!" Excessive consumption of alcohol and addiction to gambling—two fundamental sources of income for many Chinese-managed coffee bars, somewhat ironically become evidence allowing Chinese baristas, especially those who are Christian, to judge their customers as morally defective.

Hei and Shades of Blackness

"What do you call those people who are somewhat *hei*, but not that *hei*?" Jiayi asked me curiously after learning that the term *banhei* or "half black" did not make any sense to me. Growing up in China, I had never heard the word. It seems to be a colloquial expression of a local invention. The four decades of Chinese mass migration to Italy since the 1980s were part of a wider influx of immigrants to this country. The other major geographical areas of origin include Eastern Europe, the Balkans, North Africa, the Middle East, and South Asia, as well as the Philippines and Sub-Saharan Africa. Italy's racial and ethnic diversity exceeded the expectations of new Chinese arrivals, who were mostly labor migrants in search of economic prosperity. They overwhelmingly came from the hinterlands of Southern Zhejiang, where racial and ethnic social environments were highly homogeneous, the population being overwhelmingly Han Chinese. Before emigrating, they had limited knowledge of world geography and the distribution of populations, and they lacked also any lived experiences with non-Chinese racial and ethnic groups. Thus, shades of *hei* have been deployed to identify and categorize immigrant groups when drawing color lines.

Historically, China had an awareness of skin colors that comprised a hierarchy. Those with fair skin were perceived as elites who did not need to work in the field, while darker skin color was a trait of the peasantry, associated with poverty and low social and cultural status. In imperial China, the color *hei* (black) was often part of the imaginary of the most remote lands of the empire and of the ethnic minorities living there, who were not only physically different but also culturally inferior.[22] The color *hei* has also been used to denote negative qualities and immoral and illegal behaviors in Chinese vocabulary, yielding such expressions as *heigong* (illegal worker), *heishi* (illicit market), *heibang* (gangs), *heiqian* (dirty money), and so on. Yet, Chinese perceptions of skin colors never had the same racial significance or connotation as in Western societies, where race is a concept heavily influenced by their histories of colonialism and slavery.[23] The Western racial ideology associated with white supremacy and Eurocentric modernity was only introduced to China in the mid-nineteenth century, alongside Western imperialism. New racial discourses arose, centering on the yellow, white, and black races. They acknowledged white Westerners as the dominant race in modern times, but also embraced the idea that China would catch up to and again surpass Western civilization through economic development, industrial modernity, and social progress.[24] These discourses accepted Western racial classifications to situate blackness at the bottom of the global racial hierarchy, regardless of its various deployments

throughout the twentieth century, including in Maoist interna-
tionalism and in connection with contemporary African migration to Chinese cities.[25]

In Mandarin Chinese, the category of *heiren* (black people) refers to people of Sub-Saharan African descent with visibly dark skin
color. The usage of this term among my Chinese interlocutors in
Bologna was consistent with the racial terminology used in China.
Shanshan Lan's study of the African diaspora in South China shows
that instead of internalizing Western racial ideology, Chinese rural
migrants there consider nationality and the economic status of a
heiren's home country and their skin color as equally important.[26]
Mingwei Huang's study in South Africa has further suggested
that Chinese racial discourses of blackness should be understood
through the lens of racial capitalism and the racialization of labor.[27]
My Chinese interlocutors in Bologna often associated *heiren* with
poverty and the cheap labor that occupies the bottom position
in the labor market. "They often do the dirtiest and most tiring
work. Some also work for us Chinese," a Chinese woman, a child
of immigrants in her twenties told me. Yet, my Chinese interlocutors rarely associated *heiren* with crime, danger, or threats to their
personal or business security. None of them mentioned *heiren* as
particularly responsible for theft, robbery, or other violent crimes
against Chinese people or businesses in Italy. Several Chinese baristas, in fact, confessed to me that their impressions of *heiren* were
not bad, although they had rather limited interactions with them
in their everyday life. Indeed, during my entire fieldwork in Bologna between 2014 and 2015, I only met three regular customers
who would be considered *heiren* in Chinese-owned coffee bars. All
three had a degree of economic security and had taken up the habit
of frequenting coffee bars. *Heiren* therefore was not a word often
heard in our conversations.

In contrast, the term *banhei* is a racial label that my Chinese
interlocutors frequently used. All the Chinese baristas I talked to,
Chinese speakers or not, knew this local colloquialism. In their
understanding, the term referred to darker-skinned people who

did not appear phenotypically as dark as *heiren*. It served them as a convenient racial label for certain immigrant groups. Jiayi and many other Chinese interlocutors claimed that such categorization was purely based on skin color, without any negative connotations, but I quickly realized that the term is not value neutral. My initial doubts came from difficulties I encountered in my early fieldwork when I was trying to discern precisely who was meant by this color label. I learned that both North African and South Asian immigrants, such as Moroccans and Pakistanis, are typically *banhei* in this racial classification. In this sense, *banhei* is quite similar to "brown" in popular American racial parlance. However, while the term "brown" can in America also refer to Filipinos, my Chinese interlocutors claimed that Filipinos do not belong to this category, as "Filipinos are Filipinos!"

I became even more confused when I learned that a consistent definition of the word did not exist, even among my Chinese interlocutors. Lanlan's mother insisted that Romanians and Albanians, the two most populous immigrant groups in Italy, are also *banhei*, despite many of them being phenotypically the same or even lighter-colored than many native Italians. Lanlan's sister confirmed with me that her parents spoke of Eastern Europeans as *banhei* in general, even though "their skin color looks very white." In contrast, my barista teacher Letai, who migrated to Italy at the age of fifteen, made a clear distinction between immigrants from Eastern Europe and *banhei*, informing me that the latter are primarily associated with "Arabs" and "Muslim countries." Jiayi tried to provide me with an explanation about generational differences among Chinese in their use of the term. "The older generation did not go to school." He said, "They do not know that Romania and Albania are also located in Europe. I don't think younger generations like me also think Romanians are *banhei*, but Albanians . . . ? They are definitely *banhei* in the eyes of us Wenzhouese, maybe because the word 'Albanian' sounds like 'Arab' in our Wenzhou dialect?" These seemingly confusing and contradictory categorizations revealed Chinese immigrants' awareness of the differences between somatic whiteness and hegemonic whiteness. In their mind, whiteness is connected with Europeanness, Christianity, and development. It denotes membership in a dominant racial power structure that excludes phenotypically white immigrants. This phenomenon is not new. Whiteness has never been just about phenotype. In U.S. history, Irish, Italian, and Jewish immigrants from various countries were all treated initially as non-whites and were only whitened alongside their upward social mobility over generations.[28]

Chinese immigrants' construction of racial categories is also linked to their understanding of *suzhi*. In explaining how to distinguish a *banhei* from a *laowai*, my Chinese interlocutors commonly told me that *banhei* are usually ruder, more poorly dressed and lack *suzhi*, while *laowai* are, in general, more polite, dressed more decently, and possess more *suzhi*. The term *suzhi*, roughly translated as "quality," encompasses physical, intellectual, and moral aspects of individuals that can be both biological and culturally nurtured.[29] Good *suzhi* can be achieved through both prenatal biomedical and educational efforts and postnatal cultivation, educational training, and self-improvement.[30] The discourse of *suzhi*, widespread since post-Mao China, justifies social hierarchies based on notions of "high" quality, which equates to civility and modernity and implies a disposition toward self-improvement and the aspiration to improve one's economic and social status and power, as opposed to those of "low" quality who do not possess these traits.[31] It is a "value coding" used to differentiate the good from the bad, the rich from the poor, and the civilized from the uncivilized.[32] Saying that someone lacks *suzhi* is an insult in China. Urbanites in China often use the discourse of *suzhi* to discriminate against rural migrants, whose bodies are thought to exemplify a backward mentality, uncivilized social manners, and aesthetically bad taste in terms of dressing.[33]

The *suzhi* discourse is also in line with how native Italians construct class and social distinctions. Fashion and design play an important role in the symbolism of class in Italy.[34] Dress codes and various manners in social interactions also reflect *civiltà* (civility) and *educazione* (education, manners) and determine whether a person is able to fare *bella figura* (make a good impression).[35] In the postwar period, northerners used such class distinctions to racialize southern migrants, and now foreign migrants from beyond the national border are similarly categorized. Chinese baristas have learned and deployed this division to construct their own hierarchical racial perceptions. When it is impossible to make such distinctions, "then they are just *laowai*," Jiayi told me, "It does not need to be always clear." Such ambiguity further confirms that class distinctions, constructed on the basis of individuals' social behaviors and aesthetic choices in everyday racial encounters, are key indicators for Chinese residents in making racial recognitions.[36]

Triangular Racial Encounters

In a particularly notable incident, Meili's nephew, a coffee bar owner in his early thirties, was woken up around midnight by a loud noise coming from his establishment downstairs. A van had rammed into his coffee bar, breaking down the roller shutters in the process, which allowed the robbers to cart away three entire slot machines full of coins. He called the police right away and they told him to stay inside his home for his own safety. "They only registered the case and said they will try to catch them. That's it!" While saying this, Meili's nephew's face flushed red. He told me emotionally that he has been traumatized since then, but could do little to prevent it from happening again. He installed CCTV cameras at the entrance as well as inside the bar, as many other Chinese storefront owners had done, even though he understood that this would offer little beyond psychological comfort.

Chinese residents often complain about what they perceive as Italy's poor public security, and many believe that crime is associated with certain immigrant groups whom they label as *banhei*. Several Chinese-owned coffee bars that I visited had been the victims of theft and robbery, not to mention the cases that I learned about from the Chinese media. Many Chinese interlocutors had also experienced home break-ins. Indeed, one night when I came back from dinner with my second host Anna, we found that our apartment had been broken into and our belongings were scattered everywhere. It was my first experience of a burglary, and I was in shock, but Anna stayed calm and told me that it happened on average once a year and she already had learned where to stash her more precious belongings. Then she called the police to report the incident, but they only asked us if we had any weapons at home before hanging up, and nothing further was done. In another case, when Jiayi called the police after his apartment was broken into, the policeman explicitly stated that they would not be able to catch the burglar and went on to express doubt when Jiayi told him that 500 euros in cash was lost, saying "Only 500? But you Chinese must have a lot of cash at home." Retelling the experience, Jiayi burst into his trademark sarcastic laugh: "We were reporting the case, but it turned out that we ourselves became suspects."

Beyond their resentment at the Italian police's apparent incompetence and inaction, Jiayi, Meili's nephew, and many other Chinese coffee bar owners, small entrepreneurs, and residents believed that the Italian state would not provide them with adequate protection. They felt exposed to and constantly victimized by crimes such as theft, burglary, and robbery. Ever conscious of their otherness in Italy, many of my Chinese interlocutors assumed that criminals tended to target Chinese and their businesses intentionally, in part because Chinese people were known to keep cash and were economically better-off in general, but more importantly because they remained socially marginalized and powerless. This meant that the police would not take their cases as seriously and would protect them even less than they would for native Italians due to racism in law enforcement.

Indeed, in many of my Chinese interlocutors' eyes, the Italian state is a major source of racism against them. They commonly think that rather than protecting them, the Italian authorities even harass them and their businesses more than their Italian counter-parts. Many of my Chinese interlocutors claimed that they had been fined during surprise inspections and believed that these dis-proportionately targeted Chinese-owned businesses. The charges leveled against them have included tax evasion, use of unregistered family labor (which might include minors), full-time employment of a worker claimed as a part-time laborer, nonconformance to the safety rules for manufacturing workshops, failing to recycle, and malpractices in food-service. It would have been difficult for me to prove whether or not Chinese businesses in Bologna were in fact particularly targeted by local authorities, but several studies have disclosed discriminatory policies and practices against Chinese enterprises by local authorities in Prato, Rome, and Milan, among other geographical areas.[37]

Chinese baristas also sometimes found themselves caught in dilemmas involving undesirable customers' illicit behavior. Once, Liu's son, whose coffee bar I discussed earlier as a quasi-hostess club, complained to me that his business was forced to close for one week because the police discovered evidence of drug use in the trash can outside his establishment. He said, "Those *banhei* use drugs, but it's not my fault. If they smoke outside, it's not my business." He admitted that some customers often smoked in the bathroom, but continued, "What can I do? I tried to kick them out, but they just don't leave." Indeed, I often witnessed his family scolding undesirable customers, mostly immigrants, accusing them of stealing, drug use, late payment of their tabs, violations of in-door smoking regulations, messing up the bathroom, vandal-izing slot machines after gambling losses, and other forms of poor behavior. But I was told that these customers did not take their reprimands seriously, and continued to patronize the establish-ment. Liu's son had his interpretation: "They have no other places to go. They don't dare to go to a *laowai*'s place to make trouble. Only we Chinese are easy to be bullied." His perceptions of his own social vulnerability, trapped between undesirable customers and an indifferent Italian state, were widely echoed by many of my Chinese interlocutors, a further sign of how acutely self-aware they are of their social marginalization.

Immigrants develop and accumulate knowledge about racial differences and hierarchies in their everyday lives.[38] In the Italian context, the localized vernacular system of racial designation that Chinese immigrants have constructed reflects their own perceptions of racial hierarchy in Italy and of their own perceived predicament within structural inequality. Not only are they aware of Italy's racial hierarchy and extensive anti-immigrant sentiments, but many of them also share similar anti-Black and anti-Brown sentiments. As Meili and several other Chinese baristas emphasized to me in our many conversations, "*laowai* also don't like those *banhei*." The term *banhei* is the Chinese counterpart to the Italian term *extracomunitari*. Both contain pejorative and racist connotations and impose social stigmas. In Italy's anti-immigrant and white nationalist discourses, *extracomunitari* are criminalized as dangerous Others who bring disorder to Italy. From Chinese immigrants' perspectives, *banhei* symbolize the danger that threatens their business security and personal safety. In this sense, Chinese immigrants harbor the same prejudices as native Italians. The term *banhei* thus mirrors Italy's existing hierarchical color lines between native Italians and recent immigrants.

Yet, the anti-Black and anti-Brown racism that Chinese immigrants perceive differs from the traditional black and white binary. It should be situated within "the larger context of the triangular power relations" between Chinese, white Italians, and non-white residents in Italy.[39] *Laowai* and *banhei* represent two different racial Others, acting as oppositional powers in their pursuit of economic prosperity and social mobility, as well as reminders of their social vulnerability. The perceptions of these two racialized groups thus shape each other and are mutually reinforcing. "We Chinese are an attractive piece of meat coveted by all!" This is the metaphor a Chinese coffee bar owner, a child of immigrants who had lived in Italy from the age of twelve, posted on the WeChat social media platform after learning that another Chinese-managed coffee bar near his establishment had been robbed at gunpoint by a local Italian. His "all" most likely refers specifically to all non-Chinese who take money from well-off Chinese residents, including the state that levies fines while seemingly refusing to look after their security. The precariousness of their exposure to crime and conflict has fueled Chinese baristas' racialization of both *laowai* and so-called *banhei* populations, intensifying their Chinese ethnic consciousness.

Both *laowai* and *banhei*, however, are the core customers that Chinese baristas serve, interact with, and build relationships with every day. These two racialized Others constitute the major clientele for Chinese-owned coffee bars, where racial encounters take place. Together with native Italians, non-Chinese male immigrants also provide a considerable source of the business income for most of my Chinese interlocutors managing a "traditional bar." Chinese baristas thus have to manage racial encounters and negotiate, for the sake of conviviality, with all of these local populations from diverse racial, ethnic, and national backgrounds within the same social space.

In policing the customers, one of Chinese baristas' major tasks is to maintain the sociality of the space they manage, conforming to "good" customers' moral expectations while excluding "bad" customers who risk destroying such sociality. As I discussed in the previous chapter, a basic strategy is to provide service with a smile to "good" customers only, excluding "bad" customers from its benefits. The differentiation is often determined by baristas' perceptions of color lines that themselves also signal racial and class backgrounds in Italy. Normally, *laowai* are "good" customers, *banhei* are "bad" ones in their stereotypical perceptions. "There are too many *banhei* around" became a comment that I often heard from my Chinese interlocutors when they evaluated the quality of a coffee bar business. Several Chinese owners, especially those whose business targeted middle-class urbanites, told me that they had even kicked out many *banhei* in order to maintain the moral legitimacy of the space they managed. Their concerns were not unfounded. Alberto, a patron at Uncle Gumin's coffee bar and the chef from Southern Italy introduced in the Prelude, made no secret of the fact that one of the reasons he thought Uncle Gumin's place was a good one was that it was not "full of *extracomunitari.*" His attitude was in line with that of my middle-class Italian interlocutors who confessed that they would prefer not to go to a coffee bar where there were many *extracomunitari.*

Nevertheless, most Chinese baristas are well aware that immigrants are one of the main sources of patronage for their business. For this reason, they try not to see them as homogeneous. Letai explained this to me as follows: "Not all of the *banhei* are bad. There are also some good ones. Some of them are neat and tidy, polite and quiet, pay on time, and don't make trouble. Our business still relies on them. What else can we do?" Letai's reluctant inclusion of some *banhei* immigrants in his list of good clientele demonstrates Chinese baristas' racial perceptions and the everyday practice that they base on their perceptions, as well as how these fit into the racial hierarchies of both the larger Italian society and that created by their own racial classifications. Yet, their willingness to negotiate does not take them beyond either Italian moral norms for a respectful citizen or the Chinese moral criterion of *suzhi* (quality). This again highlights that their understanding of race is based not only on phenotypical distinctions, but on their understanding of civility and modernity.

The policing of customers, however, provides contexts for tensions and conflicts. Some immigrants who have expressed their discontent at the "bad" service they receive from Chinese baristas nevertheless still patronize the establishment as it is conveniently located to their home and often one of the few social spaces available to these socially marginalized residents. During my fieldwork, I never personally witnessed physical fights in any coffee bar that I regularly followed, but I heard about several cases of tensions and disputes with customers that ended in physical confrontations. One of Lanlan's family friends, who managed a coffee bar in a peripheral *quartiere* where many immigrants lived, told me that his family desperately wanted to sell their coffee bar. In less than a year of their management, he had been involved in several fights and was beaten up brutally by what he referred to as some drunk *banhei* customers.

There are also occasions of a positive nature, when Italy's racism and social marginalization can become a topic of common concern between Chinese baristas and their "good" foreign customers and hired workers. Several Chinese baristas told me that they often complained about Italy and Italians together with their non-Italian customers. Like *banhei*, Chinese immigrants also belong to the category of *extracomunitari* who are widely discriminated against in Italy. As Letai cuttingly pointed out, "In this country, *banhei* are treated as a problem of public security and we Chinese become an economic problem." Solidarity is often achieved by sharing experiences of discrimination so that the country's "problems" elicit sympathy and discursive interracial solidarity.

Chinese coffee bar owners' negotiation of triangular racial encounters is further evidenced in their choice of employees. Although they primarily rely on unpaid and flexible family labor, it is quite common to see Chinese owners hire one or several extra baristas. However, many Chinese owners find themselves in a quandary when it comes to deciding which racial or ethnic background would be preferable in an employee. They often admitted that it would be ideal if they could find a good, experienced *laowai* to work for them. But in pondering that choice, they had concerns related to the power dynamics that might arise between them and their hired laborers. Several Chinese owners confessed to me that they had experiences hiring Italian baristas in the early stages of management, but then decided not to hire Italians anymore once they had learned enough manual skills of their own. Uncle Gumin's family was one such. His three children all told me on different occasions that their family had decided to fire an Italian barista who worked for the family as she was arrogant and did not respect them as her bosses. Many Chinese owners managing a neighborhood bar would rather hire a Chinese barista to work for them when the family's workers were insufficient to meet their needs, because they believed that Chinese workers were more compliant, hardworking, and flexible when it came to their working hours. Some of them who have attained a certain degree of skill and experience in coffee bar management even prefer Chinese employees with no barista skills at all. Enbao shared his rationale: "Whether they have experience or not is not a problem. We can teach them. The most important thing is that they have to be nice and hardworking."

Some Chinese owners, however, are convinced that a *laowai* worker is important for their business, especially when theirs is an establishment that targets middle-class urbanites or offers a variety of *aperitivo* food that Chinese baristas were not able to prepare. Letai's brother and sister-in-law found their two "hardworking" Italian workers to be "very good." One was a young woman in her early twenties who was willing to work the ten-hour days that are standard for a hired Chinese worker. The other was a local young man who took on the evening shift and often brought his friends to the bar to drink "a couple of packs of beers each time." Yet, they too believed that they were "lucky" to find them, as it was quite "rare" to have such good *laowai* workers. Many other Chinese owners preferred hiring white immigrants who phenotypically looked like *laowai* or Italians. These establishments also were commonly those that targeted middle-class urbanites or tourists. Aiyue, whose coffee bar was centrally located in the *centro*, hired a Romanian barista and an Albanian waitress. I did not discover that these two hired workers were in fact immigrants until Aiyue explained to me that she and her husband preferred hiring *laowai* from countries other than Italy. She said: "It's always good to have some *laowai* to work here, but not necessarily Italians. . . . *Laowai* from other countries are good. They are also foreigners like us and they need a job to legally stay here, so they care about the job and they work harder than Italians." I never heard Aiyue use the pejorative *banhei* to refer to these two workers, although Romanians and Albanians are sometimes also considered *banhei* by first-generation Chinese immigrants. In this case, the two workers' phenotypes were more important than their immigrant identity.

Shared Space, Separate Lives

Lanlan was only 19 years old when I met her for the first time in 2014. Yet, she had already worked as the primary barista at her family's bar for more than two years. Her typical day began at 5 am and ended at around 5 pm. On the occasional days when her mother had to run errands outside of the bar, Lanlan had to work even longer hours. Her twelve-hour shifts were punctuated by a half-hour lunch break at around 11 am. On school days, she also left the bar to drop off and pick up her little brother from the nearby primary school he attended. During her long shifts, the vast majority of Lanlan's social interactions are with the bar's clientele, most of whom were retired men. Some of them absolutely adored her and her two siblings and treated them as if they were the children of a close neighbor's family. On occasion, a retired man who lived alone in the apartment above their coffee bar would invite them for lunch at his place, while another man gave Lanlan several driving lessons when she was struggling to pass her driving exam. However, these interactions were exceptional. Lanlan and her siblings rarely socialized with non-Chinese residents in their leisure time. Throughout their lives as children of Chinese immigrants in Italy, they also never had the chance to witness non-Chinese ceremonial events. Whenever I told them about Italian weddings, birthday parties, or other local events that I had attended, both girls showed intense curiosity, wanting to know all of the details.

The social gulf between Lanlan's work and her leisure time is striking. Her interactions with non-Chinese people were strictly limited to the realm of work, spatially demarcated by the boundaries of her family's bar. Even when she was not preparing drinks or chatting with the clientele, Lanlan would retreat into an online

Chinese world. She likes to scroll through her WeChat feed, chat with her Chinese friends, read online Chinese novels, watch Mandarin TV dramas, or, as a beauty lover, browse through Chinese websites on cosmetics products. If not for her presence in a peripheral bar in Bologna surrounded by non-Chinese customers, Lanlan's downtime during her shifts would look little different from the leisure time of other teenage girls in China. The four to five hours from 5 pm to her bedtime at around 9:30 pm or 10 pm were her personal time, although even then she tutored her little brother to help him with his homework. Most of this time, she spent time upstairs at home without setting foot in the bar again. She sometimes hung out with her Chinese friends or took her brother and sister for a walk in the *centro*, which is only twenty minutes away by bus. Even so, she was usually back home before sunset. Occasionally, she took some days off for holidays or to travel with her Chinese friends, even once spending a week with them in Greece in the summer of 2016. Her socio-spatial segregation from native Italians and non-Chinese immigrants of her age was such that, despite having lived in Bologna for years, she had no inkling of the popular *aperitivo* bars or clubs popular with local youth. Almost all the trendy Chinese restaurants in the city frequented by her Chinese peers, however, were well known to her.

Like Lanlan, most of my Chinese interlocutors who had immigrated to Italy in their teenage years did not have any Italian friends. Instead, they only socialized with their Chinese peers and conducted their social lives within the Chinese community. This segregation is not purely volitional on the part of these young Chinese immigrants but rather reflects a deep social and cultural alienation from mainstream Italian culture that is shared by children of Chinese immigrants of Lanlan's generation. In Lanlan's, the differences in their respective national and sociocultural backgrounds while growing up made her interactions with her Italian peers difficult. They had such drastically different life experiences. As Lanlan told me, "It's hard to make friends with *laowai*. We just

don't get along with each other. We have different interests. . . .
I usually hang out with Chinese friends. It makes me feel more
comfortable." Several other Chinese young people confessed similar feelings to me.

Lanlan's younger sister Beibei became more *laowai*-ized, or
laowaihua to borrow Lanlan's word, which means "assimilated."
She started school in Italy in the third grade and speaks Italian like
a native. Beibei even claims that her Italian is better than her Chinese. I was unable to determine whether this was the case, since
she always socialized with Chinese speakers both in-person and
on social media in Chinese. When I first met her in the summer
of 2014, Beibei had just enrolled in an *istituto tecnico economico*
or "technical economic institute." It was the same upper secondary school which her sister and many other Chinese children had
attended. While Lanlan had dropped out after her first year due
to language difficulties, Beibei was an A student in school and
planned to continue on to college. She was the only Chinese
student in her class. During breaks between classes, she often accompanied her Italian classmates as they stood outside smoking,
despite not being a smoker herself. Nevertheless, she claimed to
have few Italian friends and her interactions with her classmates
were mostly limited to school. "Maybe because I am too shy and
introverted" she said in her low and soft voice.

As our conversations went deeper, Beibei also admitted that her
family situation might be a key factor that discouraged her from
making friends with non-Chinese peers. Ever the docile daughter
in the eyes of her parents, Beibei always went straight back home
after school and rarely joined in extracurricular events or activities
with other students. She and many other children of Chinese immigrants in Italy with similar family and migration backgrounds
still shared their parents' sense of profound vulnerability as relative newcomers in an unfamiliar society. In the early stages of
settlement and capital accumulation in Italy, these children of
immigrants thus lacked the same opportunities to enjoy leisure
time as native Italian students. On school days, Beibei took the bus

home, typically showed up at the bar at 2 pm.[40] After school, she spent most of the rest of her day behind the bar counter together with her sister or mother and often did her homework there. Years later, when Beibei was a university student in law, she once told me that she had become very excited after learning about the Erasmus exchange program that allowed millions of European college-aged students to study abroad in other participating EU countries. She wanted to enroll in Erasmus so that she too could spend several months or a year on exchange. However, after reflecting on her family's situation, Beibei ultimately decided not to bring up the exchange program with her parents. She concluded that her family needed her labor in the bar, and it was not worth troubling her parents over something so frivolous. Like many other Chinese teenagers in Italian schools, Beibei and her sister rarely informed their parents of parent-teacher conferences or any school events involving parents. They regarded such engagements as, at best, an unnecessary distraction and, at worst, an occasion for embarrassment as their parents would likely be unable to communicate with either the teachers or the other parents.

Unlike his sisters, Lanlan and Beibei's younger brother Xiaochun was born in Italy. His parents then sent their infant son back to China as they were both working full time in an Italian-run leather workshop and had no means of taking care of the boy. Xiaochun stayed with his grandparents in China until 2012, when his parents brought him back to Italy just in time to start primary school. At that point, the family had just bought their bar and were finally able to care for their son. Like his sisters, Xiaochun spends many hours at the bar where he reads, does schoolwork, and plays pool with some Italian teenagers from the neighborhood. He also helps his parents and sisters clearing tables, collecting empty beer bottles, and doing other chores around the family establishment. Unlike his older sister Beibei, however, Xiaochun is not good at school despite having quickly learned fluent Italian. Given his lack of promise or interest in formal education, Xiaochun's parents are looking to set their son up with his own small business after he graduates from the same *Istituto tecnico economico* where his two sisters had studied, possibly a sushi restaurant or a coffee bar. However, while his parents have not pushed Xiaochun to study harder in school, they are insistent that he must learn to read and write Mandarin Chinese.

Xiaochun's parents' emphasis on their children mastering Mandarin reflects a wider trend among the Chinese residents in Italy who increasingly regard Mandarin fluency as an indispensable skill. I noticed that the children of Chinese immigrants who were born in the 1980s and had spent their childhoods in Italy usually either could not speak fluent Mandarin Chinese or did not speak it at all. Those born in the 1990s or later, however, usually speak, read, and write the language as if they had never left China. I often saw Meili's elder son reading Chinese E-novels, even though he had only completed one year of primary school in China. Since then, he had learned Chinese partly in the Chinese Church by reading the Bible and partly through self-study. His family also kept the *Xinhua zidian* (New Chinese Dictionary), a best-selling Chinese dictionary close at hand. Indeed, the presence of that Chinese dictionary on the bar's side table, sometimes opened to a particular page, is one of my enduring memories of Meili's establishment. Another example is Uncle Gumin's second daughter Enhua. She enjoyed watching Korean dramas with Chinese subtitles, despite never having attended any Chinese-language school. She instead learned to speak and read Mandarin Chinese to the level of a native speaker while living in Bologna.

The increasing prevalence of Mandarin use among children of Chinese immigrants in Italy reflects both disillusionment on the part of Chinese residents with their Italian host society and their shifting relationship with China. Mandarin Chinese, which has increasingly replaced local dialects as the means of communication between family members and within Chinese diasporic institutions, affords accessibility to China's vast consumer market and entertainment industry, offering an alternative to the mainstream Italian media and consumer culture. Fluent Mandarin speakers who feel alienated and marginalized in Italy can easily access a comfortable cultural space in a Chinese-language digital universe that offers entertainment, community, and a sense of belonging. Besides its being the linguistic entryway into this digital cultural space, Chinese residents in Italy increasingly see Mandarin fluency as economically beneficial. Many who do not know the language have also started learning it as adults. As Uncle Gumin commented, "Mandarin Chinese is important. Even many *laowai* are learning it now. . . . It's our advantage as Chinese. If the economic situation in Italy gets even worse, at least we can leave here and maybe go back to China."

Lanlan's mother's shifts starts at 5 pm and ends at 11 pm, or midnight, depending on when the last customers drift out. Her husband often stays with her after dark. In the daytime, when it's Lanlan's shift, they often stay at home and sometimes go downstairs to their bar. Her mother walks behind the bar counter to check if everything is in order, while her father goes around to "check the security," as Lanlan puts it. After an early lunch, the parents often go to stock up on needs for the bar, buy groceries for the family, visit their friends or relatives, or deal with other daily errands. The two of them have meanwhile kept up frequent transnational connections with their relatives who are now spread across Spain, Brazil, and China. The extended family members keep one another updated by phone on the latest news about the business situations in their respective host societies. They also travel to visit their relatives on occasion, usually to take part in important life moments such as weddings. Thanks to the social media app WeChat, their transnational interactions became even more frequent after 2011 when the app became available. They spend much of their time on WeChat every day, chatting or playing virtual games with friends and relatives around the world. Lanlan's mother was especially captivated by the social game WeChat Red Packet when it became popular in 2014. Every Chinese immigrant I know, regardless of their age, from teenagers to the elderly, use WeChat in their everyday life. It offers a reprieve from the tedium of twelve-hour or longer shifts behind the bar counter, while also helping to reinforce transnational connections and the collective Chinese identity of its diasporic users. Without this essential social tool, Chinese baristas would have a much harder time keeping up transnational family solidarity and might be less fully included in Chinese communities in Italy and beyond.

When moving to Bologna, the only friends that Lanlan's family had in the city were two Chinese families, who both managed coffee bars. One was a Christian family from their same village in China. The other was a Buddhist couple who had previously worked with Lanlan's parents in the same factory in the central Italian region of Marche on the east coast of Italy. Lanlan's mother is a devout Christian and mostly goes online to listen to sermons through a Chinese Christian WeChat group. She pushed her three children to attend Sunday worship and other religious activities at the Chinese Church, and despite initial resistance, the three siblings became quite active in the Church. This was not only because it provides a good excuse for them to escape from a monotonous life trapped in the bar, but also because they found many Chinese peers with similar family and migration backgrounds and became good friends with some of them. Indeed, both Lanlan and Beibei eventually met their future husbands in the Church.

The social presence of the Chinese Evangelical Christian Church of Bologna thus offers an alternative diasporic community for many Chinese immigrant families. Several scholars have emphasized the role of Chinese immigrant religious institutions in helping mobilize ethnic resources and negotiate on behalf of the diaspora in the oftentimes precarious and xenophobic social environments of predominantly white societies.[41] Lanlan's family's case makes evident also the role of the Chinese Church plays as an emotional anchor for its members. By providing a ready space and community for Chinese Christians in Bologna and its surrounding areas, the Chinese Church plays an important role in mitigating the loneliness and sense of marginalization common to recent immigrants and their children. However, as an alternative community separate from that of mainstream Italian social life, the Chinese Christian network in Bologna also contributes to the stark social segregation between Chinese and non-Chinese residents by lessening the need or desire of Chinese immigrants to socialize with those outside of their ethnic communities. This social facet of the Chinese Church, more so than any religious doctrine, helps explain the vast social chasm that exists between Chinese Christians and non-Chinese local populations.

The Limits of Conviviality

I attended Uncle Gumin's second daughter Enhua's graduation ceremony from the University of Bologna in March 2015. In a huge lecture theatre, Enhua and other graduates-to-be sat in the first row, waiting for their turn to present their theses to three white professors sitting behind a long table. Enhua occasionally exchanged some words with the students around her. Groups of friends and relatives scattered about the room had come to offer support. Enhua's team included her siblings and several Chinese friends. After the oral defense, we went to the *piazza* outside to celebrate her graduation. Unlike graduation ceremonies in other places in the world, the Italian-style rite of passage is designed to embarrass the celebrated graduate. Enhua's siblings also adopted this Italian ritual, adding to it some uniquely Chinese elements. They forced her to pull an "ancient" light blue Chinese stage costume on top of her elegant black dress and completed the look with a pink paper umbrella that she was to hold in one hand and a big paper fan to be held in the other. They also prepared a laurel wreath which they put on her head. Prosecco toasts followed. This brief cross-cultural ritual, however, was not shared with any non-Chinese friends or classmates, as none of them showed up (nor were they invited). Afterwards, Enhua and her Chinese friends went to have an early dinner in a Chinese restaurant, while I decided to leave for her family-managed bar to have a conversation with her father.

As we have seen, while they shared their convivial coffee bar space, Chinese baristas and their families lived quite rigidly separate social and cultural lives outside this site of everyday interaction. Their sociability with their customers usually stopped when they stepped out of their business space. None of them invited their customers to attend weddings, birthday parties, family events, or other ritual life moments. The Chinese baristas I knew also rarely shared their personal experiences or family stories with their customers, not even with those with whom they had a good relationship. An ethnographic study of Chinese entrepreneurs from a Chinese state-owned construction firm in Angola shows that interpersonal relationships were built on reliable mutual benefits rather than on a more generalized trust.[42] When Chinese owners sell their business and move out of the neighborhood, their site-specific personal relationships with their customers terminate. This retreat occurs not only among recent Chinese immigrants, but also commonly among their children. Here the conviviality that Chinese baristas cultivate manifests its spatial boundary.

The coffee bar space has become a kind of prism through which Chinese baristas acquire racial knowledge and produce a racialized worldview. Their racialization of both *laowai* and *banhei* reflects their double disenchantment with Italy, as well as the insecurity of their lives in this host country. On the one hand, they are disillusioned with Italy's pluralistic society and structural inequalities in terms of race, ethnicity, and class. They have come to associate Italy's racial and ethnic heterogeneity with crime and public peril. As for the *laowai*, on the other hand, their laziness, sloppiness, and other perceived negative "qualities" simply do not match what, in their imaginary, white people from a "developed country" should be like. These are the traits that they had long associated with people from the so-called "developing world." (Ironically, such perceptions of Italians echo certain intra-Western tropes about Italy within the Global North.) Italy's economic stagnation is another issue, especially as it stands in such sharp contrast to China's meteoric rise that many Chinese question their decision to emigrate to the supposedly affluent and more developed "West." Against this backdrop of shifting geopolitics, Chinese residents questioned the Western-dominated racial hierarchy and formed their own racial understandings. These new racial formations are symptomatic of China's ongoing wider challenge to the established global hierarchy.

Moreover, Chinese baristas and many other Chinese entrepreneurs in Italy have been disappointed that their increasing economic prosperity did not translate into social respectability but, ironically, resulted in even more insecurity. Conviviality and conflicts are not mutually exclusive in barista-customer interactions. Indeed, conflicts are even embedded in day-to-day social interactions and emerge against the backdrop of prosaic routine.[43] Everyday racism—or at least the perceived racism that Chinese baristas experience in their social encounters at the coffee bar— further enhance their sense of otherness. The jarring experience of being both socially vulnerable and economically privileged has thus contributed to a pronounced Chinese ethnic consciousness in Italy, reinforcing racialized perceptions of both native Italians and non-Chinese immigrants.

To be fair, the prejudices regarding the so-called *laowai* and *banhei* that Chinese immigrants hold are not necessarily shared by their children. As I surveyed the forty years of mass Chinese migration to Italy, I noticed that the Chinese have grown to be increasingly heterogeneous in terms of their economic power, social class, generational traits, education, culture, citizenship status, and language preferences.[44] Several children of Chinese immigrants, baristas or not, have expressed to me their concerns about the blatant anti-Black and anti-Brown racism of Chinese residents in Italy. I personally know that some of them have become more vocal and socio-politically engaged in the pursuit of racial and ethnic justice. However, the racism and social exclusion that the younger-generation Chinese have encountered in one form or another for being *i cinesi* remains a lived experience that they share with the older generation. These tensions and conflicts solidify the younger generations' ethnic consciousness and work to justify social, ethnic, and even national boundaries.[45] Most of the children of Chinese immigrants, regardless of their place of birth, have decided to maintain their Chinese citizenship rather than going through the Italian naturalization process, even though China is a place where they have barely or never lived.[46]

Therefore, the conviviality that Chinese bricoleurs strive to construct around Chinese Espresso tends to be both spatialized and contingent. Chinese-managed coffee bars have become a place where a certain sense of community and solidarity is constructed among established Italian residents, Chinese immigrant families, and other diverse immigrant populations through shared food and taste. Yet, this conviviality does not constitute a romanticized cultural harmony nor the reductionist reproduction of power.[47] On the one hand, Chinese baristas strategically negotiate and even exploit for their own benefit various forms of structural inequality within the larger society in which they are embedded, as well as the complex power dynamics between diverse actors. On the other hand, the structural elements they deploy in constructing their convivial coffee bar communities also set the spatial limits of that very conviviality.

Coda

CLOSING TIME

I RETURNED TO BOLOGNA AGAIN in October of 2022. It had been nearly three years since my last visit to the city in December 2019, just a few months before the outbreak of the Covid-19 pandemic in Italy. For Chinese residents, the country's surging infection rate at the start of the pandemic brought about both renewed anxieties over rising Sinophobia, as well as an upsurge of pride of their own Chinese identity. Under the double fear of viral contagion and anti-Chinese racism, Chinese residents typically took more serious and disciplined precautions than did the Italians to combat the spread of the virus. This resulted in a very low rate of infection among Chinese communities, in contrast to the situation in Italy as a whole, at least in the early stage of the pandemic.[1] Several Chinese interlocutors I contacted via WeChat understood their success in containing the spread of the virus as further evidence of China's cultural superiority over Italy. Indeed, the pandemic seemed to have exacerbated the disillusionment already felt by many Chinese residents towards Italy, even prior to Covid-19.

Among the Chinese owners I know, some left the coffee bar niche, while others stayed on over the last decade. My barista teacher Letai was one of those who stayed. One afternoon, I walked into Letai's bar without having given him any notice of my arrival. Not surprisingly, Letai was there. "You are back!" Letai laughed after standing there stunned for a second. The retired wine dealer, a regular customer in his seventies, ran to give me a big hug. "Welcome back!" He called out excitedly. As I entered, two young Italian women came in, purchased two packs of cigarettes and left. Three elderly Italian men sat around a table in their usual separate wing of the bar playing cards, while a fourth stood and watched them. A middle-aged man, whose nationality was unclear to me, was trying his luck at a slot machine. Letai stole a glance at his watch. "It's time to prepare some free snacks for the *keren* (customers, guests) who drink." As he said this, he began cutting into squares two salty croissants leftover from earlier in the day and some bits of soft cheese. He placed them in two square white bowls, then filled another two bowls with olives and chips. He lined up the four bowls at the corner of the bar counter. This was the exact combination he had taught me when I was training to be a barista several years earlier. Along with the new customers, another noticeable difference was the presence of a large transparent plastic divider installed over the bar counter as a measure against Covid transmission. Like several other Chinese coffee bar owners whom I talked to, Letai remarked that he had no plans to remove it, at least in the near future, citing its use in helping him avoid unintentional spittle flying across the bar counter. On top of that, "it was just nice to have some distance from the customers," he concluded.

Covid had also made its presence felt with a line of tables placed under the porticoes outside the bar. There, much of the current clientele seemed to be composed of more recent immigrants instead of the older retired Italian regulars. The bar, on the whole, had transformed into an establishment more receptive of passersby, as many older customers stopped showing up. Some of them had passed away during the pandemic. The last major update that Letai announced to me was the news that he finally had received his Italian citizenship, so that the *tabaccheria* attached to the coffee counter no longer needed to be registered under an Italian collaborator's name. As his mother now likes to tease, "Letai is Italian now!"

Uncle Gumin's family also chose to remain in the coffee bar business. His family owned the property of the storefront where they had opened a new bar in 2016. Being freed from paying the rent, his small bar was able to survive the economic winter that accompanied the Covid lockdown. The second daughter Enhua and her husband were the baristas there. They had married just a year before. Her husband had migrated to Italy in his teenage years from China and had dropped out of high school. While working at Uncle Gumin's coffee bar, the young couple was also looking for a new business of their own. Once when Enhua was not around, her husband remarked that "it is a great pity" that she had given up her hopes of a white-collar office job, as she had a university degree in economics and also some working experience in an accounting firm. Nevertheless, he went on to lament the low pay of wage laborers in the white-collar labor market and predicted a gloomy future for her had she become an accountant. Enhua's younger brother Enbao now worked in an Italian design studio after graduating from a Master's program in industrial design, but he still helped out in the family business on weekends. His fiancée, a Chinese woman who had recently received a degree in law, worked as an intern in a law firm focusing on labor consultancy. As the only Chinese in their workplaces, they both claimed to have experienced frequent discrimination and casual racism from their coworkers. Both are now also uncertain whether they should open a small business like most of their fellow Chinese for the economic autonomy that it affords them, or stick to their office jobs in pursuit of a middle-class lifestyle after marriage.

On my last trip to Bologna before Covid, I also encountered some new Chinese entrepreneurs. Achen was one of them. He had opened a bar—a combination of a coffeehouse and a wine bar—in an upper middle-class *bolognese* neighborhood in the summer of 2015, a few days after I had completed my major fieldwork. I first met him at a dinner meeting organized by the *Associazione dei bar cinesi* (Chinese Coffee Bar Association) in Bologna.[2] The other participants, mostly Chinese coffee bar owners and the committee members of the Association, unanimously praised Achen's business as "the most successful and profitable" among all of the Chinese-managed coffee bars in Bologna and feted Achen himself as an excellent barista who had also managed to earn a professional wine tasting certificate. They told me that Achen's place was exceptionally high-end, targeting "rich" *laowai*. They also said that even though Achen's "upgraded" establishment was rather exceptional, it nonetheless exemplified a new generation of Chinese-managed coffee bars that were no longer dependent on slot machines, which had come under increasingly strict state regulation. Achen noted that this "upgraded" business was not the first bar that he and his wife had managed. The couple, both in their early thirties, are also children of immigrants who arrived in Italy in their teenage years. Both of their families entered the coffee bar business around 2010, as had many other Chinese families. After marriage, he and his wife bought their own "traditional bar" and sold it before they opened this "upgraded" one.

I went to Achen's place on several occasions and at different times in the next few days, trying to piece together the story of this upscale version of Chinese Espresso. The bar was not very big, but three large French windows made it look more spacious than it actually was. The décor, the light, the music, and a variety of well-presented food offerings and drinks had garnered favorable online comments from Italian customers, who described the space as *elegante* (elegant) and *invitante* (inviting). To achieve this, Achen told me, he had hired a "professional" Italian team to design and decorate the space, and had created proper Spotify playlists for the background music. The bar also had a Facebook page where he often shared photos and menus of lunches and of the trendy *apericena* (pre-dinner drink and buffets). While Achen and his wife were also self-employed baristas, the three *laowai* baristas they hired were the major laborers preparing lunch and the buffet. As Achen expected, the bar became a gender-balanced social space for more educated middle-class professionals. Retired men, immigrants, and slot machines—the three mainstays of the stereotypical *bar cinese*—were nowhere in sight. Since it was so different from the stereotype, an Italian friend from Bologna living in that neighborhood initially mistook Achen and his wife for paid laborers working for an Italian owner.

One night, I went to Achen's place at nearly 10 pm, their closing time, as I wanted to have an uninterrupted conversation with him. After the last customer left, a Chinese man in his sixties, whom I had never seen during business hours and who seemed, based on his attire and appearance quite out of place in this chic environment, suddenly made an appearance. Achen told me that the man was his father, who came to clean the bar every day, and that this was how their family divided the labor. For the next two hours, while I was talking with Achen, his father silently cleaned the entire place inch by inch. Achen's father reminded me of the numerous invisible migrant workers who toil late at night to make cities the clean spaces we inhabit.

While his father was preparing to close up the storefront, Achen began talking about his plans for the business, his entrepreneurial ambitions, and his desire for social mobility. He brought up his hopes for his three daughters. He sent them to learn alpine skiing from a private instructor every winter, as it was a skill that children from a "good," middle-class *laowai* family ought to learn. Several times he insisted on the importance of *rongru* or "integration." If they acted respectable like *laowai*, he was convinced that his family and Chinese people in Italy in general would gain respect from Italians. During this conversation, I was struck by the incongruity between a Chinese immigrant who had successfully submerged the Chinese ownership of a quintessentially Italian social space and the scene playing in the background where his father was so meticulously cleaning the bar, just as I had seen so many other Chinese owners doing at closing time.

The entire episode reminded me of the story of Cinderella. When the *laowai* left and midnight was approaching, Achen's bar seemed to magically revert to the original Chinese look that Achen seemed so keen to conceal, while he himself dreamed of joining the ranks of the affluent middle-class Italians whom he served on a daily basis. As we left at midnight to the sound of the metal shutters closing on Achen's business for that day, a thought came to me that I did not share with him. In the future, would Achen's bar, alongside the other small Chinese businesses in Italy, help their children realize their own Cinderella stories of achieving social respectability and racial equality, the goals to which Achen still aspired? Or would the children and grandchildren of the Italy's Chinese immigrants become even more disillusioned with the country their parents or grandparents had adopted?

NOTES

Prelude

1. All of the names used in this book are pseudonyms.

Chapter One: The Paradox of Chinese Espresso

1. Coffee bars are called *bar* in Italian. Like many other culturally embedded terms or concepts, a literal translation cannot always adequately explain the cultural implications that this word embodies. As the Italian adage puts it, *Traduttore, traditore* (Translator, traitor). There is no corresponding word in English or in Chinese that can precisely convey the complexity of *bar* in Italian. I therefore use the term "coffee bar" in this book to refer to Italy's establishments where coffee is the most central drink and business is conducted primarily during the daytime. On the one hand, the term "coffee bar" highlights the particularity of this culturally embedded business, in which coffee is the primary and representative product, while on the other it shows that *bar* in the Italian understanding shares one of the fundamental features of bars in their English definition, namely, that these places with bar counters for the social consumption of drinks that include alcoholic beverages. When indicating a type of coffee bar, I often omit the word "coffee" for the sake of simplicity, for instance, "neighborhood bar," "dairy bar," "tobacco bar," etc. My Chinese interlocutors usually use the term *jiuba* as a generic term to refer to a *bar* in the Italian sense, even if *jiuba* literally means "alcohol bar." When they need to specify a "bar" that corresponds to the English definition, they would emphasize this aspect by calling it a "night-time *jiuba*."

2. More official statistics and numbers about coffee bar businesses in Italy can be found in the annual reports provided by the FIPE (*Federazione Italiana Pubblici Esercizi* or the Italian Federation of Food Service Businesses). See the FIPE's website: www.fipe.it.

3. As above, see FIFE's annual reports on the website: www.fipe.it.

4. Some examples of provocative headlines that I translated include: "Italian Entrepreneurship Collapses, Chinese Immigrants Celebrate!" published by *Il Giornale*

on August 9, 2014; "The Long March of the Chinese in Italy: We will Win!" published by *Panorama*, October 10, 2010; "Immigrants, Chinese Invasion, Enterprises like Mushrooms: +232%!" published by *La Repubblica*, December 10, 2012.

5. The Italian article has the translated title "The Chinese Bosses of the Coffee Bars. In Milan one out of ten is theirs. In this way, we lose pieces of our identity." It was written by the Italian journalist and writer Antonio Galdo and was published on a website focusing on lifestyle and sustainability, *Nonsprecare.it.*, where he was the director in 2019. It is one of the articles that advocated resistance to Chinese coffee bars and to Chinese capital in general.

6. See the original article in Italian that I translated as "When China Approaches the Bar, Some Sell and Others Resist" in *Ravenna & Dintorni*, written by Matteo Pezzani and published on July 17, 2013.

7. Hall 2017: 31–79.

8. Zhou 2012: 221–36.

9. See more discussions about the representation of espresso as a national beverage in Italian popular culture in Pojmann (2021: 47–62). Recently, Italy has applied to UNESCO to add Italian espresso to its official list of Intangible Heritages of Humanity (Fassino 2020). See also the news at https://www.theguardian.com/world/2022/jan/21/italy-seeks-unesco-heritage-status-espresso-coffee.

10. Lévi-Strauss 2021: 20–22.

11. Altglas 2014: 476.

12. de Certeau 1984: xv.

13. Deleuze and Guattari 1983: 1–8.

14. Gilroy 2004; Amin 2012: 59–82; Hemer et al. 2020; Cheng 2022.

15. Taha 2022: 2.

16. Nowicka and Vertovec 2014; Padilla et al. 2015; Berg and Nowicka 2019: 1–14; Cory 2020.

17. Erickson 2011.

18. See further discussion in Valentine (2008), Wise and Noble (2016), and Nowicka (2020).

19. Çaglar and Glick Schiller 2018: 26–28.

20. Muehlebach 2012: 205.

21. Carney 2021: 102–24.

22. Schiller 2016. Everts (2010) also discussed immigrant-run corner shops in Germany as a meaningful space where local consumers and immigrant shopkeepers engage with each other through shared practices revolving around selling and buying.

23. Massey 1994: 146–56.

24. Portes 1995: 1–41; Brettell 2003: 127–38; Zhou 2004.

25. Yanagisako 2002.

26. Counihan and Højlund 2018: 1.

27. Pratt 1991: 34.

28. For example, Tuckett (2018) has described ways in which people strategically navigate Italy's restrictive immigration bureaucracy, ambiguous laws, and complex documentation regime; Giordano (2008) explored how some female immigrants pass through institutional settings to obtain legal rights and social services granted to qualified "victims" in Italy.

29. Moretti's (2015: 133–58) ethnographic study in Milan provides another example of how immigrant groups utilize urban spaces in alternative ways to re-envision the city and claim their legitimate presence in it.

30. Tsing 2005: 13.

31. Cheng 2013.

32. Portelli 2003; Lombardi-Diop 2012.

33. Kopytoff 1986.

34. As Lombardi-Diop (2012) argued, whiteness used to be limited to the middle class and intellectual elites, typically from Northern Italy, during the fascist period, but it began to extend to average Italians and eventually to mass society under the visual regimes of advertising and TV broadcasting during the post-war economic take-off, which saw huge improvements in people's living standard. This whitening process further excluded non-white people who were economically deprived and socially marginalized. During my fieldwork in Bologna, my Italian interlocutors were often shocked when I told them that Italians were not considered white in the United States historically.

35. The Italian term *immigrato*, as well as its plural form *immigrati*, is a racialized term widely used in public discourse in Italy to refer to immigrants / non-Europeans / Others in contrast to *italiani* who were natives / white Europeans / Us, regardless of the person's self-identification, citizenship, birthplace, or how long ago their ancestors had settled in Italy. In this book, I use the terms "native Italians" in contrast to "immigrants" to signal the dichotomy of Us and Others and to underscore the otherness in Italian society of more recent residents with an immigration background, regardless of the subjects' actual citizenship (Glick Schiller 2015).

36. Mullings 2004.

37. Balibar and Wallerstein 1991: 222.

38. Morning and Maneri 2022: 84.

39. Social scientists have extensive discussions about this form of racism, which is widespread in Western Europe. They described it as "cultural racism" or "neo-racism" (Balibar and Wallerstein 1991: 17–28), "new racism" (Cole 1997), "cultural fundamentalism" (Stolcke 1995), or "unmarked racisms" (Harrison 2000). Also see Harrison 1995; Grillo 2003; Vertovec 2011.

40. Mahmud 2020.

41. Greenland 2021: 4–6.

42. Mahmud 2014: 129–33.

43. Krause 2001.

44. Rofel and Yanagisako 2018: 65.

45. Forgacs 2014.

46. Labanca 2002: 473–76.

47. Allen and Russo 1997: 7.

48. Schneider 1998: 1–23.

49. Pugliese 2008: 3.

50. Pinkus 2003.

51. Del Boca 2003.

52. Fogu 2006; Patriarca 2010: 189.

53. Portelli 2003.

54. Colombo and Dalla-Zuanna 2019.

55. Oliveri 2018.

56. Pugliese 2008: 21.

57. ibid: 25.

58. Angel-Ajani 2000.

59. Gilroy 1991: 74.

60. Carter 1997: 195–203; Angel-Ajani 2000; Ambrosini 2013.

61. Colombo and Dalla-Zuanna 2019: 18.

62. ibid: 23.

63. Barbagli 1998: 136–40.

64. Mezzadra 2012.

65. Mai 2002.

66. Maher 1996.

67. Stanley 2008.

68. Romania is the most common country of origin of the immigrants in Italy. As an EU country, it is not included in the statistics about non-EU immigration. However, Romanians, as well as other immigrants from Eastern Europe, are also ambiguously considered *extracomunitari* in the everyday parlance.

69. Marsden 2022: 173.

70. In Italy, there are no racially segregated communities or ethnic enclaves like the Chinatowns that exist in many American cities. Yet, Italians often use the term "Chinatown" to refer to neighborhoods or districts with highly concentrated Chinese populations and visible Chinese cultural markers, for example, in Prato, Milan, and Rome. The term often carries pejorative connotations (Raffaetà and Baldassar 2015, Ravagnoli 2022: 29).

71. Essed 1991: 3; Bracci 2015; Latham 2015; Krause and Li 2022.

72. Douglas 1966: 36.

73. In this book, I use Southern Zhejiang to refer to Wenzhou Prefecture and neighboring Qingtian County in Zhejiang Province. Geographically, Qingtian County shares borders with Yongjia, Wencheng, and Ruian, which are the three

counties of Wenzhou. Qingtian became a part of Lishui Prefecture, rather than Wenzhou, only after an administrative reorganization in 1963.

74. The "Wenzhou model" as an innovative economic system has four distinctive features: "it consists of numerous private enterprises, small-scale cottage industries, and petty commerce;" it is "composed of large numbers of specialized wholesale petty commodity markets controlled by the Wenzhouese;" "it is built on a network of tens of thousands of mobile Wenzhou traders throughout the country who facilitate smooth flows of raw materials and finished products from one place to another;" and it is "made possible by various forms of nongovernmental financial arrangements created by people themselves to support private businesses" (Zhang 2001: 53).

75. Zhang 2001; Xiang 2005.

76. Xiang 2003; Nyíri 2004.

77. Examples regarding Chinese international migration include Watson (1975), Liu (1998), Guest (2003), Hamilton (2006), and Kuhn (2008). Non-Chinese examples include, for example, Massey and Espinosa (1997) and Brettell (2003).

78. The term *baihuo* means "general merchandise" (literally a "hundred goods"). Baihuo shops sell miscellaneous low-cost consumer goods. It is a common business model that many Wenzhou Chinese operate in various parts of the world, Italy included. See Haugen and Carling (2005) on *baihuo* shops in Cape Verde; Silva (2018) on Chinese wholesale markets in Brazil; and Hessler (2015) on Chinese merchants selling lingerie in Egypt.

79. Zhang 2001: 23–46.

80. The term *qiaoxiang* is widely used in Chinese academic literature to refer to areas known for emigration, usually rural areas characterized by high numbers of emigrants abroad with close ties to their hometowns or villages. The traditional major *qiaoxiang* are concentrated in particular districts, towns, or villages in the three coastal provinces of Zhejiang, Fujian, and Guangdong. Kuhn (2008: 43–51) uses the model of "corridor + niche" to characterize a cultural formation in *qiaoxiang* in which emigrants and their kin groups remaining in their original home communities fit into local ecologies at both ends and form "a system of labor distribution" through continuous transnational connections. See Li and Wong's (2018) article for an extensive introduction to Chinese *qiaoxiang* migration models.

81. Gates 1996: 42–61.

82. Wang 1991: 3–21.

83. See examples in the Philippines (Omohundro 1981), Latin America (HuDeHart 2002), the United States (Siu 1987), Europe (Pieke et al. 2004, Watson 1975), and India (Oxfeld 1993).

84. Rofel and Yanagisako 2018: 41.

85. Glick Schiller and Çağlar 2013.

86. Skeldon 2007.

87. This definition also helps differentiate these laborers and small entrepreneurs from Chinese transnational capitalists, professionals and expats, the emerging second or third generation middle-class Chinese, and *liuxuesheng* (Chinese international students), as well as other people of Chinese descent who together constitute the increasingly heterogeneous Chinese population of Italy.

88. Chinese residents also manage the local bar businesses and tobacco shops in Spain and in France, while in Belgium Chinese residents run local chip shops (van Dongen 2019).

89. Kuhn 2008.

90. Zhou 1992.

91. Bonacich 1973.

92. van Dongen 2019.

93. Nyíri 2011; Wang 2020: 87–117.

94. Sheridan 2019.

95. Park 2017.

96. Racial tensions between minority communities had already generated a great deal of scholarly discussion following the Los Angeles race riots in 1992. See Abelmann and Lie (1995), Min (1996), Kim (2000), Lee (2002), and Park (2019).

97. Colombo and Dalla-Zuanna 2019.

98. According to Resca (1995), Umberto Sun was among the first Chinese men to settle in Bologna between the 1920s and 1930s. These Chinese men virtually all came from southern Zhejiang Province of China, which is also the place of origin for the mass migration to Italy since the 1980s. Umberto Sun and many other Chinese men married Italian women from rural backgrounds and opened family workshops and businesses, sometimes producing and selling ties or leather goods. The Chinese residents in Bologna had reached a population of 1,000 by the time the Second Sino-Japanese War began in 1937 (Resca 1995: 28). At that point, most Chinese citizens in Bologna went back to China by taking advantage of free trips provided by various international organizations. Thus, only around 100 Chinese residents were still living in Bologna by the end of the 1940s, a number that remained stable through the 1950s and 1960s (Resca 1995: 28). Large-scale Chinese migration to Bologna did not resume until the mid-1980s. See Chapter Two for more discussion of Chinese mass migration to Italy.

99. The annual reports about foreign citizens in Bologna can be found at the official website of the *Comune di Bologna* (Municipality of Bologna) at www.comune .bologna.it. The number of registered Chinese citizens does not include those who are naturalized, undocumented immigrants, or those who work and live in Bologna but have their residence registered outside of the city.

100. The demographic statistics of Italy can be found on the website of the ISTAT (*Istituto Nazionale di Statistica* or Italian National Institute of Statistics) at www.istat.it.

101. Sociologist Arnaldo Bagnasco (1977) suggested that there is not one Italy, but three "Italies" coexisting within Italian territory. The first is the Northwest, characterized by modern industries with Fordist-scale mass production, while the second is the less-developed South. The third Italy consists of the Northeast and Central regions, including Emilia-Romagna, of which Bologna is the capital. It is characterized by decentralized production in highly specialized small-scale manufacturing workshops and family enterprises with low technology, but high craftsmanship that were developed in the 1970s. However, there have been debates about whether the "third Italy" acts as a unique economic model for regional development or just a constructed myth; see i.e., Bianchini (1991) and Hadjimichalis (2006).

102. The demographic composition of Bologna might explain why Italian, rather than the local *bolognese*, has become the common language used throughout the city. See more statistics about migrant flows in Bologna on the Municipality of Bologna's website at www.comune.bologna.it.

103. For more demographic statistics about foreign citizens in Bologna, see the Municipality of Bologna's website at www.comune.bologna.it.

104. Salih and Riccio 2011.

105. Anthropologist and historian David Kertzer has extensively discussed the rise and fall of the Italian Communist Party. See Kertzer (1980, 1996).

106. Kertzer 1980: 169–83.

107. Però 2007: 119–36.

108. Riccio 2000.

109. These statistics come from a 2011 FIPE report that specifically addresses foreign entrepreneurship in the Italian food service industry. See the full report "Rapporto sull'imprenditoria straniera nella ristorazione italiana" on their website at www.fipe.it.

110. My estimate is based on the number of *imprese individuali* or "sole proprietorships," provided by the Chamber of Commerce of Bologna. In 2014, there were 119 that were Chinese-owned, which is nearly half of the 240 coffee bars owned by foreign citizens and 11% of all coffee bar sole proprietorships in Bologna. This form of ownership and *società di persone* or "partnership firms" are the two major forms of coffee bar enterprises, which are usually small and family-owned; around 90% of all types of coffee bars in Bologna and in Italy in general fall into these categories. My own findings during my fieldwork also show that Chinese-owned coffee bars were registered either as "partnership firms," in which adult family members were all business partners, or "sole proprietorship," in which one family member was registered as the self-employed owner while others were employees.

111. My fieldwork was not limited to Bologna. I made regular weekly visits to Cesena, a provincial town of 90,000 residents in Emilia-Romagna, between April and June of 2015. A key interlocutor I met in Bologna introduced me to two Chinese

families managing coffee bars there. I also took the opportunity while visiting my Italian or Chinese friends in other places in Northern and Central Italy to stop by Chinese-owned coffee bars there, including in Rome, Milan, and provincial towns in the regions of Lombardy, Marche, and Emilia-Romagna. These visits enabled me to obtain a more complete picture of Chinese-managed coffee bars while comparing the regional differences between them.

112. Hom 2015: 6.

113. Mills 1959: 5–8.

114. Cowan 1991: 181.

115. Wacquant 2004: 6.

116. Marchand 2010: S2.

117. Glick Schiller 2009.

118. Pink 2015: 27–28.

119. Faier and Rofel 2014: 364.

120. Krause and Bressan 2018: 573–74.

121. Herzfeld 2016: 165–79.

122. The Chinese Evangelical Christian Church of Bologna is the largest of the three Chinese Protestant Christian churches in the city. It is a branch of the Chinese Evangelical Church in Italy, which is a diasporic religious institution attended almost exclusively by Chinese residents. Wenzhou was often called "China's Jerusalem," as around ten percent of its total population was estimated to be Christians (Cao 2011: 1). In Bologna, around 200 Chinese from nearly 70 households, people who had been Christian prior to emigration, regularly attended Sunday worship during my 2014–2015 fieldwork, a number that doubled for the Christmas celebration. Around a dozen of these Christian families managed coffee bar businesses, accounting for around ten percent of the Chinese ownership in Bologna. This percentage is consistent with my estimation of the Christians in the total Chinese population in Bologna. For more about Chinese Christian entrepreneurs in Wenzhou, see Cao (2011) and Cao (2013). A discussion about the deeply intertwined relations between business ethics, religious prescriptions, and family values among Chinese Christian entrepreneurs and how they negotiated ethical practices in their everyday lives can be found in Deng (2021).

123. Geertz 1971: 3–30; Rabinow 1977.

124. Geertz 1971: 3–30; Clifford 1986; Abu-Lughod 1991; Narayan 1993.

125. Trouillot 1991: 22; Harden 2011.

126. Appadurai 1988: 39.

127. Gupta and Ferguson 1992; De Genova 2016.

128. Dominguez 1994; Kusow 2003.

129. Wimmer and Glick Schiller 2003.

130. Ong 1996: 351.

131. Rosaldo 1989: 19.

132. Foucault 1977: 171.

133. Sunder Rajan 2021: 10.

134. Abu-Lughod 1991: 52.

135. Tsing 2005: 13.

136. Pieke 2000.

Chapter Two: Becoming Baristas

1. The full report *Rapporto sull'imprenditoria straniera nella ristorazione italiana* (March 2011) is available on the FIPE's official website at www.fipe.it. It is on page 11, as I translated from the original text in Italian: "It is a fact that it could have more value for an immigrant than an Italian. Yet, at the same time, it is possible that the start-up of a business is not purely the result of a choice for subsistence living and social mobility, but more generally connected to the availability of capital from suspicious sources."

2. Stewart and Strathern 2004: 56.

3. Schneider and Schneider 1994.

4. Zhang 2019.

5. Cole 1997: 129.

6. It is not my intention to suggest that no underground or criminal organizations operate in the Chinese communities in Italy or that no unlawful practices occur in regard to Chinese migration or economic activities.

7. Biehl and Locke 2017.

8. The numbers were included in the 2021 industry report from the *Associazione bar cinesi in Italia* or the "Chinese Coffee Bar Association in Italy." The original report is in the format of short video available on Youtube at the link https://www.youtube.com/watch?v=fVIZwxTkdV8.

9. For more discussions about the "Made in Italy" model of capitalist development, see Bagnasco (1977), Blim (1990), Yanagisako (2002), Della Sala (2004), and Gaggio (2007).

10. Wolf 1982; Yanagisako 2002.

11. Sandalj 2013.

12. The first Starbucks, which was the company's high-end Reserve Roastery, only opened in Milan's city center in 2018. Since then, the American brand has continued expanding across the major cities in Northern and Central Italy and around twenty Starbucks have opened by 2022.

13. Gibson-Graham 2014.

14. A rich sociological literature has provided structural framework in understanding ethnic and immigrant entrepreneurship, including Aldrich and Waldinger (1990), Waldinger (1996), Kloosterman et al. (1999), and Rath and Swagerman (2016). They have examined the role of the economic, social, and political structures

and institutions of the host society in immigrant entrepreneurship, contending that immigrants' economic activities are deeply embedded in larger opportunity structures and sociological contexts beyond mere ethnic communities.

15. Coffee bar operators also had to contend with the steady decline in coffee consumption at coffee bars since the 1980s due to the increasing use of new technological innovations, such as coffee vending machines and single-serving coffee machines for domestic and office use (Sandalj 2013).

16. Ingold 2000: 323–38.

17. Campagna and Venturelli 2013: 103.

18. ibid: 105.

19. ibid: 109.

20. Herzfeld 2009: 40.

21. The term *maisan* literally means "sell scattered" in Southern Zhejiang dialects. It is used to indicate all kinds of small-scale ambulant selling without a fixed shop, covering street peddling, itinerant trading, and market vending within a fixed stall. The term *shiye*, like the English word "enterprise," has two meanings. It refers to either a company or business, or a project or undertaking that is difficult and requires much effort.

22. In 2015, a hired skilled worker in a Chinese-owned coffee bar working for 10 to 12 hours a day could usually earn a monthly salary of around 1200 euros after tax. When I returned to Bologna in July 2018, several Chinese interlocutors claimed that it had risen to around 1500 euros due to the shortage of Chinese labor.

23. Giambelli 1984; Brigadoi Cologna 2017: 16.

24. Carchedi and Ferri 1998.

25. For example, an article that discourages interracial marriage between Chinese and Italians was published by *Corriere della Sera*, one of the major newspapers in Italy, on August 11, 1938, three months before the Italian racial laws were promulgated by the fascist regime.

26. Brigadoi Cologna 2019: 61–82.

27. ibid: 87.

28. In addition to those from Southern Zhejiang, there were also Chinese people from Taiwan and Hong Kong who migrated to Italy through the networks of the established Chinese-Italian families during the 1960s and 1970s (Giambelli 1984).

29. Li 1999.

30. Similar to Chinese emigrants from a village in Fujian Province to the United States that Julie Chu (2010) studied in in the early 2000s, my interlocutors from Southern Zhejiang also widely accepted human smuggling as part of their "moral career" and perceived legality as a flexible resource rather than a moral valuation. This is consistent with the findings of an earlier investigation, which concluded that forced labor did not typically apply to Chinese migration to Prato, Italy (Ceccagno et al 2008).

31. Brigadoi Cologna 2017: 15.

32. ibid: 15.

33. The Fujianese, mostly from rural areas of Sanming and Fuqing, started joining the mass migration to Italy in the late 1980s through their connections with Wenzhou migrants (Pieke et al. 2004). Chinese citizens from *Dongbei* began arriving in Italy in the mid-1990s. These immigrants were mostly dislocated workers who had lost their jobs in the restructuring of Chinese state-owned enterprises during the late 1980s and early 1990s (Paul 2020). These later arrivals usually started their immigrant lives by filling the bottom economic positions together with other later arrivals from Zhejiang (Pedone 2013). While some of them also achieved economic mobility, their number, social networks, and economic power in Italy have been much weaker than their co-nationals from Zhejiang.

34. Benton and Pieke 1998.

35. Tomba 1999.

36. Ceccagno 2007; Lan 2014.

37. Krause 2018: 166–88.

38. Redi 1997.

39. Abate 2018.

40. Nowadays vast wholesale markets and malls, owned by Chinese family entrepreneurs from Southern Zhejiang, have also emerged in other European cities, supplying low-cost Chinese consumer goods to both native and immigrant entrepreneurs (Ma Mung 2015).

41. The *hukou* system divides China's entire population into two categories of residence in order to police population movement within China. Individuals hold either urban or rural *hukou* residence and their internal migration does not change their residence status. Rural *hukou* holders do not have the same access to social services and benefits, including housing, employment, and children's education, as do urban *hukou* holders. Set up in the 1950s, the *hukou* system has relaxed in the post-Mao era through a series of reforms, but the labels and asymmetrical economic and political differentiation still exist.

42. Rofel 2007: 1–25.

43. Thunø 2001; Nyíri 2004.

44. Lem 2007: 383; Chu 2010: 63–68.

45. Lem's (2010) study shows that Chinese immigrants in France, who were marginalized in the country's labor market, similarly valued and actively adopted small entrepreneurship as an effective strategy for sustaining a livelihood.

46. Bologna, like many other European cities, has kept numerous open-air marketplaces, which were a part of the cityscape and everyday urban life. These local markets have helped many small entrepreneurs and immigrants to make a living. Black's (2012) ethnographic study on a local market in Turin shows that such markets are important places of everyday sociability where social relations are negotiated.

They are often the first places in cities where immigrants and established residents come in contact with each other. The vendors and shoppers are frequently engaged with social interactions for the purpose of exchange, trade and socializing.

47. Ceccagno 2012.

48. Italy's Ministry of Labor and Social Policies has published annual reports on the major immigrant groups in the country since the year of 2012 on the website www .integrazionemigranti.gov.it. The annual reports about Chinese immigrants were entitled "La comunità cinese in Italia."

49. Krause 2018: 166–88.

50. Rumbaut 1991; Zhou 1997.

51. Compulsory education in Italy is from six to sixteen years of age. Primary school lasts five years from ages six to eleven, lower secondary school lasts three years from eleven to fourteen, and upper secondary schools last three to five years. This means that compulsory education can cover the first two years of upper secondary schools for a student, assuming the student has not suspended schooling or been held back previously. All types of upper secondary schools lasting five years allow students to take the *Esame di Maturità* (Graduation Exam) or *Esame di Stato* (State Exam) that grant access to universities.

52. Also see Ceccagno 2004; Brigadoi Cologna 2011. Yet, the contribution of Chinese children's labor to their immigrant families from Southern Zhejiang is not unique. For instance, Flores's (2018) study of Latino, immigrant-origin families in the Unites States illustrated that older sisters also bear significant caretaking responsibilities for their younger siblings' educations and their educational care work are often vital to forging socioeconomic mobility and kinship obligations in these immigrant families.

53. Pieke 1991.

54. See more stories of "eating bitterness" among Chinese rural migrants in Loyalka (2012).

55. He 2021.

56. For this reason, in this book, the owner of the Chinese-managed coffee bar business usually refers to a patrilineal family, consisting of the parents, unmarried children, and married sons and their wives, if any, regardless of whose name the coffee bar is registered under.

57. Portes and Sensenbrenner 1993; Brettell 2003; Zhou 2004.

58. That said, the practice of *orario continuato* has become more common than before, especially in the large urban centers and among big supermarkets, international brand shops, and other large corporations.

59. Patriarca 2010: 20–50.

60. Hom 2015: 53–59.

61. The term *laowai* literally means "foreigners," but my Chinese interlocutors commonly use it to refer to native Italians, excluding immigrants. See more discussions about Chinese immigrants' racial perceptions in Chapter Six.

62. A study of the interactions between Chinese managers and African communities in Zambia and in Tanzania reveals similar findings. Chinese managers racialized different work ethics between Chinese and Africans. They also explained China's rapid economic development through Chinese people's devotion to work (Lee 2009: 654–56).

63. Piore 1979: 86–114; Portes and Bach 1985: 240–266; Cole and Booth 2007.

Chapter Three: Situating Space

1. Del Negro's (2004) ethnographic study of the public lives of people in a small town in Central Italy shows that *passeggiata*, literally meaning "promenade, strolling," appears to be a cultural performance central to the local culture and urban lives. This cultural performance is highly gendered. While all the town people participate in *passeggiata*, young women are the most active participants. Men typically sit and relax in a bar watching people walk by.

2. Lefebvre 1991.

3. Low 2009: 26.

4. Roseberry 1996.

5. Pojmann 2021: 13.

6. Billig 1995: 38.

7. Low 1996.

8. Several historical studies discussed the gendered nature of early European coffeehouses. For instance, in Britain, women were not entirely absent, as they worked in the business as owners, employees, or sex workers (Ellis 2004); in France, respectable women were not expected to show up in cafés alone (Haine 1996). In Vienna, while the coffeehouses were primarily a masculine space, some open-air coffeehouses with high visibility were also respectable spaces for bourgeois women to visit unaccompanied, as their behavior was open to monitoring (Ashby 2013). Several Italian interlocutors in Bologna told me that it was more common to see middle-class women go to a *caffè storico* to enjoy desserts with coffee or hot chocolate and to spend their leisure time there in the regions of Friuli and Veneto in Italy, due to their close historical connections with the Austrian Empire.

9. Habermas 1991.

10. Garvin 2021.

11. In the comedy *La bottega del caffè* (The Coffee House, 1750), written by the Venetian playwright Carlo Goldoni, a waiter is amused to see hotel porters enter the *caffè* trying to follow the fashion of coffee-drinking in Venice. The historian William Ukers also noticed temporal segregation in the early Venetian *caffè*, where the new bourgeois often went in the mornings and the leisure classes in the afternoons and then on into the late hours of the night. Thus, customers from different social

backgrounds did not necessarily have a chance to communicate with one another or partake in the same discussions (Ukers 1935: 25–30).

12. Mintz 1986: 109–12.

13. Parasecoli 2014: 178.

14. Bologna was a city where *osterie* flourished for centuries. The *Osteria del Sole*, now an iconic wine bar in Bologna's *centro storico* has been serving clientele since 1465. In contrast, none of the *bar storici* in the city date back before the twentieth century.

15. Coffee consumption in Italy was relatively low in the early twentieth century. Italians were more familiar with coffee surrogates made from *orzo* (barley), which have remained popular decaffeinated beverages to this day. During the fascist regime, actual coffee consumption further declined due to the Great Depression, the fascist campaigns against imported luxury commodities, the country's shift towards a wartime economy, and the loss of Italy's African colonies and the sea-borne trade routes. Coffee shortages only gradually eased in the post-war period.

16. Historian Jonathan Morris wrote about the effect of state regulations on the price of coffee in Italy (Morris 2010). A maximum price for "a cup of coffee without service" was established by Italian local authorities, often in discussion with local trade federations, and had been imposed intermittently since 1911 to counter inflation in the cost of living. Some coffee bars attempted to charge more for their coffee during the inflationary decade of the 1970s following the "economic miracle." They were quickly met with boycotts and protests from consumers. The retail price of a cup of coffee was still regulated by local authorities together with the coffee bar proprietors' association in the 1990s.

17. There are extensive scholarly discussions about the colonial history and the political economy of the global coffee trade; see especially Bates (1999), Sick (1999), Jaffee (2007), West (2012), Tucker (2017), and Reichman (2018).

18. Morris 2010.

19. Sociologist Ray Oldenburg (1989) described coffeehouses as the "third place," separated from the two usual social environments of home and workplace, that could offer friendship and a sense of community.

20. Mintz 1986: 146–50.

21. Gilmore 1985.

22. Kertzer 1980: 34–39.

23. Willson 2010: 174.

24. Fraser 1990.

25. Baldoli 2006: 16.

26. Black 2001: 82; Guano 2007.

27. Cowan 1991.

28. Baldoli 2006: 19.

29. Hobsbawm 1983.

30. Krause 2018: 59–64.

31. Baldoli 2006.

32. Xiang 2021: 149.

33. Giddens 1991: 18.

34. Reed-Danahay 2020: 7.

35. The term *banhei* is a racial label that my Chinese interlocutors commonly use to vaguely refer to brown people. See more discussion on Chinese immigrants' racial perceptions in Chapter Six.

36. More recently, local authorities have introduced more regulations governing the placement of slot machines in terms of time and space. For instance, bars close to schools are not allowed to have slot machines. They have also regulated time spans for playing. See more reports, debates, and discussions about slot machines and gambling policies in Italy in Fiasco (2010), Dotti (2013), La Rosa (2016), and Rolando and Scavarda (2017).

37. See the original post in Italian at the link: https://www.puntarellarossa.it /2015/07/08/fermento-a-bologna-in-bolognina-il-bar-che-mancava/.

Chapter Four: Reproducing Taste

1. Behar 1997: 1–33.

2. The term *barista*, referring to either gender, appeared in Italian as an alternative to the English word *barman* during the period of Italy's fascist regime, and was a part of the nationalist desire to purify the language of foreign influences (Panzini 1931: 56, Ben-Ghiat 1997).

3. Bourdieu 1984.

4. Guyer 2004: 203–205; Besky 2020: 155–60.

5. Taussig 1993; Bhabha 1994: 83–84.

6. Vann 2006; Paxson 2010; Cavanaugh and Shankar 2014.

7. Apart from espresso-based coffee, Italy's coffee bars commonly sell *caffè d'orzo* (barley coffee), often shortened to simply *orzo*, and *caffè al ginseng* (ginseng coffee), often just called *ginseng*. These two types of instant coffee are made through small automatic machines, independent of espresso machines.

8. Garvin (2021) shows that the "coffee triangle," the transnational exchange of coffee beans and labor between Italy, Brazil, and Ethiopia during the fascist period, continues to impact today's coffee farming models in Ethiopia and Brazil, as well as the global coffee bar culture.

9. Morris 2010: 159.

10. See Poggioli's report on NPR radio, published on July 14, 2017 at the link https://www.npr.org/transcripts/535638587.

11. Baldoli 2006: 24.

12. Spackman and Lahne 2019.

13. Besky 2020.

14. Roseberry 1996.

15. This is called SAB certification (*Somministrazione Alimenti e Bevande* or Food and Beverage Administration). More information about SAB and other legal documentation for coffee bar management can be found on the Italian website *Aprire un bar* (Opening a Coffee Bar): https://aprireunbar.com/.

16. A macchiato can be considered a variation of cappuccino. The Italian word *macchiato* literally means "stained" in English. A *latte macchiato* is a cup of steamed, foamless milk mixed with a shot of espresso that "stains" the milk. A *caffè macchiato*, often referred to simply as a *macchiato*, is an espresso with a dash of milk. The milk can be steamed with or without foam, or simply served cold. More commonly, the steamed milk with foam used in a cappuccino is also incorporated into a macchiato. While a cappuccino is generally served in a larger ceramic cup, a macchiato may be served in the same ceramic cup as a shot of espresso, or in a glass cup of similar size. The milk is added to the cup until it is almost full.

17. Spackman and Lahne 2019.

18. Grasseni 2004: 41.

19. Latour 2004: 207.

20. ibid: 207.

21. de Certeau and Giard 1998.

22. *Caffè* or *caffè normale* (normal coffee) refers to a "standard" single shot of espresso, while *caffè basso / ristretto* (short / narrow coffee) means an extra-strong single shot of espresso with less water passing through the grounds. *Caffè alto / lungo* (tall / long coffee) refers to a single shot of espresso with more water in the cup, providing a weaker coffee but a few more sips to drink, and *caffè doppio* means two shots of espresso. *Caffè americano* refers to a shot of espresso with hot water, while *caffè corretto* (corrected coffee) means a shot of espresso with a small amount of liquor. The meanings of some terms, such as *cappuccino* and *macchiato*, remained virtually unchanged when they were introduced into the English vocabulary. Latte, which is popular in American coffeehouse chains, is not considered to be a type of coffee, as the term simply means "milk" in Italian, while *caffè latte*, which is the Italian drink referred to in English as "latte," is usually understood to be a drink taken at home for breakfast.

23. Spritz is a mixture of a bitter liqueur and prosecco wine, which is then topped off with club soda or sparkling water. Other mixed drinks relatively common in a "traditional bar" managed by Chinese include the Americano, the Negroni, and the Negroni Sbagliato.

24. Wong 2013: 81–113.

25. Jasanoff 2004.

26. Miller 1997.

27. Korff 2003: 9.

28. Appadurai 1996: 178.

29. Terrio 2000; Trubek 2008; Beriss 2019.

30. Pink 2015: 32–34.

31. Savaş 2014.

32. Appadurai 1986.

33. Douglas and Isherwood 1996: xv.

Chapter Five: Performing Sociability

1. Radice 2016: 435.

2. Hochschild 1983: 3–23. See more discussions about how service workers as emotional laborers navigate the power grid of gender hegemony, economic control, labor regulations, surveillance techniques, rigid job routines, and racial hierarchy in Paules (1991), Bayard de Volo (2003), Leidner (1993), and Kang (2010).

3. Hochschild 1983: 18.

4. Baldoli 2006: 25. The original text that Baldoli (2006) discussed is *Il manuale del barista, con i consigli di undici famosi barman*, Maria. P. De Benedetti, ed., published by the Milanese Imprint Rizzoli in 1979.

5. Baldoli 2006: 24.

6. Goffman 1967: 5.

7. Goffman 1956.

8. Herzfeld 2016: 166.

9. Simmel 1949: 255.

10. Sillander 2021.

11. Jeffrey and McFarlane 2008: 420.

12. Glick Schiller et al. 2011.

13. Mauss 1985.

14. Bodenhorn and vom Bruck 2006.

15. A variety of local dialects exist in Italy, Bologna included. Most of them, which have their own local variations, are not mutually intelligible. These local languages are often associated with strong regional and local identities (see i.e., Cavanaugh 2012).

16. Bernard 2011: 272–73.

17. Morgan 2004.

18. Lindenfeld 1990: 91.

19. Held 2005.

20. Wu 2020: 159–92.

21. Cavanaugh 2016.

22. ibid: 41.

23. Black 2012: 23.

24. Sheridan 2018.

25. Mauss 2002.

26. Kipnis 1997. See more discussions about gift economy and *guanxi* production in post-Mao China in Yang (1994) and Yan (1996).

27. *Zingara* is feminine form of the word *zingaro*, which is a pejorative and racialized term for the Roma, corresponding to "Gypsies" in English.

28. Wise 2016.

29. Said 2016; Wise 2016.

30. Hostess clubs are a rather distinctive night-time entertainment industry among East Asian countries. They employ primarily female staff to cater to male clients seeking drinks and attentive conversation. See Allison (1994) for more about sexuality in hostess clubs in the context of Japan.

31. Hall 1993.

32. Hanser 2012.

33. The full report is entitled "Il Bar Italiano: Focus on Caffetteria." It is available on the FIPE's website at www.fipe.it.

34. Leidner 1991; Kang 2010: 133–64.

35. The boundary between flirtation and harassment is often a fine one and can be very vague. Here, I use the term "flirting" to imply friendly sexual banter and distinguish it from "harassment," which is considered offensive and inappropriate by the receiving party.

36. Hochschild 1983: 7.

37. Kaspar and Landolt 2016.

38. Tsing 2005: 4.

39. Since 2005, Italy has implemented an anti-smoking law that bans indoor smoking in public places including bars, restaurants, discotheques, and offices. Naturally, some customers ignore this ban.

40. Kang 2010.

41. Black 2012: 7.

Chapter Six: Contesting Racialization

1. This tragedy only received a few passing reports in the local media. Some of the coverage focused on it as a crime of passion, speculating about a toxic romance between the desperate Moroccan man and the attractive Chinese woman. Some spotlighted the murderer's identity as an undocumented *extracomunitario* (non-EU immigrant) from North Africa. Other media outlets used it as an opportunity to give the public a glimpse into the barista's funeral and the mysterious *comunità cinese* or "Chinese community" in Italy, describing the barista's funeral, which was attended by hundreds of Chinese people. Most Italians had never encountered a Chinese funeral, much less one on such a large scale. In Italy there was even a saying: *Non muoiono mai i cinesi* or "The Chinese never die." The media reports and public reactions to this

tragedy in mainstream Italian society reified the social marginalization of Chinese and other immigrants, as well as their highly racialized images.

2. Vertovec 2007.

3. Brubaker 2009.

4. Harrison 1995; Trouillot 1991; Silverstein 2005.

5. Omi and Winant 2015: 109.

6. Mullings 2004. An example is Sautman and Yan's (2016) study of Chinese investment in Africa, in which the authors discussed how Chinese employers and African workers racialize each other while both are racialized in the Western racial discourse.

7. Joseph 2015.

8. Roth 2012.

9. Ong 2003.

10. Louie 2004: 20.

11. Ravagnoli 2022: 10.

12. I have followed the official WeChat account of *Huarenjie* (Chinatown), one of the most popular Chinese digital media in Italy. Virtually all my Chinese interlocutors whose primary language is Chinese followed this media. Together with other information shared in WeChat posts and group chats, this digital media constitutes one of the major channels through which Chinese residents receive daily news and information concerning the interests of Chinese communities in Italy, including job advertisements, updates on business and immigration regulations, news about crime against Chinese residents, and reports of state inspections against Chinese enterprises, etc.

13. Butler 2009: 13–16; Muehlebach 2011; Allison 2013: 6–7; Millar 2014; Tsing 2015: 2.

14. Allison 2016.

15. Parla 2019: 31; Lan 2022.

16. *Laowai* is an informal term or slang for *waiguo ren* (foreigner). It is usually neutral, but can also be somewhat pejorative in some circumstances. Anthropologist Pál Nyíri suggested that the word *laowai* be translated as "whitey" as recent Chinese immigrants in Europe and other white-majority societies usually use the term in referring to locals of European origin (Nyíri 2006: 104).

17. Mao 2015, Liu and Self 2019.

18. Lan 2022.

19. Lee 2002: 93.

20. Lan 2012: 5–6.

21. Park 2019.

22. Dikötter 2015: 9.

23. ibid: 8–10.

24. Cheng 2019: 15–16.

25. ibid: 161–238.

26. Lan 2017: 191.

27. Huang 2021.

28. Brodkin 1998; Guglielmo and Salerno 2012; Ignatiev 2012.

29. Kipnis 2006.

30. Wahlberg 2018; Hizi 2021.

31. Kipnis 2006.

32. Anagnost 2004: 194.

33. Yan 2008: 114–38.

34. Carter 1997: 190–92.

35. Silverman (1975) has extensive descriptions about the complex cultural implications of the term *civiltà* in her ethnographic account of life in a hill town in Central Italy in the 1970s. She notes that the term has a broader meaning than the English word "civility." It refers to "ideas about a civilized way of life" that implies "an ideology about civilization" that associates civility with urbanity (Silverman 1975: 2). The meaning of *cilvità* is associated with class distinctions. To say someone is *civile* may have various meanings according to the context. It may intend someone's good education, manners, how they dress and speak or refer to social behaviors such as being gentle, polite, generous, or able to present a *bella figura*.

36. Bourdieu 1984.

37. See Lucchini (2008), Bressan and Krause (2017), and Marsden (2022). What happened in Prato was particularly significant. The local authorities there had largely intensified security measures and surprise inspections and instated a new inspection regime after a tragic factory fire that took the lives of seven Chinese workers in 2013. Krause (2018: 251) noted that the tragedy brought together members from the xenophobic right-wing party and the liberal center-left party. Both positioned themselves as social justice supporters and accused Chinese immigrants of exploitive working conditions in violation of human rights. Yet, as Krause (2018) also pointed out, this tragedy was highly politicized and became an excuse to justify selective inspections of Chinese enterprises.

38. A good example is Sheridan's (2022) study of Chinese residents' *Heiren* talk in Tanzania, which both reflects their tense relations with Tanzanians and contributes to constructing an African Other.

39. Lan 2017: 5. Racial triangulation was originally a notion that political scientist Claire J. Kim (1999) raised to explain racial dynamics beyond Black and White in the United States. She argued that Asian Americans were located in triangularized racial positions with reference to these two racial points. They were relatively valorized compared to black Americans and civically obstracized compared to white Americans. These processes of racialization ultimately reinforced white dominance. Among the

tremendous heated scholarly debates that have followed, Park (2019) developed the concept of a multi-tiered "racial cartography" to understand how race at the intersection of citizenship, class, culture, and other forms of structural inequality impacts interracial dynamics between minority groups.

40. Schools in Italy commonly have about five hours of morning lessons beginning at 8:00 or 8:30 am every day from Monday to Saturday. School ends after the morning session and students can then go back home. Some schools with special afternoon programs and activities may be open until 4:00 or 4:30 pm, like the primary school that Lanlan and Beibei's little brother attended.

41. Guest 2003; Cao 2013.

42. Schmitz 2021.

43. Lee 2002.

44. My ethnographic study for this book focuses on Chinese baristas and other Chinese small business owners who were attached to Chinese ethnic economies in Italy. Some children of Chinese immigrants have already distanced themselves from their ethnic communities. They tend to speak Italian as their primary language, have received higher education, have little knowledge about or connections with China, and are more integrated into mainstream society in terms of occupation and lifestyle. Their perceptions of structural inequality and their construction of racial ideology amid ambiguous power dynamics in the context of social transformation and the changing geopolitical landscape warrants further investigation.

45. Min 1996: 218–22.

46. According to the statistics that I requested from the ISTAT (*Istituto Nazionale di Statistica* or Italian national Institute of Statistics,) there were only 12,920 Chinese citizens who became naturalized Italian citizens in all of Italy from 2012 to 2021, comprising less than five percent of Italy's total Chinese population and less than one percent of all the foreigners who became naturalized in the same period. Even in Bologna, where Chinese residents tend to be more established immigrants running small family businesses, only 559 or less than ten percent of Chinese residents changed their citizenship from 2012 to 2021, which is less than two percent of the foreign citizens who were naturalized during the same period. Obtaining Italian citizenship would have entailed giving up their Chinese citizenship, as China does not recognize dual citizenship. My Chinese interlocutors commonly held permanent residency permits that allowed them to live in Italy while retaining their Chinese citizenship. They claimed that it is for practical reasons, as they would not need to apply for a Chinese visa to travel to China. Many also explained that they valued their Chinese identity and would not feel comfortable giving up Chinese citizenship. Some who had obtained Italian citizenship claimed that, for them, naturalization was also for practical reasons. For example, only Italian citizens were permitted to purchase a license to sell tobacco products. These practical concerns echo Aihwa Ong's (1999)

concept of "flexible citizenship." Citizenship has become a transnational strategy that mobile subjects deploy to "respond fluidly and opportunistically to changing political-economic conditions" (Ong 1999: 6).

47. Wise and Noble 2016.

Coda

1. Krause and Bressan 2020.

2. The Association is a branch of the *Associazione bar cinesi* in Italy, founded in 2016. It is the first Chinese ethnic association based around a single business sector. When I was there in December 2019, the president of the Association in Bologna told me that more than one hundred Chinese coffee bar owners had joined in the first six months after it was founded.

REFERENCES

Abate, Roberta. "Perché gli Imprenditori Cinesi hanno Iniziato ad Aprire Ristoranti Giapponesi?" *Vice Italia*, February 16, 2018. https://www.vice.com/it/article/a347gj/ristoranti-giapponesi-aperti-da-imprenditori-cinesi.

Abelmann, Nancy, and John Lie. 1995. *Blue Dreams: Korean Americans and the Los Angeles Riots*. Cambridge, MA: Harvard University Press.

Abu-Lughod Lila. 1991. "Writing against Culture." In *Recapturing Anthropology: Working in the Present*, Richard G. Fox, ed., 137–62. Santa Fe, NM: School of American Research Press.

Aldrich, Howard E., and Roger Waldinger. 1990. "Ethnicity and Entrepreneurship." *Annual Review of Sociology* 16 (1): 111–135.

Allen, Beverly and Mary Russo, eds. 1997. *Revisioning Italy: National Identity and Global Culture*. Minneapolis: University of Minnesota Press.

Allison, Anne. 1994. *Nightwork: Sexuality, Pleasure, and Corporate Masculinity in a Tokyo Hostess Club*. Chicago, IL: University of Chicago Press.

———. 2013. *Precarious Japan*. Durham, N.C.: Duke University Press.

———. 2016. "Precarity: Commentary by Anne Allison." Curated Collections. *Cultural Anthropology*. https://journal.culanth.org/index.php/ca/precarity-commentary-by-anne-allison.

Altglas, Véronique. 2014. "'Bricolage': Reclaiming a Conceptual Tool": *Culture and Religion* 15 (4): 474–93.

Ambrosini, Maurizio. 2013. "Immigration in Italy: Between Economic Acceptance and Political Rejection." *International Migration and Integration* 14: 175–194.

Amin, Ash. 2012. *Land of Strangers*. Cambridge: Polity Press.

Anagnost, Ann. 2004. "The Corporeal Politics of Quality (Suzhi)." *Public Culture* 16 (2): 189–208.

Angel-Ajani, Asale. 2000. "Italy's Racial Cauldron: Immigration, Criminalization and the Cultural Politics of Race." *Cultural Dynamics* 12 (3): 331–52.

Appadurai, Arjun. 1986. "Introduction: Commodities and the Politics of Value." In *The Social Life of Things: Commodities in Cultural Perspective*, Arjun Appadurai, ed., 3–63. Cambridge: Cambridge University Press.

Appadurai, Arjun. 1988. "Putting Hierarchy in Its Place." *Cultural Anthropology* 3 (1): 36–49.

———. 1996. *Modernity at Large: Cultural Dimensions of Globalization*. Minneapolis, MN: University of Minnesota Press.

Ashby, Charlotte. 2013. "The Café of Vienna: Space and Sociability." In *The Viennese Café and Fin-de-siècle Culture*, Charlotte Ashby, Tag Gronberg, and Simon Shaw-Miller, eds., 9–31. Oxford and New York: Berghahn Books.

Bagnasco, Arnaldo. 1977. *Tre Italie: La problematica territoriale dello sviluppo italiano*. Bologna: Il Mulino.

Baldoli, Claudia. 2006. "L'espresso: Modernità e tradizione nell'Italia del caffè." *Memoria e ricerca* 2006 (23): 13–26.

Balibar, Etienne, and Immanuel Wallerstein. 1991. *Race, Nation, Class: Ambiguous Identities*. London: Verso.

Barbagli, Marzio. 1998. *Immigrazione e criminalità in Italia*. Bologna: Il Mulino.

Bates, Robert H. 1999. *Open-economy Politics: The Political Economy of the World Coffee Trade*. Princeton, NJ: Princeton University Press.

Bayard de Volo, Lorraine. 2003. "Service and Surveillance: Infrapolitics at Work among Casino Cocktail Waitresses." *Social Politics: International Studies in Gender, State & Society* 10 (3): 346–76.

Behar, Ruth. 1997. *The Vulnerable Observer: Anthropology that Breaks Your Heart*. Boston: Beacon Press.

Ben-Ghiat, Ruth. 1997. "Language and the Construction of National Identity in Fascist Italy." *The European Legacy* 2 (3): 438–43.

Benton, Gregor, and Frank N. Pieke, eds. 1998. *The Chinese in Europe*. Basingstoke: Macmillan Press.

Berg, Mette Louise, and Magdalena Nowicka. 2019. *Studying Diversity, Migration and Urban Multiculture: Convivial Tools for Research and Practice*. London: UCL Press.

Beriss, David. 2019. "Food: Location, Location, Location." *Annual Review of Anthropology* 48: 61–75.

Bernard, H. Russell. 2011. *Research Methods in Anthropology: Qualitative and Quantitative Approaches*, 5th edition. Lanham, MD: AltaMira Press.

Besky, Sarah. 2020. *Tasting Qualities: The Past and Future of Tea*. Berkeley, CA: University of California Press.

Bhabha, Homi. 1994. *The Location of Culture*. London & New York: Routledge.

Bianchini, Franco. 1991. "The Third Italy: Model or Myth?" *Ekistics* 58 (350 / 351): 336–45.

Biehl, João, and Peter Locke. 2017. "Foreword: Unfinished." In *Unfinished: The Anthropology of Becoming*, João Biehl, and Peter Locke, eds., ix–xiii. Durham, NC: Duke University Press.

Billig, Michael. 1995. *Banal Nationalism*. London: Sage.

Black, Christopher. 2001. *Early Modern Italy: A Social History*. London: Routledge.

Black, Rachel E. 2012. *Porta Palazzo: The Anthropology of an Italian Market.* Philadelphia: University of Pennsylvania Press.

Blim, Michael L. 1990. *Made in Italy: Small-Scale Industrialization and Its Consequences.* New York: Praeger.

Bodenhorn, Barbara, and Gabriele vom Bruck. 2006. "'Entangled in Histories': An Introduction to the Anthropology of Names and Naming." In *The Anthropology of Names and Naming,* Gabriele vom Bruck and Barbara Bodenhorn, eds., 1–30. Cambridge: Cambridge University Press.

Bonacich, Edna. 1973. "A Theory of Middleman Minorities." *American Sociological Review* 38 (5): 583–94.

Bourdieu, Pierre. 1984. *Distinction: A Social Critique of the Judgement of Taste.* Cambridge, MA: Harvard University Press.

Bracci, Fabio. 2015. "The 'Chinese Deviant': Building the *Perfect Enemy* in a Local Arena." In *Chinese Migration to Europe: Prato, Italy, and Beyond,* Loretta Baldassar, Graeme Johanson, Narelle McAuliffe, and Massimo Bressan, eds., 83–100. London: Palgrave Macmillan.

Bressan, Massimo, and Elizabeth L. Krause. 2017. "La cultura del controllo: Letture subalterne di un conflitto urbano." *Antropologia* 2017: 131–51.

Brettell, Caroline B. 2003. *Anthropology and Migration: Essays on Transnationalism, Ethnicity, and Identity.* Walnut Creek, CA.: Altamira Press.

Brigadoi Cologna, Daniele. 2011 "Giovani cinesi d'Italia: Una scommessa che non dobbiamo perdere." In *Cross Generation Marketing,* Luca Massimiliano Visconti, and Enzo Napolitano, eds., 259–78. Milano: Egea.

———. 2017. "Un secolo di immigrazione cinese in Italia." *Mondo Cinese* 163, Anno XLV, n.3: 13–22.

———. 2019. *Aspettando la fine della guerra: Lettere dei prigionieri cinesi nei campi di concentramento fascisti.* Rome: Carocci.

Brodkin, Karen. 1998. *How Jews Became White Folks and What that Says about Race in America.* New Brunswick: Rutgers University Press.

Brubaker, Rogers. 2009. "Ethnicity, Race, and Nationalism." *Annual Review of Sociology* 35 (1): 21–42.

Butler, Judith. 2009. *Frames of War: When is Life Grievable?* New York: Verso.

Çaglar, Ayse, and Nina Glick Schiller. 2018. *Migrants and City-Making: Dispossession, Displacement, and Urban Regeneration.* Durham, NC: Duke University Press.

Campagna, Angiolino, and Angela Venturelli. 2013. *Quando Bologna veniva al Bar Campagna: Storia cittadina di una dinastia contadina.* Bologna: Pendragon.

Cao, Nanlai. 2011. *Constructing China's Jerusalem: Christians, Power, and Place in Contemporary Wenzhou.* Stanford, CA: Stanford University Press.

———. 2013. "Renegotiating Locality and Morality in a Chinese Religious Diaspora: Wenzhou Christian Merchants in Paris, France." *Asia Pacific Journal of Anthropology* 14 (1): 85–101.

Carchedi, Francesco, and Marica Ferri. 1998. "The Chinese Presence in Italy: Dimensions and Structural Characteristics." In *The Chinese in Europe*, Gregor Benton and Frank Pieke, eds., 261–80. Basingstoke: Macmillan Press.

Carney, Megan A. 2021. *Island of Hope: Migration and Solidarity in the Mediterranean.* Berkeley, CA: University of California Press.

Carter, Donald Martin. 1997. *States of Grace: Senegalese in Italy and the New European Immigration.* Minneapolis: University of Minnesota Press.

Cavanaugh, Jillian R. 2012. *Living Memory: The Social Aesthetics of Language in a Northern Italian Town.* Hoboken, NJ: John Wiley & Sons.

———. 2016. "Talk as Work: Economic Sociability in Northern Italian Heritage Food Production." *Language & Communication* 48: 41–52.

Cavanaugh, Jillian R., and Shalini Shankar. 2014. "Producing Authenticity in Global Capitalism: Language, Materiality, and Value." *American Anthropologist* 116 (1): 51–64.

Ceccagno, Antonella. 2004. *Giovani migranti cinesi: La seconda generazione a Prato.* Milan: Franco Angeli.

———. 2007. "Compressing Personal Time: Ethnicity and Gender within a Chinese Niche in Italy." *Journal of Ethnic and Migration Studies* 33 (4): 635–54.

———. 2012. "The Hidden Crisis: The Prato Industrial District and the One Thriving Chinese Garment Industry." *Revue Européenne des Migrations Internationales* 28(4): 43–65.

Ceccagno, Antonella, Renzo Rastrelli, and Alessandra Salvati. 2008. *Ombre cinesi?: Dinamiche migratorie della diaspora cinese in Italia.* Rome: Carocci.

Cheng, Sealing. 2022. "The Poetics of Togetherness: Conviviality of Asylum-Seekers in the Shadow of Hong Kong." *Migration Studies* 10 (2): 130–51.

Cheng, Wendy. 2013. *The Changs Next Door to the Díazes: Remapping Race in Suburban California.* Minneapolis, MN: University of Minnesota Press.

Cheng, Yinghong. 2019. *Discourses of Race and Rising China.* Cham: Springer International Publishing.

Chu, Julie Y. 2010. *Cosmologies of Credit.* Durham, DC: Duke University Press.

Clifford, James. 1986. "Introduction: Partial Truths." In *Writing Culture: The Poetics and Politics of Ethnography*, James Clifford, and George E. Marcus, eds., 1–26. Berkeley, CA: University of California Press.

Cole, Jeffrey. 1997. *The New Racism in Europe: A Sicilian Ethnography.* Cambridge: Cambridge University Press.

Cole, Jeffrey, and Sally S. Booth. 2007. *Dirty Work: Immigrants in Domestic Service, Agriculture, and Prostitution in Sicily.* Plymouth: Lexington Books.

Colombo, Asher D., and Gianpiero Dalla-Zuanna. 2019. "Immigration Italian Style, 1977–2018." *Population and Development Review* 45(3): 585–615.

Cory, Erin. 2020. "Bringing Conviviality into Methods in Media and Migration Studies." In *Conviviality at the Crossroads: The Poetics and Politics of Everyday Encoun-

ters, Oscar Hemer, Maja Povrzanović Frykman, and Per-Markku Ristilammi, eds., 145–64. Cham: Springer Nature.

Counihan, Carole, and Susanne Højlund, 2018. "Making Taste Public: An Ethnographic Approach." In *Making Taste Public: Ethnographies of Food and the Senses*, Carole Counihan, and Susanne Højlund, eds., 1–10. London & New York: Bloomsbury Publishing.

Cowan, Jane K. 1991. "Going Out for Coffee? Contesting the Grounds of Gendered Pleasures in Everyday Sociability." In *Contested Identities: Gender and Kinship in Modern Greece*, Peter Loizos and Euthymios Papataxiarchēs, eds., 180–202. Princeton, NJ: Princeton University Press.

De Certeau, Michel. 1984. *The Practice of Everyday Life*. Berkeley, CA: University of California Press.

De Certeau, Michel, and Luca Giard. 1998. "Ghosts in the City." In *The Practice of Everyday Life, vol.2: Living and Cooking*, Michel de Certeau, Luca Giard, and Pierre Mayol, eds., 133–44. Minneapolis: University of Minnesota Press.

De Genova, Nicolas. 2016. "The 'Native's Point of View' in the Anthropology of Migration." *Anthropological Theory* 16 (2–3): 227–40.

Del Boca, Angelo. 2003. "The Myths, Suppressions, Denials, and Defaults of Italian Colonialism." In *A Place in the Sun: Africa in Italian Colonial Culture fromPost-Unification to the Present*, Patrizia Palumbo, ed., 17–36. Berkeley: University of California Press.

Del Negro, Giovanna P. 2004. *The Passeggiata and Popular Culture in an Italian Town: Folklore and Performance of Modernity*. Montreal: McGill-Queen's Press.

Deleuze, Gilles, and Félix Guattari. 1983. *Anti-Oedipus: Capitalism and Schizophrenia*. Minneapolis, MN: University of Minnesota Press.

Della Sala, Vicent. 2004. "The Italian Model of Capitalism: On the Road between Globalization and Europeanization?." *Journal of European Public Policy* 11 (6): 1041–1057.

Deng, Grazia Ting. 2021. "Bargaining with God in the Name of Family: Chinese Christian Entrepreneurs in Italian Coffee Bars." In *Chinese Religions Going Global*, Nanlai Cao, Giuseppe Giordan, and Fenggang Yang, eds., 1–19. Leiden & Boston: Brill.

Dikötter, Frank. 2015. *The Discourse of Race in Modern China*. Oxford: Oxford University Press.

Dominguez, Virginia R. 1994. "A Taste for 'the Other': Intellectual Complicity in Racializing Practices." *Current Anthropology* 35 (4): 333–48.

Dotti, Marco. 2013: *Slot City, Brianza-Milano e Ritorno*. Roma: Round Robin.

Douglas, Mary. 1966. *Purity and Danger: An Analysis of Concepts of Pollution and Taboo*. London: Routledge & Kegan Paul.

Douglas, Mary, and Baron Isherwood. 1996. *The World of Goods: Towards an Anthropology of Consumption*. London: Routledge.

Ellis, Markman. 2004. *The Coffee-House: A Cultural History*. London: Hachette UK.

Erickson, Brad. 2011. "Utopian Virtues: Muslim Neighbors, Ritual Sociality, and the Politics of Convivència." *American Ethnologist* 38 (1): 114–31.

Essed, Philomena. 1991. *Understanding Everyday Racism: An Interdisciplinary Theory*. Newbury Park: Sage Publications.

Everts, Jonathan. 2010. "Consuming and Living the Corner Shop: Belonging, Remembering, Socializing." *Social and Cultural Geography* 11 (8): 847–863.

Faier, Lieba, and Lisa Rofel. 2014. "Ethnographies of Encounter." *Annual Review of Anthropology* 43: 363–77.

Fassino, Gianpaolo. 2020. "Il caffè espresso: Un tratto costitutivo della vita degli italiani." *Palaver* 9 (2): 167–88.

Fiasco, Maurizio. 2010. "Breve Storia del Gioco in Italia: Tre Epoche per Tre Strategie." *Narcomafie* 9 / 10: 22–30.

Flores, Andrea. 2018. "The Descendant Bargain: Latina Youth Remaking Kinship and Generation through Educational Sibcare in Nashville, Tennessee." *American Anthropologist* 120 (3): 474–86.

Fogu, Claudio. 2006. "Italiani Brava Gente: The Legacy of Fascist Historical Culture on Italian Politics of Memory." In *The Politics of Memory in Postwar Europe*, Richard N. Lebow, Wulf Kansteiner, and Claudio Fogu, eds., 147–76. Durham and London: Duke University Press.

Forgacs, David. 2014. *Italy's Margins: Social Exclusion and Nation Formation since 1861*. Cambridge: Cambridge University Press.

Foucault, Michel. 1977. *Discipline and Punish: The Birth of the Prison*. New York, NY: Vintage Book.

Fraser, Nancy. 1990. "Rethinking the Public Sphere: A Contribution to the Critique of Actually Existing Democracy." *Social Text* 25 / 26: 56–80.

Gaggio, Dario. 2007. *In Gold We Trust: Social Capital and Economic Change in the Italian Jewelry Towns*. Princeton, NJ: Princeton University Press.

Garvin, Diana. 2021. "The Italian Coffee Triangle: From Brazilian *Colonos* to Ethiopian *Colonialisti*." *Modern Italy* 26 (3): 291–312.

Gates, Hill. 1996. *China's Motor: A Thousand Years of Petty Capitalism*. Ithaca: Cornell University Press.

Geertz, Clifford. 1973. *The Interpretation of Culture: Selected Essays by Clifford Geertz*. New York, NY: Basic Books.

Giambelli, Rodolfo A. 1984. "L'emigrazione cinese in Italia: Il caso di Milano." *Mondo Cinese* 48: https://www.tuttocina.it/Mondo_cinese/048/048_giam.htm.

Gibson-Graham. 2014. "Rethinking the Economy with Thick Description and Weak Theory." *Current Anthropology* 55 (Supplement 9): S147–S153.

Giddens, Anthony. 1991. *Modernity and Self-Identity: Self and Society in the Late Modern Age*. Cambridge: Polity Press.

Gilmore, David D. 1985. "The Role of the Bar in Andalusian Rural Society: Observations on Political Culture under Franco." *Journal of Anthropological Research* 41 (3): 263–77.

Gilroy, Paul. 1991. *Ain't No Black in the Union Jack: The Cultural Politics of Race and Nation*. Chicago, IL: Chicago University Press.

———. 2004. *After Empire: Melancholia or Convivial Culture?* London: Routledge.

Giordano, Cristiana. 2008. "Practices of Translation and the Making of Migrant Subjectivities in Contemporary Italy." *American Ethnologist* 35 (4): 588–606.

Glick Schiller, Nina. 2009. "A Global Perspective on Migration and Development." *Social Analysis* 53 (3): 14–37.

———. 2015. "Diasporic Cosmopolitanism: Migrants, Sociabilities and City Making." In *Whose Cosmopolitanism?: Critical Perspectives, Relationalities and Discontents*, Nina Glick Schiller and Andrew Irving, eds., 103–20. New York and Oxford: Berghahn Books.

Glick Schiller, Nina, and Ayşe Çağlar. 2013. "Locating Migrant Pathways of Economic Emplacement: Thinking beyond the Ethnic Lens." *Ethnicities* 13 (4): 494–514.

Glick Schiller, Nina, Tsypylma Darieva, and Sandra Gruner-Domic. 2011. "Defining Cosmopolitan Sociability in a Transnational Age: An introduction." *Ethnic and Racial Studies* 34 (3): 399–418

Goffman, Erving. 1956. *The Presentation of Self in Everyday Life*. New York: Anchor Books.

———. 1967. *Interaction Ritual: Essays on Face-to-Face Behavior*. New York, NY: Pantheon Books.

Grasseni, Cristina. 2004. "Skilled Vision: An Apprenticeship in Breeding Aesthetics." *Social Anthropology* 12 (1): 41–55.

Greenland, Fiona. 2021. *Ruling Culture: Art Police, Tomb Robbers, and the Rise of Cultural Power in Italy*. Chicago: University of Chicago Press.

Grillo, Ralph D. 2003. "Cultural Essentialism and Cultural Anxiety." *Anthropological Theory* 3 (2): 157–73.

Guano, Emanuela. 2007. "Respectable Ladies and Uncouth Men: The Performative Politics of Class and Gender in the Public Realm of an Italian City." *Journal of American Folklore* 120 (475): 48–72.

Guest, Kenneth J. 2003. *God in Chinatown: Religion and Survival in New York's Evolving Immigrant Community*. New York and London: New York University Press.

Guglielmo, Jennifer, and Salvatore Salerno. 2012. *Are Italians White?: How Race Is Made in America*. New York & London: Routledge.

Gupta, Akhil, and James Furguson. 1992. "Beyond 'Culture': Space, Identity, and the Politics of Difference." *Cultural Anthropology* 7 (1): 6–23.

Guyer, Jane I. 2004. *Marginal Gains: Monetary Transactions in Atlantic Africa*. Chicago, IL: University of Chicago Press.

Habermas, Jürgen. 1991. *The Structural Transformation of the Public Sphere: An Inquiry into a Category of Bourgeois Society*. Cambridge: MIT Press.

Hadjimichalis, Costis. 2006. "The End of Third Italy as We Knew It?" *Antipode* 38 (1): 82–106.

Haine, W. Scott. 1996. *The World of the Paris Café: Sociability among the French Working Class, 1789–1914*. Baltimore, MA: John Hopkins University Press.

Hall, Elaine. 1993. "Waitering / Waitressing: Engendering the Work of Table Servers." *Gender and Society* 7 (3): 329–46.

Hall, Stuart. 2017. "Race: The Sliding Signifier." In *The Fateful Triangle: Race, Ethnicity, Nation*, Kobena Mercer, ed., 31–79. Cambridge, MA: Harvard University Press.

Hamilton, Gary G. 2006. *Commerce and Capitalism in Chinese Societies*. London: Routledge.

Hanser, Amy. 2012. "Class and the Service Encounter: New Approaches to Inequality in the Service Work-place." *Sociology Compass* 6 (4): 293–305.

Harden Jacalyn. 2011. "Native like Me: Confessions of an Asiatic Black Anthropologist." *Critique of Anthropology* 31 (2): 139–55.

Harrison, Faye V. 1995. "The Persistent Power of 'Race' in the Cultural and Political Economy of Racism." *Annual Review of Anthropology* 24: 47–74.

———. 2000. "Facing Racism and the Moral Responsibility of Human Rights Knowledge." *Annals of the New York Academy of Sciences* 925 (1): 45–69.

Haugen, Heidi Østbø, and Jørgen Carling. 2005. "On the Edge of the Chinese Diaspora: The Surge of *Baihuo* Business in an African City." *Ethnic and Racial Studies* 28 (4): 639–662.

He, Xiao. 2021. "Between Speaking and Enduring: The Ineffable Life of Bitterness among Rural Migrants in Shanghai." *HAU: Journal of Ethnographic Theory* 11 (3): 1016–28.

Held, Gudrun. 2005. "Politeness in Italy: The Art of Self-Representation in Requests." In *Politeness in Europe*, Leo Hickey and Miranda Stewart, eds., 292–305. Clevedon: Multilingual Matters Ltd.

Hemer, Oscar, Maja Povrzanović Frykman, and Per-Markku Ristilammi, eds. 2020. *Conviviality at the Crossroads: The Poetics and Politics of Everyday Encounters*. Cham: Springer Nature.

Herzfeld, Michael. 2009. *Evicted from Eternity: The Restructuring of Modern Rome*. Chicago and London: The University of Chicago Press.

———. 2016. *Cultural Intimacy: Social Poetics and the Real Life of States, Societies, and Institutions*, 3rd edition. London: Routledge.

Hessler, Peter. 2015. "Learning to Speak Lingerie: Chinese Merchants and the Inroads of Globalization." *New Yorker*: August 10 & 17 Issue at https://www.newyorker.com/magazine/2015/08/10/learning-to-speak-lingerie.

Hizi, Gil. 2021. "Against Three 'Cultural' Characters Speaks Self-Improvement: Social Critique and Desires for 'Modernity' in Pedagogies of Soft Skills in Contemporary China." *Anthropology & Education Quarterly* 52 (3): 237–53.

Hobsbawm, Eric. 1983. "Introduction: Inventing Traditions." In *The Invention of Tradition*, Eric Hobsbawm, and Terence Ranger, eds., 1–14. Cambridge: Cambridge University Press.

Hochschild, Arlie R. 1983. *The Managed Heart: Commercialization of Human Feeling*. Berkeley: University of California Press.

Hom, Stephanie M. 2015. *The Beautiful Country: Tourism and the Impossible State of Destination Italy*. Toronto: University of Toronto Press.

Huang, Mingwei. 2021. "The Chinese Century and the City of Gold: Rethinking Race and Capitalism." *Public Culture* 33 (2): 193–217.

Hu-DeHart, Evelyn. 2002. "Huagong and Huashang: The Chinese as Laborers and Merchants in Latin America and the Caribbean." *Amerasia Journal* 28 (2): 64–91.

Ignatiev, Noel. 2012. *How the Irish Became White*. New York & London: Routledge.

Ingold, Tim. 2000. *The Perception of the Environment: Essays on Livelihood, Dwelling and Skill*. London & New York: Routledge.

Jaffee, Daniel. 2007. *Brewing Justice: Fair Trade Coffee, Sustainability, and Survival*. Berkeley, CA: University of California Press.

Jasanoff, Sheila. 2004. "The Idiom of Co-production." In *States of Knowledge: The Co-Production of Science and the Social Order*, Sheila Jasanoff, ed., 1–12. London & New York: Routledge.

Jeffrey, Craig, and Colin McFarlane. 2008. "Performing Cosmopolitanism." *Environment and Planning D: Society and Space* 26 (3): 420–27.

Joseph, Tiffany D. 2015. *Race on the Move: Brazilian Migrants and the Global Reconstruction of Race*. Stanford, CA: Stanford University Press.

Kang, Miliann. 2010. *The Managed Hand: Race, Gender, and the Body in Beauty Service Work*. Berkeley, CA: University of California Press.

Kaspar, Heidi, and Sara Landolt. 2016. "Flirting in the Field: Shifting Positionalities and Power Relations in Innocuous Sexualisations of Research Encounters." *Gender, Place & Culture* 23 (1): 107–19.

Kertzer, David I. 1980. *Comrades and Christians: Religion and Political Struggle in Communist Italy*. Cambridge: Cambridge University Press.

———. 1996. *Politics and Symbols: The Italian Communist Party and the Fall of Communism*. New Haven, CT: Yale University Press.

Kim, Claire Jean. 2000. *Bitter Fruit: The Politics of Black-Korean Conflict in New York City*. New Haven, CT: Yale University Press.

Kipnis, Andrew B. 1997. *Producing Guanxi: Sentiment, Self, and Subculture in a North China Village*. Durham, NC: Duke University Press.

———. 2006. "*Suzhi*: A Keyword Approach." *The China Quarterly* 186 (June): 295–313.

Kloosterman, Robert, Joanne Van Der Leun, and Jan Rath. 1999. "Mixed Embeddedness: (In) formal Economic Activities and Immigrant Businesses in the Netherlands." *International Journal of Urban and Regional Research* 23 (2): 252–66.

Kopytoff, Igor. 1986. "The Cultural Biography of Things: Commoditization as Process." In *The Social Life of Things: Commodities in Cultural Perspective*, Arjun Appadurai, ed., 64–91. Cambridge: Cambridge University Press.

Korff, Ruediger. 2003. "Local Enclosures of Globalization: The Power of Locality." *Dialectical Anthropology* 27: 1–18.

Krause, Elizabeth L. 2001. "Empty Cradles and the Quiet Revolution: Demographic Discourse and Cultural Struggles of Gender, Race and Class in Italy." *Cultural Anthropology* 16 (4): 576–611.

———. 2018. *Tight Knit: Global Families and the Social Life of Fast Fashion*. Chicago: Chicago University Press.

Krause, Elizabeth L, and Massimo Bressan. 2018. "Circulating Children, Underwriting Capitalism: Chinese Global Households and Fast Fashion in Italy." *Current Anthropology* 59 (5): 572–595.

———. 2020. "Viral Encounters: Xenophobia, Solidarity, and Place-based Lessons from Chinese Migrants in Italy." *Human Organization* 79 (4): 259–70.

Krause, Elizabeth L., and Ying Li. 2022. "Out of Place: Everyday Forms of Marginalization, Racism, and Resistance among Chinese Migrants in Italy." *Journal of Ethnic and Migration Studies* 48 (9): 2023–55.

Kuhn, Philip A. 2008. *Chinese among Others: Emigration in Modern Times*. Lanham, MD: Rowman & Littlefield.

Kusow, Abdi M. 2003. "Beyond Indigenous Authenticity: Reflections on the Insider / Outsider Debate in Immigration Research." *Symbolic Interaction* 26 (4): 591–599.

Labanca, Nicola. 2002. *Oltremare. Storia dell'espansione coloniale Italiana*. Bologna: Il Mulino.

Lan, Shanshan. 2012. *Diaspora and Class Consciousness: Chinese Immigrant Workers in Multiracial Chicago*. New York & London: Routledge.

———. 2017. *Mapping the New African Diaspora in China: Race and the Cultural Politics of Belonging*. New York & London: Routledge.

———. 2022. "Between Privileges and Precariousness: Remaking Whiteness in China's Teaching English as a Second Language Industry." *American Anthropologist* 124: 118–29.

Lan, Tu. 2014. "Made in Italy, by Chinese: How Chinese Migration Changed the Apparel Production Networks in Prato." Ph.D. dissertation. Department of Geography, University of North Carolina at Chapel Hill.

La Rosa, Fabio. 2016. *Il gioco d'azzardo in Italia: Contributi per un approccio interdisciplinare*. Milan: FrancoAngeli.

Latham, Kevin. 2015. "Media and Discourses of Chinese Integration in Prato, Italy: Some Preliminary Thoughts." In *Chinese Migration to Europe: Prato, Italy, and Beyond*, Loretta Baldassar, Graeme Johanson, Narelle McAuliffe, and Massimo Bressan, eds., 139–58. London: Palgrave Macmillan.

Latour, Bruno. 2004. "How to Talk About the Body? The Normative Dimension of Science Studies." *Body and Society* 10 (2 / 3): 205–29.

Lee, Ching Kwan. 2009. "Raw Encounters: Chinese Managers, African Workers, and the Politics of Casualization in Africa's Chinese Enclaves." *The China Quarterly* 199: 647–66.

Lee, Jennifer. 2002. *Civility in the City: Blacks, Jews, and Koreans in Urban America.* Cambridge, MA: Harvard University Press.

Lefebvre, Henri. 1991. *The Production of Space.* Oxford: Blackwell.

Leidner, Robin. 1991. "Serving Hamburgers and Selling Insurance: Gender, Work, and Identity in Interactive Service Jobs." *Gender & Society* 5 (2): 154–77.

———. 1993. *Fast Food, Fast Talk: Service Work and the Routinization of Everyday Life.* Berkeley, CA: University of California Press.

Lem, Winnie. 2007. "William Roseberry, Class and Inequality in the Anthropology of Migration." *Critique of Anthropology* 27 (4): 377–94.

———. 2010. "Mobilization and Disengagement: Chinese Migrant Entrepreneurs in Urban France." *Ethnic and Racial Studies* 33 (1): 92–107.

Lévi-Strauss, Claude. 2021. *Wild Thought: A New Translation of "La Pensée Sauvage."* Chicago, IL: University of Chicago Press.

Li, Minghuan. 1999. "'To Get Rich Quickly in Europe!': Reflections on Migration Motivation in Europe." In *Internal and International Migration: Chinese Perspectives,* Frank N. Pieke, and Hein Mallee, eds., 181–98. Richmond, Surrey: Curzon.

Li, Minghuan, and Diana Wong. 2018. "Moving the Migration Frontier: A Chinese *Qiaoxiang* Migration Model?" *International Migration* 56 (1): 63–77.

Lindenfeld, Jacqueline. 1990. *Speech and Sociability at French Urban Marketplaces.* Amsterdam & Philadelphia: John Benjamins.

Liu, Hong. 1998. "Old Linkages, New Networks: The Globalization of Overseas Chinese Voluntary Associations and Its Implications." *The China Quarterly* 155: 588–609.

Liu, Yang, and Charles C. Self. 2019. "*Laowai* as a Discourse of Othering: Unnoticed Stereotyping of American Expatriates in Mainland China." *Identities* (2019): 1–19.

Lombardi-Diop, Cristina. 2012. "Postracial / Postcolonial Italy." In *Postcolonial Italy: Challenging National Homogeneity,* Cristina Lombardi-Diop and Caterina Romeo, eds., 175–90. London: Palgrave Macmillan.

Louie, Andrea. 2004. *Chineseness across Borders: Renegotiating Chinese Identities in China and the United States.* Durham and London: Duke University Press.

Low, Setha M. 1996. "Spatializing Culture: The Social Production and Social Construction of Public Space in Costa Rica." *American Ethnologist* 23 (4): 861–79.

———. 2009. "Towards an Anthropological Theory of Space and Place." *Semiotica* 175–1 / 4: 21–37.

Loyalka, Michelle. 2012. *Eating Bitterness: Stories from the Front Lines of China's Great Urban Migration*. Berkeley, CA: University of California Press.

Lucchini, Giulio. 2008. "Luoghi di residenza e di lavoro della comunità cinese a Roma." In *Il vicino cinese*, Valentina Pedone, ed., 27–44. Roma: Nuove Edizioni Romane.

Maher, Vanessa. 1996. "Immigration and Social Identities." In *Italian Cultural Studies: An Introduction*, David Forgacs and Robert Lumley, eds., 160–77. Oxford: Oxford University Press.

Mahmud, Lilith. 2014. *The Brotherhood of Freemason Sisters: Gender, Secrecy, and Fraternity in Italian Masonic Lodges*. Chicago, IL: University of Chicago Press.

———. 2020. "Fascism, a Haunting: Spectral Politics and Antifascist Resistance in Twenty-First-Century Italy." In *Beyond Populism: Angry Politics and the Twilight of Neoliberalism*, Jeff Maskovsky and Sophie Bjork-James, eds., 141–66. Morgantown, WV: West Virginia University Press.

Mai, Nicola. 2002. "Myths and Moral Panics: Italian Identity and the Media Representation of Albanian Immigration." In *The Politics of Recognizing Difference: Multiculturalism in Italy*, Ralph Grillo, and Jeff Pratt, eds., 77–94. Aldershot, England, and Burlington, VT: Ashgate.

Ma Mung, Emmanuel. 2015. *"Migrants of Chinese Origin in France: Economic and Social Integration."* In *Chinese Migration to Europe: Prato, Italy, and Beyond*, Loretta Baldassar, Graeme Johanson, Narelle McAuliffe, and Massimo Bressan, eds., 49–54. London: Palgrave Macmillan.

Mao, Yanfeng. 2015. "Who is a *Laowai*? Chinese Interpretations of *Laowai* as a Referring Expression for Non-Chinese." *International Journal of Communication* 9: 2119–40.

Marchand, Trevor H. J. 2010. "Making Knowledge: Explorations of the Indissoluble Relation between Minds, Bodies, and Environment." *Journal of the Royal Anthropological Institute* 16: S1–S21.

Marsden, Anna. 2022. "Racism in Italy and the Italian-Chinese Minority." In *Languages of Discrimination and Racism in Twentieth-Century Italy: Histories, Legacies and Practices*, Marcella Simoni and Davide Lombardo, eds, 155–76. Cham: Palgrave Macmillan.

Massey, Doreen. 1994. *Space, Place, and Gender*. Minneapolis: University of Minnesota Press.

Massey, Douglas S., and Kristin E. Espinosa. 1997. "What's Driving Mexico–US Migration? A Theoretical, Empirical, and Policy Analysis." *American Journal of Sociology* 102 (4): 939–999.

Mauss, Marcel. 1985. "A Category of Human Mind: The Notion of Person; the Notion of Self." In *The Category of the Person: Anthropology, Philosophy, History*, Michael Carrithers, Steven Collins, and Steven Lukes, eds., 1–25. Cambridge: Cambridge University Press.

———. 2002. *The Gift: The Form and Reason for Exchange in Archaic Societies.* London: Routledge.

Mezzadra, Sandro. 2012. "The New European Migratory Regime and the Shifting Patterns of Contemporary Racism." In *Postcolonial Italy: Challenging National Homogeneity,* Cristina Lombardi-Diop and Caterina Romeo, eds., 37–50. London: Palgrave Macmillan.

Millar, Kathleen. 2014. "The Precarious Present: Wageless Labor and Disrupted Life in Rio de Janeiro, Brazil." *Cultural Anthropology* 29 (1): 32–53.

Miller, Daniel. 1997. "Why Some Things Matter." In *Material Cultures: Why Some Things Matter,* Daniel Miller, ed., 3–21. London: UCL Press.

Mills, C. Wright. 1959. *The Sociological Imagination.* Oxfold: Oxford University Press.

Min, Pyong Gap. 1996. *Caught in the Middle: Korean Communities in New York and Los Angeles.* Berkeley, CA: University of California Press.

Mintz, Sidney W. 1986. *Sweetness and Power: The Place of Sugar in Modern History.* New York: Viking Penguin.

Moretti, Cristina. 2015. *Milanese Encounters: Public Space and Vision in Contemporary Urban Italy.* Toronto: University of Toronto Press.

Morgan, Marcyliena. "Speech Community." In *A Companion to Linguistic Anthropology,* Alessandro Duranti, ed., 3–22. Oxford: Blackwell.

Morning, Ann, and Marcello Maneri. 2022. *An Ugly Word: Rethinking Race in Italy and the United States.* New York: Russell Sage Foundation.

Morris, Jonathan. 2010. "Making Italian Espresso, Making Espresso Italian." *Food and History* 8 (2): 155–83.

Muehlebach, Andrea. 2011. "On Affective Labor in Post-Fordist Italy." *Cultural Anthropology* 26 (1): 59–82.

———. 2012. *The Moral Neoliberal: Welfare and Citizenship in Italy.* Chicago, IL: University of Chicago Press.

Mullings, Leith. 2004. "Race and Globalization: Racialization from Below." *Souls: A Critical Journal of Black Politics, Culture, and Society* 6 (2):1–9.

Narayan, Kirin. 1993. "How Native is a 'Native' Anthropologist?" *American Anthropologist* 95 (3): 671–686.

Nowicka, Magdalena. 2020. "Fantasy of Conviviality: Banalities of Multicultural Settings and What We Do (Not) Notice When We Look at Them." In *Conviviality at the Crossroads: The Poetics and Politics of Everyday Encounters,* Oscar Hemer, Maja Povrzanović Frykman, and Per-Markku Ristilammi, eds., 15–42. Cham: Springer Nature.

Nowicka, Magdalena, and Steven Vertovec. 2014. "Comparing Convivialities: Dreams and Realities of Living-with-Difference." *European Journal of Cultural Studies* 17 (4): 341–56.

Nyíri, Pál. 2004. "Expatriating Is Patriotic? The Discourse on 'New Migrants' in the People's Republic of China and Identity Construction among Recent Migrants from the PRC." In *State / Nation / Transnation: Perspectives on Transnationalism in the Asia-Pacific*, Brenda S.A. Yeoh, and Katie Willis, eds., 138–61. London: Routledge.

———. 2006. "The Yellow Man's Burden: Chinese Migrants on a Civilizing Mission." *China Journal* 56: 83–106.

———. 2011. "Chinese Entrepreneurs in Poor Countries: A Transnational 'Middleman Minority' and Its Futures." *Inter-Asia Cultural Studies* 12 (1): 145–53.

Oldenburg, Ray. 1989. *The Great Good Place: Cafés, Coffee Shops, Community Centers, Beauty Parlors, General Stores, Bars, Hangouts, and How They Get You Through the Day*. St Paul: Paragon House Publishers.

Oliveri, Federico. 2018. "Racialization and Counter-racialization in Times of Crisis: Taking Migrant Struggles in Italy as a Critical Standpoint on Race." *Ethnic and Racial Studies* 41 (10): 1855–73.

Omi, Michael, and Howard Winant. 2015 [1986]. *Racial Formation in the United States*. 3rd edition. New York: Routledge / Taylor & Francis Group.

Omohundro, John T. 1981. *Chinese Merchant Families in Iloilo: Commerce and Kin in a Central Philippine City*. Athens, OH: Ohio University Press.

Ong Aihwa. 1996. "Traveling Tales and Traveling Theories in Postcolonial Feminism." In *Women Writing Culture*, Ruth Behar, and Deborah A. Gordon, eds., 350–72. Berkeley and Los Angeles: University of California Press.

———. 1999. *Flexible Citizenship: The Cultural Logics of Transnationality*. Durham and London: Duke University Press.

———. 2003. *Buddha is Hiding: Refugees, Citizenship, the New America*: Berkeley, Los Angeles and London: University of California Press.

Oxfeld, Ellen. 1993. *Blood, Sweat, and Mahjong: Family and Enterprise in an Overseas Chinese Community*. Ithaca, NY: Cornell University Press.

Padilla, Beatriz, Joana Azevedo, and Antonia Olmos-Alcaraz. 2015. "Superdiversity and Conviviality: Exploring Frameworks for Doing Ethnography in Southern European Intercultural Cities." *Ethnic and Racial Studies* 38 (4): 621–635.

Panzini, Alfredo. 1931. *Supplemento ai dizionari italiani*, 6th edition. Milan: Hoepli.

Parasecoli, Fabio. 2014. *Al Dente: A History of Food in Italy*. London: Reaktion Books.

Park, Kyeyoung. 2019. *LA Rising: Korean Relations with Blacks and Latinos after Civil Unrest*. Lanham, Boulder, New York, and London: Lexington Books.

Park, Yoon Jung. 2017. "The Politics of Chineseness in South Africa from Apartheid to 2015." In *Contemporary Chinese Diasporas*, Min Zhou, ed., 29–51. London: Palgrave Macmillan.

Parla, Ayse. 2019. *Precarious Hope: Migration and the Limits of Belonging in Turkey*. Stanford, CA: Stanford University Press.

Patriarca, Silvana. 2010. *Italian Vices: Nation and Character from the Risorgimento to the Republic*. Cambridge: Cambridge University Press.

Paul, Marc. 2020. "The *Dongbei*: The New Chinese Immigration in Paris." In *Globalizing Chinese Migration*, Pál Nyíri, and Igor Saveliev, eds., 120–26. London & New York: Routledge.

Paules, Greta. 1991. *Dishing It Out: Power and Resistance among Waitresses in a New Jersey Restaurant*. Philadelphia, PA: Temple University.

Paxson, Heather. 2010. "Locating Value in Artisan Cheese: Reverse Engineering Terroir for New World Landscapes." *American Anthropologist* 112 (3): 444–57.

Pedone Valentina. 2013. "*Chuguo*, uscire dal paese: Breve quadro dei flussi migratori dalla Cina verso l'estero." In Berti, Fabio, Valentina Pedone, and Andrea Valzania. *Vendere e comprare: Processi di mobilità sociale dei cinesi a Prato*, 59–84. Pisa: Pacini Editore.

Però, Davide. 2007. *Inclusionary Rhetoric, Exclusionary Practices: Left-Wing Politics and Migrants in Italy*. New York and Oxford: Berghahn Books.

Pieke, Frank N. 1991. "Chinese Educational Achievement and 'Folk Theories of Success." *Anthropology and Education Quarterly* 22 (2): 162–80.

———. 2000. "Serendipity: Reflections on Fieldwork in China." In *Anthropologists in a Wider World: Essays on Field Research*, Dresch Paul, Wendy James, and David Parkin, eds., 129–50. New York and Oxford: Berghahn.

Pieke, Frank N., Pál Nyíri, Mette Thunø, and Antonella Ceccagno, eds. 2004. *Transnational Chinese: Fujianese Migrants in Europe*. Stanford, CA: Stanford University Press.

Pink, Sarah. 2015. *Doing Sensory Ethnography*, 2nd edition. London: SAGE Publications Ltd.

Pinkus, Karen. 2003. "Empty Spaces: Decolonization in Italy." In *A Place in the Sun: Africa in Italian Colonial Culture from Post-Unification to the Present*, Patrizia Palumbo, ed., 299–320. Berkeley, CA: University of California Press.

Piore, Michael J. 1979. *Birds of Passage: Migrant Labor and Industrial Societies*. Cambridge: Cambridge University Press.

Pojmann, Wendy. 2021. *Espresso: The Art and Soul of Italy*. New York, NY: Bordighera Press.

Portelli, Alessandro. 2003. "The Problem of the Color Blind: Notes on the Discourse of Race in Italy." In *Crossroutes: The Meaning of Race for the 21st Century*, Paola Boi, and Sabine Broeck, eds., 29–39. Münster: LIT Verlag.

Portes, Alejandro, ed. 1995. *The Economic Sociology of Immigration: Essays on Networks, Ethnicity, and Entrepreneurship*. New York, NY: Russell Sage Foundation.

Portes, Alejandro, and Robert Bach. 1985. *Latin Journey: Cuban and Mexican Immigrants in the United States*. Berkeley, CA: University of California Press.

Portes, Alejandro, and Julia Sensenbrenner. 1993. "Embeddedness and Immigration: Notes on the Social Determinants of Economic Action." *American Journal of Sociology* 98 (6). 1320–50.

Pratt, Mary L. 1991. "Arts of the Contact Zone." *Profession* 1991: 33–40.

Pugliese, Joseph. 2008. "Whiteness and the Blackening of Italy: La Guerra Cafona, Extracommunitari and Provisional Street Justice." *Portal: Journal of Multidisciplinary International Studies* 5 (2): 1–35.

Rabinow, Paul. 1977. *Reflections on Fieldwork in Morocco*. Berkeley, CA: University of California Press.

Radice, Martha. 2016. "Unpacking Intercultural Conviviality in Multiethnic Commercial Streets." *Journal of Intercultural Studies* 37 (5): 432–48.

Raffaetà, Roberta, and Loretta Baldassar. 2015. "Spaces Speak Louder than Words: Contesting Social Inclusion through Conflicting Rhetoric about Prato's Chinatown." In *Chinese Migration to Europe: Prato, Italy, and Beyond*, Loretta Baldassar, Graeme Johanson, Narelle McAuliffe, and Massimo Bressan, eds., 119–38. London: Palgrave Macmillan.

Ravagnoli, Violetta. 2022. *The Building of Chinese Ethnicity in Rome: Networks without Borders*. London: Palgrave Macmillan.

Rath, Jan, and Anna Swagerman. 2016. "Promoting Ethnic Entrepreneurship in European Cities: Sometimes Ambitious, Mostly Absent, Rarely Addressing Structural Features." *International Migration* 54 (1): 152–66.

Redi, Federica. 1997. "Bacchette e forchette: La diffusione della cucina cinese in Italia." *Mondo Cinese* 95: https://www.tuttocina.it/Mondo_cinese/095/095_redi.htm.

Reed-Danahay. 2020. *Bourdieu and Social Space: Mobilities, Trajectories, Emplacements*. Oxford and New York: Berghahn Publishers.

Reichman, Daniel R. 2018. "Big Coffee in Brazil: Historical Origins and Implications for Anthropological Political Economy." *Journal of Latin American and Caribbean Anthropology* 23 (2): 241–61.

Resca, Andrea. 1995. "Cultura e struttura: L'analisi delle relazioni economiche e sociali nella comunità cinese a Bologna." Thesis of *Laurea*, Faculty of Social Sciences, University of Bologna.

Riccio, Bruno. 2000. "The Italian Construction of Immigration: Sedentarist and Corporatist Narratives: Facing Transnational Migration in Emilia-Romagna." *Anthropological Journal on European Cultures* 9 (2): 53–74.

Rofel, Lisa. 2007. *Desiring China: Experiments in Neoliberalism, Sexuality, and Public Culture*. Durham: NC: Duke University Press.

Rofel, Lisa, and Sylvia J. Yanagisako. 2018. *Fabricating Transnational Capitalism: A Collaborative Ethnography of Italian-Chinese Global Fashion*. Durham & London: Duke University Press.

Rolando, Sara, and Alice Scavarda. 2017. "Gambling Policy in European Welfare Regimes: A European Research Project on the Profitability of Gambling. Italian Report." Publications of the Faculty of Social Sciences 30 / 2016, University of Helsinki.

Rosaldo, Renato. 1989. *Culture and Truth: The Remaking of Social Analysis.* Boston, MA: Beacon.

Roseberry, William. 1996. "The Rise of Yuppie Coffees and the Reimagination of Class in the United States." *American Anthropologist* 98 (4): 762–775.

Roth, Wendy. 2012. *Race Migrations: Latinos and the Cultural Transformation of Race.* Stanford, CA: Stanford University Press.

Rumbaut, Ruben G. 1991. *The Agony of Exile: A Study of the Migration and Adaptation of Indochinese Refugee Adults and Children.* Baltimore, MD: Johns Hopkins University Press.

Said, Maurice. 2016. "Humour and Lying: Male Sociality among Coastal Sinhalese." *Etnofoor* 28 (1): 97–109.

Salih, Ruba, and Bruno Riccio. 2011. "Transnational Migration and Rescaling Processes. The Incorporation of Migrant Labor." In Nina Glick Schiller and Ayse Çaglar, eds., *Locating Migration: Rescaling Cities and Migrants*, 123–42. Ithaca, NY: Cornell University Press.

Sandalj, Vincenzo. 2013. "Italy." In Robert W. Thurston, Jonathan Morris, and Shawn Steiman, eds., *Coffee: A Comprehensive Guide to the Bean, the Beverage, and the Industry*, 184–87. Lanham, MD: Rowman & Littlefield Publishers.

Sautman, Barry, and Hairong Yan. 2016. The Discourse of Racialization of Labor and Chinese Enterprises in Africa." *Ethnic and Racial Studies* 39 (12): 2149–68.

Savaş, Özlem. 2014. "Taste Diaspora: The Aesthetic and Material Practice of Belonging." *Journal of Material Culture* 19 (2): 185–208.

Schiller, Anne. 2016. *Merchants in the City of Art: Work, Identity, and Change in a Florentine Neighborhood.* Toronto: University of Toronto Press.

Schmitz, Cheryl Mei-ting. 2021. "Making Friends, Building Roads: Chinese Entrepreneurship and the Search for Reliability in Angola." *American Anthropologist* 123 (2): 343–54.

Schneider, Jane, ed. 1998. *Italy's "Southern Question": Orientalism in One Country.* Oxford: Berg.

Schneider, Jane, and Peter Schneider. 1994. "Mafia, Antimafia, and the Question of Sicilian Culture." *Politics and Society* 22: 237–58.

Sheridan, Derek. 2018. "If You Greet Them, They Ignore You": Chinese Migrants, (Refused) Greetings, and the Inter-Personal Ethics of Global Inequality in Tanzania." *Anthropological Quarterly* 91 (1): 237–65.

———. 2019. "Weak Passports and Bad Behavior: Chinese Migrants and the Moral Politics of Petty Corruption in Tanzania." *American Ethnologist* 46 (2): 137–49.

———. 2023. "The Semiotics of *Heiren* (黑人): Race, Everyday Language, and Discursive Complicities in a Chinese Migrant Community." *Journal of Ethnic and Migration Studies* 49 (13): 3308–26.

Sick, Deborah. 1999. *Farmers of the Golden Bean: Costa Rican Households and the Global Coffee Economy.* Dekalb, IL: Northern Illinois University Press.

Sillander, Kenneth. 2021. "Introduction: Qualifying Sociality through Values." *Anthropological Forum* 31 (1): 1–18.

Silva, Carlos Freire da. 2018. "Brazil-China Connections: The Chinese Migration in Downtown São Paulo." *Cadernos Metrópole* 20 (41): 223–43.

Silverman, Sydel. 1975. *Three Bells of Civilization: The Life of an Italian Hill Town.* New York, NY: Columbia University Press.

Silverstein, Paul A. 2005. "Immigrant Racialization and the New Savage Slot: Race, Migration, and Immigration in the New Europe." *Annual Review of Anthropology* 34 (1): 363–84.

Simmel, Georg. 1949. "The Sociology of Sociability." *American Journal of Sociology* 55 (3): 254–61.

Siu, Paul C.P. 1987. *The Chinese Laundryman: A Study of Social Isolation.* New York, NY: NYU Press.

Skeldon, Ronald. 2007. "The Chinese Overseas: The End of Exceptionalism?" In *Beyond Chinatown: New Chinese Migration and the Global Expansion of China,* Mette Thunø, ed., 35–48. Copenhagen: NIAS Press.

Spackman, Christy, and Jacob Lahne. 2019. "Sensory Labor: Considering the Work of Taste in the Food System." *Food, Culture & Society* 22 (2): 142–51.

Stanley, Flavia. 2008. "On Belonging in / to Italy and Europe: Citizenship, Race, and the 'Immigration Problem.'" In *Citizenship, Political Engagement, and Belonging: Immigrants in Europe and the United States,* Deborah Reed-Danahay and Caroline B. Brettell, eds., 43–59. New Brunswick and London: Rutgers University Press.

Stewart, Pamela J., and Andrew Strathern. 2004. *Witchcraft, Sorcery, Rumors and Gossip.* Cambridge: Cambridge University Press.

Stolcke V. 1995. "Talking Culture: New Boundaries, New Rhetorics of Exclusion in Europe. *Current Anthropology* 36 (1):1–24.

Sunder Rajan, Kaushik. 2021. *Multisituated: Ethnography as Diasporic Praxis.* Durham and London: Duke University Press.

Taha, Maisa. 2022. "Introduction to Theme Issue: Dignity, Conviviality, and Moral Contests of Belonging." *Anthropologica* 64 (2): 1–5.

Taussig, Michael. 1993. *Mimesis and Alterity: A Particular History of the Senses.* New York: Routledge.

Terrio, Susan J. 2000. *Crafting the Culture and History of French Chocolate.* Berkeley, CA: University of California Press.

Thunø, Mette. 2001. "Reaching Out and Incorporating Chinese Overseas: The Trans-Territorial Scope of the PRC by the End of the 20th Century." *The China Quarterly* 168 (December): 910–929.

Tomba, L. 1999. "Exporting the 'Wenzhou Model' to Beijing and Florence: Suggestions for a Comparative Perspective on Labor and Economic Organization in Two Migrant Communities." In *Internal and International Migration: Chinese Perspectives,* Frank N. Pieke, and Hein Mallee, eds., 280–94. Richmond, Surrey: Curzon.

Trouillot, M. 1991. "Anthropology and the Savage Slot: The Poetics and Politics of Otherness." In *Recapturing Anthropology*, Richard G. Fox, ed., 17–44. Santa Fe, NM: School of American Research Press.

Trubek, Amy B. 2008. *The Taste of Place: A Cultural Journey into Terroir*. Berkeley, CA: University of California Press.

Tsing, Anna Lowenhaupt. 2005. *Friction: An Ethnography of Global Connection*. Princeton, NJ: Princeton University Press.

———. 2015. *The Mushroom at the End of the World: On the Possibility of Life in Capitalist Ruins*. Princeton, NJ: Princeton University Press.

Tucker, Catherine M. 2017. *Coffee Culture: Local Experiences, Global Connections*. New York: Routledge.

Tuckett, Anna. 2018. *Rules, Paper, Status: Migrants and Precarious Bureaucracy in Contemporary Italy*. Stanford, CA: Stanford University Press.

Ukers, William H. 1935. *All About Coffee*. New York: The Tea and Coffee Trade Journal.

Valentine, Gill. 2008. "Living with Difference: Reflections on Geographies of Encounter." *Progress in Human Geography* 32 (3): 323–37.

Van Dongen, Els. 2019. "Localizing Ethnic Entrepreneurship: 'Chinese' Chips Shops in Belgium, 'Traditional' Food Culture, and Transnational Migration in Europe." *Ethnic and Racial Studies* 42 (15): 2566–84.

Vann, Elizabeth F. 2006. "The Limits of Authenticity in Vietnamese Consumer Markets." *American Anthropologist* 108 (2): 286–96.

Vertovec, Steven. 2007. "Super-Diversity and Its Implications." *Ethnic and Racial Studies* 30 (6): 1024–54.

———. 2011. "The Cultural Politics of Nation and Migration." *Annual Review of Anthropology* 2011 (40): 241–56.

Wacquant, Loïc. 2004. *Body and Soul: Notebooks of an Apprentice Boxer*. Oxford: Oxford University Press.

Wahlberg, Ayo. 2018. *Good Quality: The Routinization of Sperm Banking in China*. Berkeley, CA: University of California Press.

Waldinger, Roger David. 1996. *Still the Promised City? African-Americans and New Immigrants in Postindustrial New York*. Cambridge, MA: Harvard University Press.

Wang, Gungwu. 1991. *China and the Chinese Overseas*. Singapore: Times Academic Press.

Wang, Yuting. 2020. *Chinese in Dubai: Money, Pride, and Soul-Searching*. Leiden & Boston: Brill.

Watson, James L. 1975. *Emigration and the Chinese Lineage: The "Mans" in Hong Kong and London*. Berkeley, CA: University of California Press.

West, Paige. 2012. *From Modern Production to Imagined Primitive*. Durham, NC: Duke University Press, 2012.

Willson, Perry. 2010. *Women in Twentieth-Century Italy*. London: Palgrave Macmillan.

Wimmer, Andreas, and Nina Glick Schiller. 2003. "Methodological Nationalism, the Social Sciences, and the Study of Migration: An Essay in Historical Epistemology." *International Migration Review* 37 (3): 576–610.

Wise, Amanda. 2016. "Convivial Labour and the 'Joking Relationship': Humour and Everyday Multiculturalism at Work." *Journal of Intercultural Studies* 37 (5): 481–500.

Wise, Amanda, and Greg Noble. 2016. "Convivialities: An Orientation." *Journal of Intercultural Studies* 37 (5): 423–31.

Wolf, Eric. 1982. *Europe and the People without History*. Berkeley, CA: University of California Press.

Wong, Winne Won Yin. 2013. *Van Gogh on Demand: China and the Readymade*. Chicago, IL: University of Chicago Press.

Wu, Di. 2020. *Affective Encounters: Everyday Life among Chinese Migrants in Zambia*. London: Routledge.

Xiang, Biao. 2003. "Emigration from China: A Sending Country Perspective." *International Migration* 41 (3): 21–48.

———. 2005. *Transcending Boundaries: Zhejiangcun: The Story of a Migrant Village in Beijing*. Leiden & Boston: Brill.

———. 2021. "The Nearby: A Scope of Seeing." *Journal of Contemporary Chinese Art* 8 (2–3): 147–65.

Yan, Hairong. 2008. *New Masters, New Servants: Migration, Development, and Women Workers in China*. Durham, NC: Duke University Press.

Yan, Yunxiang. 1996. *The Flow of Gifts: Reciprocity and Social Networks in a Chinese Village*. Stanford: Stanford University Press.

Yanagisako, Sylvia J. 2002. *Producing Culture and Capital: Family Firms in Italy*. Princeton, NJ: Princeton University Press.

Yang, Mayfair Mei-hui. 1994. *Gifts, Favors, and Banquets: The Art of Social Relationships in China*. Ithaca, NY: Cornell University Press.

Zhang, Gaoheng. 2019. *Migration and the Media: Debating Chinese Migration to Italy, 1992–2012*. Toronto: University of Toronto Press.

Zhang, Li. 2001. *Strangers in the City: Reconfigurations of Space, Power, and Social Networks within China's Floating Population*. Stanford: Stanford University Press.

Zhou, Min. 1992. *Chinatown: The Socioeconomic Potential of an Urban Enclave*. Philadelphia, PA: Temple University Press.

———. 1997. "Growing Up American: The Challenge Confronting Immigrant Children and Children of Immigrants." *Annual Review of Sociology* 23: 63–95.

———. 2004. "Revisiting Ethnic Entrepreneurship: Convergencies, Controversies, and Conceptual Advancements." *International Migration Review* 38 (3): 1040–74.

———. 2012. *Contemporary Chinese America: Immigration, Ethnicity, and Community Transformation*. Philadelphia, PA: Temple University Press.

INDEX

aesthetics, 90, 93, 110, 127, 187
Africa, 14, 182, 231n6, 226n15
aging, 9, 11, 25, 41, 44, 67
Albania /Albanians, 17, 163, 185, 194
alien, 6, 9, 141
alienation, 91, 111, 196
amnesties, 16, 45, 50, 53
anti-southernism, 14–15, 37–38, 176
Appadurai, Arjun, 137
apprenticeship, 30, 109, 112–13, 119–20,
    124–27
Arabs, 185
artisanship, 28, 44, 124, 128, 135, 219n101
Asian Americans, 22, 232n39
aspirations, 8, 10, 34, 52, 63, 67, 130, 186
Associazione bar cinesi (Chinese Coffee
    Bar Association), 208–9, 221n8,
    234n2
austerity, 8, 15
Austrian Empire, 225n8
authenticity, 5–6, 73, 93, 103, 111, 118;
    and taste, 6, 118–19, 128

backwardness, 12, 14, 20, 53, 186
Balkans, 13, 96, 182
banhei (half black, "brown" immigrants),
    96, 129, 171–72, 176, 182, 184–87,
    189–95, 203–4, 227n35. See also *hei*;
    racism: anti-Black and anti-Brown
banter, 157–58, 162, 166, 230n35
bar (coffee bar): *bar cinesi*, 69, 71, 101–2,
    140, 210; *bar di passaggio* (passersby

bar), 79–80, 88–92, 97, 99, 142, 145,
    148, 164; *bar di quartiere* (neighbor-
    hood bar), 79–85, 94, 99, 117, 134, 142,
    146, 148, 155, 157, 193; *bar di tendenza*
    (trendy bar), 94–95, 103–4, 123,
    209–10; *bar tradizionale* (traditional
    bar), 26, 69, 93–96, 99, 101–4, 110,
    123–24, 151, 191, 209, 228n23; *circoli*
    (cooperative bar), 76, 84, 94; defini-
    tion and translation of, 213n1; female
    patronage of, 76–77; history of,
    72–77; peripheral, 85, 142, 145, 178,
    196; and social class, 99, 162; typology
    of, 79–80. See also *caffè*; *osteria*
Barbagli, Marzio, 16
baristas: and cappuccino-making, 124–28;
    and certification, 123; definition of,
    110, 227n2; and espresso-making,
    120, 122; and gender, 141, 160–61,
    163–67; and language skills, 60, 62,
    164, 166–68; and sensory skills,
    125–128, 138; and social skills, 110, 139,
    148, 167; and training, 111–13, 121–23,
    126, 129, 131
Behar, Ruth, 109
bella figura (good impression), 96, 142,
    148, 187, 232n35
Bel Paese (the Beautiful Country), 28
Black, Rachael, 149
blackness, 22; and global racial hierar-
    chy, 193; shades of, 182, 187. See also
    hei; racism: anti-Black and anti-Brown

255

A NOTE ON THE TYPE

This book has been composed in Arno, an Old-style serif typeface in the classic Venetian tradition, designed by Robert Slimbach at Adobe.

Printed in the USA
CPSIA information can be obtained
at www.ICGtesting.com
JSHW021629240324
59808JS00003B/3

9 780691 245799